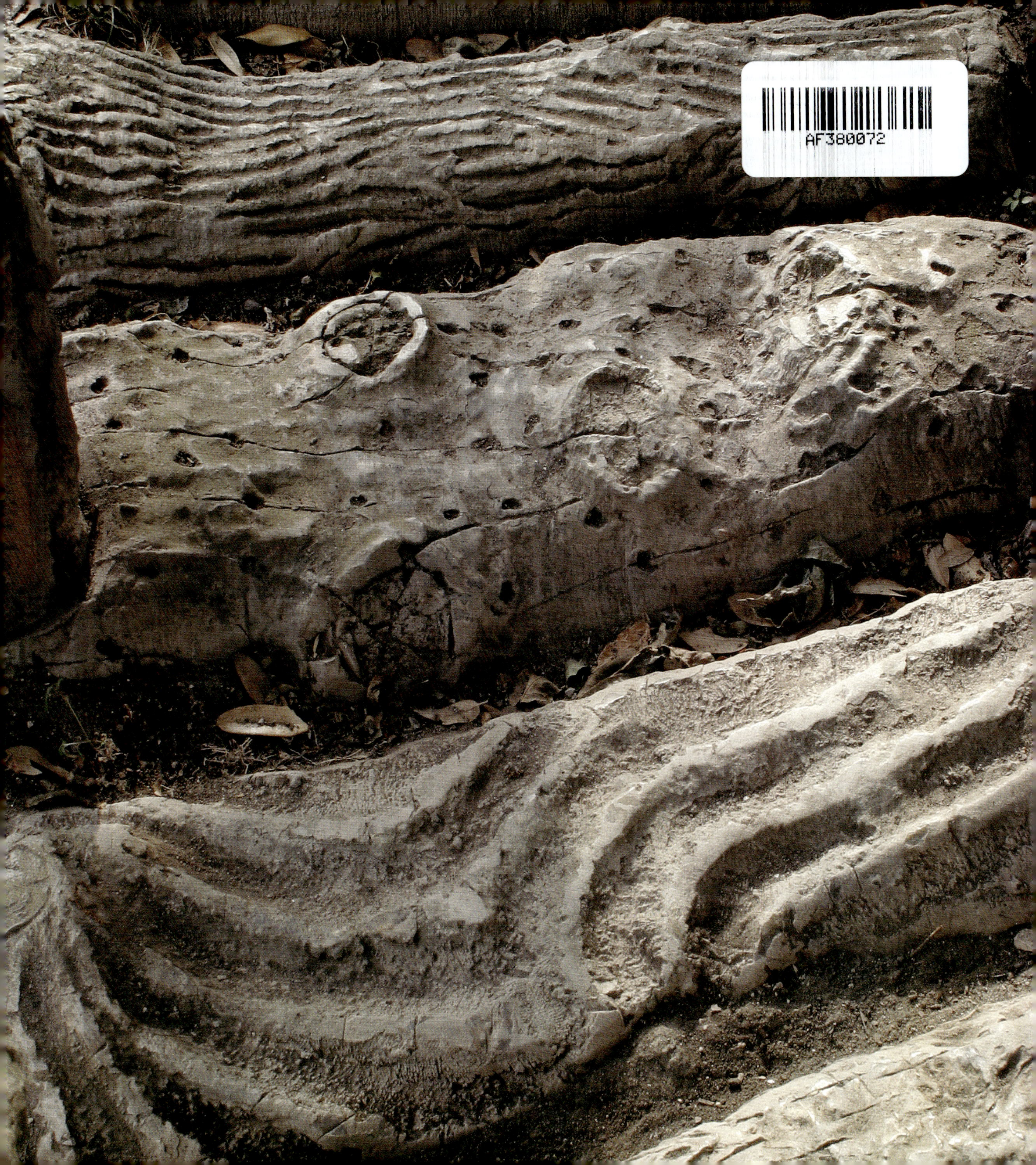
AF380072

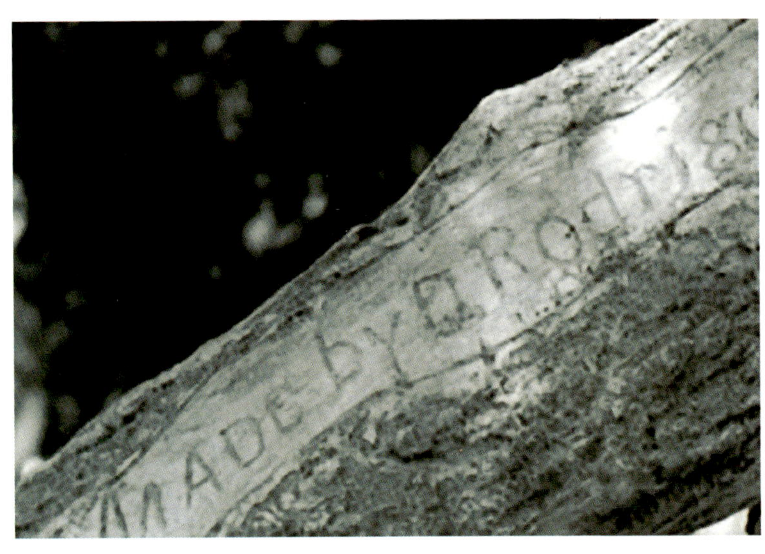

CAPTURING NATURE

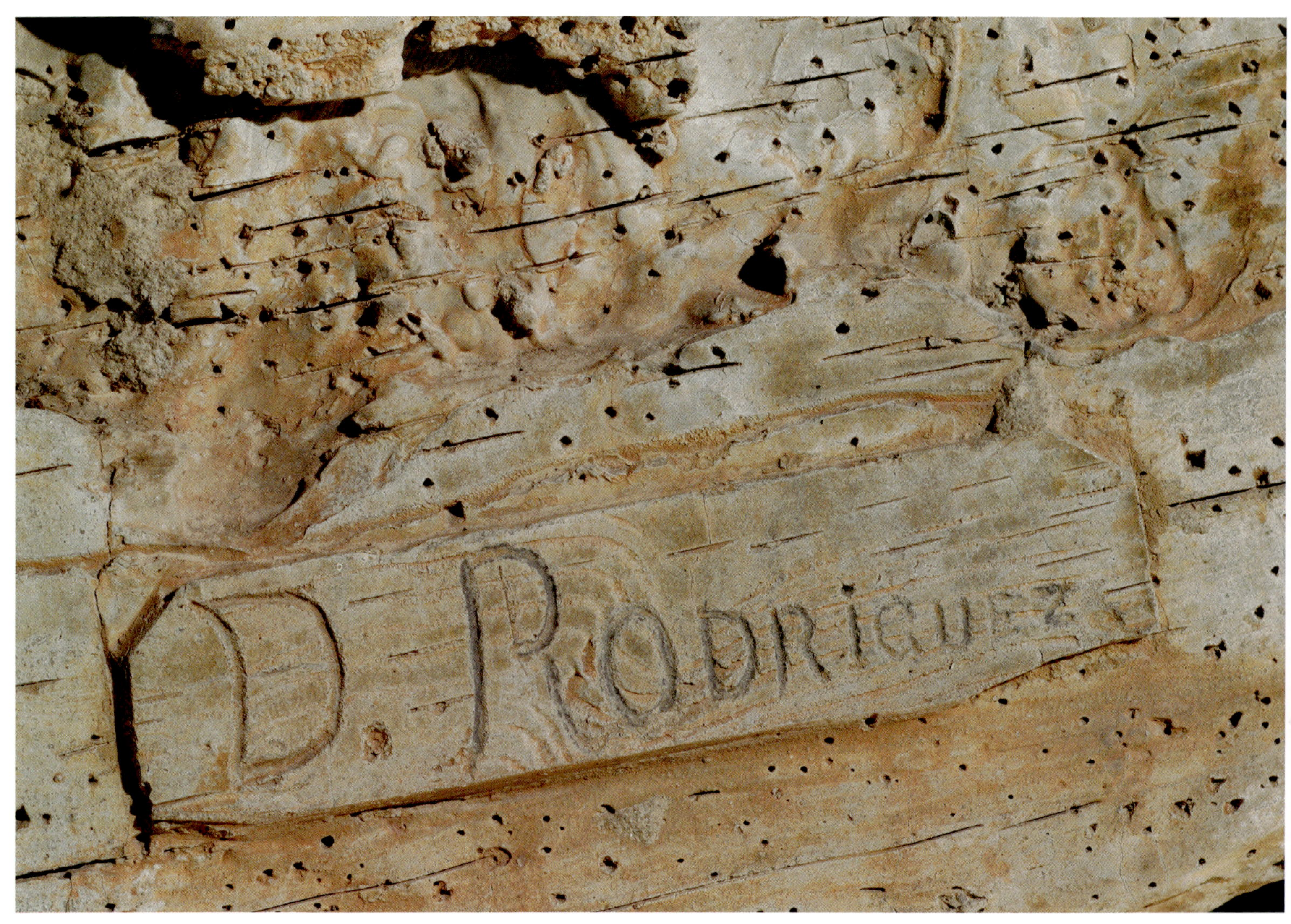

NUMBER TWELVE:

Rio Grande / Río Bravo

Borderlands Culture and Traditions

Norma E. Cantú, *General Editor*

CAPTURING NATURE

The Cement Sculpture of Dionicio Rodríguez

Patsy Pittman Light

Texas A&M University Press
College Station

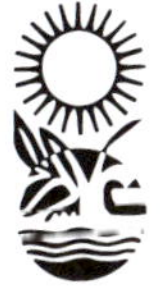

This paper meets the requirements of ANSI/NISO Z39.48-1992
(Permanence of Paper). Binding materials have been chosen for durability.

Texas A&M University Press joins the author in expressing appreciation
to those whose financial support has contributed to the publication
of this book. These donors are listed in the Acknowledgment of
Donors at the back of the book.

Library of Congress Cataloging-in-Publication Data

Light, Patsy Pittman.
    Capturing nature : the cement sculpture of Dionicio Rodríguez /
Patsy Pittman Light.
        p.   cm. — (Rio Grande/Río Bravo ; no. 12)
    Includes bibliographical references and index.
    ISBN-13: 978-1-58544-610-0 (cloth : alk. paper)
    ISBN-13: 978-1-62349-248-9 (flex bound with flaps)
    ISBN-13: 978-1-60344-844-4 (ebook)
    1. Rodríguez, Dionicio, 1891–1955. 2. Concrete sculpture—United
States. 3. Outdoor sculpture—United States. 4. Nature in art.
    5. Garden ornaments and furniture—United States. I. Rodríguez,
Dionicio, 1891–1955. II. Title.
NB237.R635L54 2007
730.92—dc22
                                                    2007020593

Design by Barbara Mathews Whitehead

Frontmatter photographs without captions are by Patsy Light (p. i),
Bob Parvin (p. ii), and courtesy of Manuela Vargas Theall (p. v).
Endsheets are by Bob Parvin.

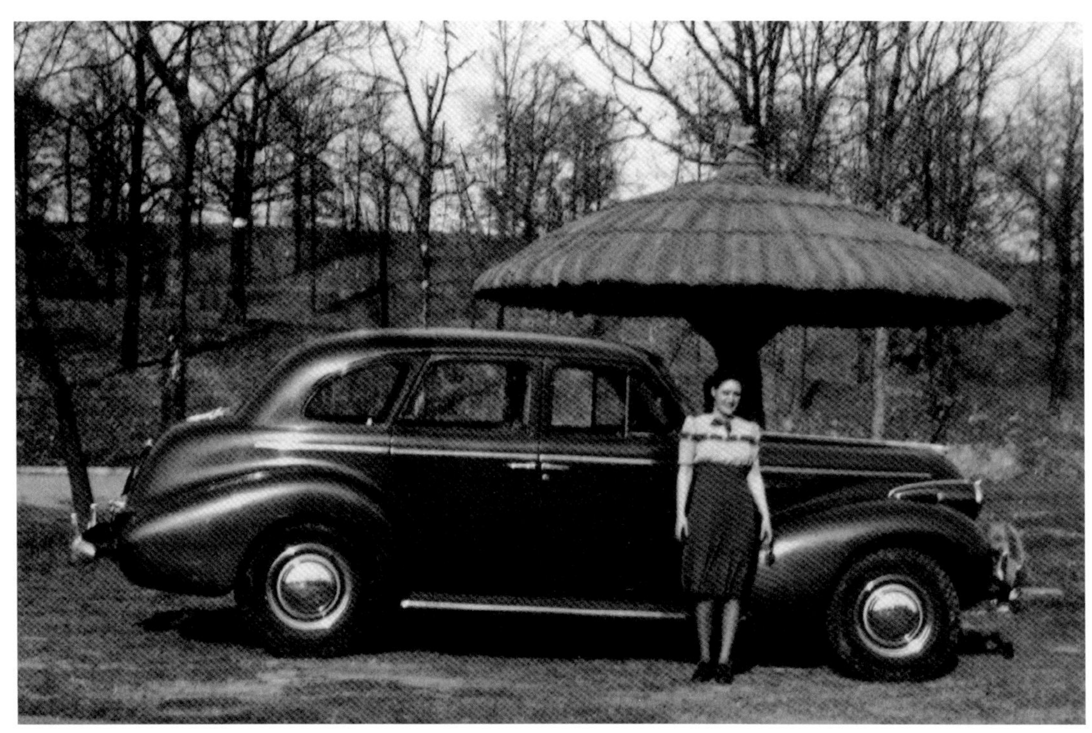

This book is dedicated to
Manuela Vargas Theall,
whose shared memories of her uncle,
Dionicio Rodríguez,
made this story come alive.

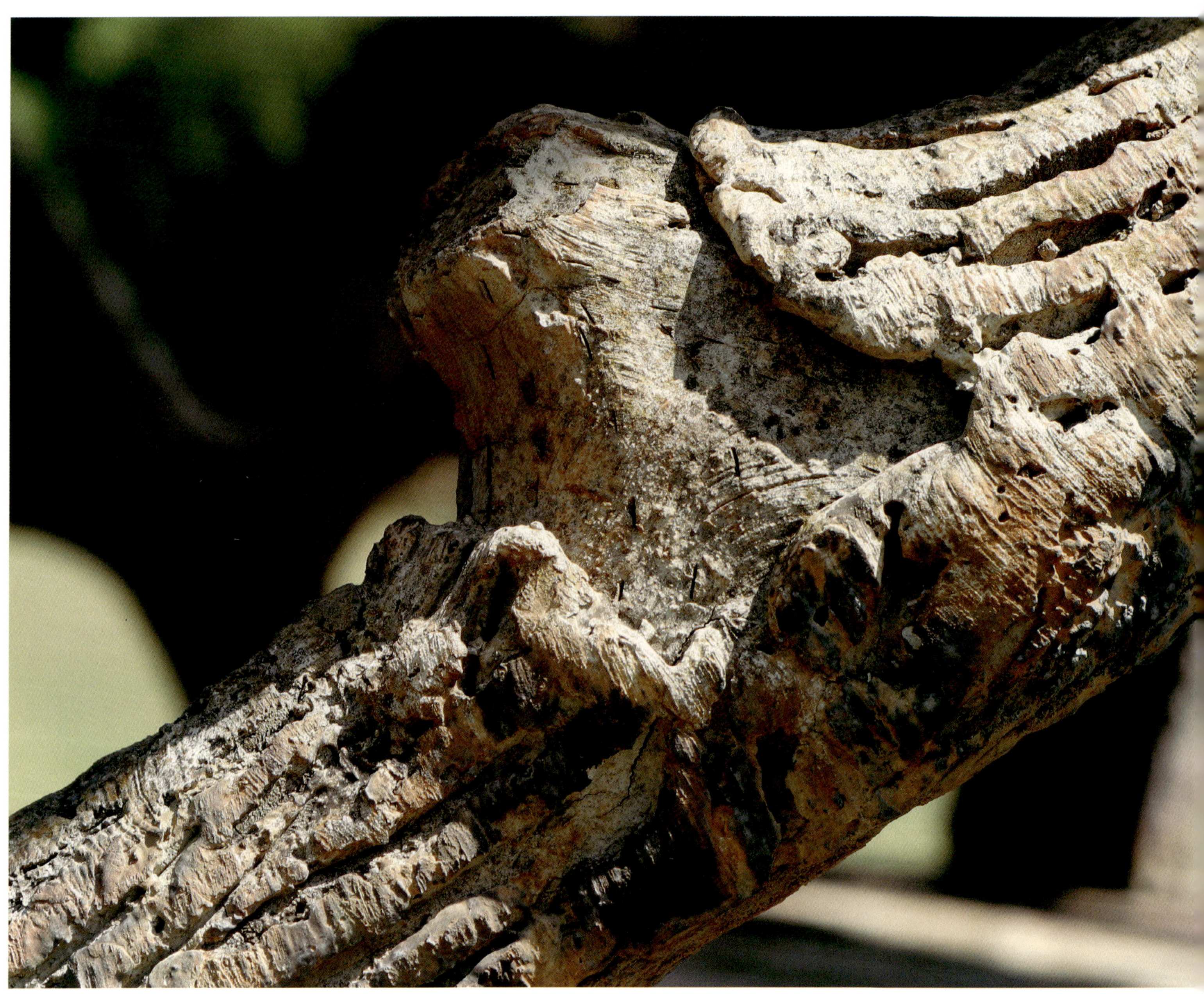

Peach tree branch, Albert Steves gazebo, Comfort, Texas.
Photo: Bob Parvin.

Contents

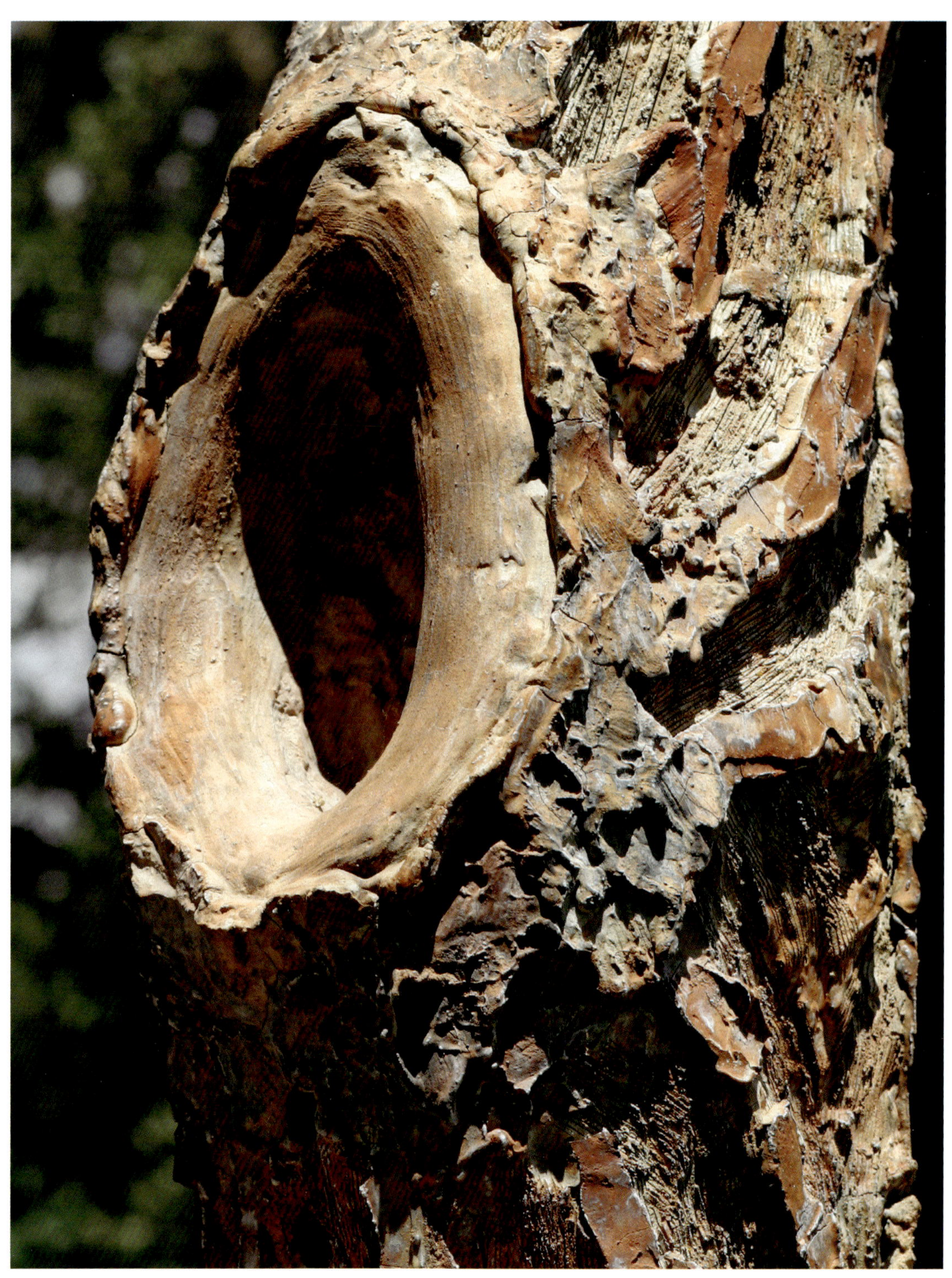

Hackberry knothole, Albert Steves gazebo,
Comfort, Texas. Photo: Bob Parvin.

Preface

Ifirst became acquainted with the cement *faux bois* of Mexican sculptor Dionicio Rodríguez after moving to San Antonio in the early 1960s. As an artist and art historian, I was intrigued by his ability to mimic the shapes, colors, and textures in nature. As I learned more about him through the years, I began to appreciate what it meant for him to work in the hot Texas sun, to mix the cement to the proper consistency, to struggle with his homemade tools to create his very realistic sculptures, and to perfect their appropriate coloring by applying chemical solutions before the cement became too dry.

To those unfamiliar with the genre or Rodríguez's interpretation of it, it may seem incongruous that a utilitarian material ordinarily used for foundations, streets, and sidewalks could be employed to create artistic forms. The use of cement as a creative medium is not unique to Rodríguez: examples by others exist in the United States, Europe, Mexico, Central and South America, and Asia.

Although the cement buildings and sculpture of early twentieth-century Spanish architect Antoni Gaudi are on a grander scale, his curvilinear shapes and textures echo those in nature, similar to those which inspired Rodríguez. On a national level, the works of artisans who utilized cement are numerous: grottos by Joseph Zoetl, Father Paul Dobberstein, Father Mathias Wernerus, and Father Philip Wagner; Watts Towers by Simon Rodia; Land of Pasaquan, the cement-faced stone and brick constructions by St. EOM (Eddie Owens Martin); the human and animal sculptures by Fred Smith, and Thunder Mountain Monument by Frank Van Zant. A discussion of additional cement artisans working in Texas during Rodríguez's time can be found in the text.

For several years, I had been involved in writing nominations for sites and buildings to be listed on the National Register of Historic Places, a process that documents entities in perpetuity. It suddenly dawned on me that Rodríguez's *trabajo rústico* (rustic work) in San Antonio merited official recognition. One summer day in 1995, I grabbed my camera and began photographing his sculptures in my immediate neighborhood. Realizing that Dionicio's story needed to be told, I enlisted the aid of fellow historian Maria Pfeiffer.

This book and its illustrations are the result of an eight-year investigation by Maria Pfeiffer and me. In 1997 we were awarded a grant by the San Antonio Conservation Society to assist in the initial cost of film and processing of photographs. Although the documentation of the life and work of Rodríguez is interesting and important, the real story is found in the sculpture itself, and photographs, both archival and contemporary, evidence the uniqueness of his artistry. Our original goal was to record Dionicio Rodríguez's large body of work in San Antonio for a National Register listing, but as we proceeded with our research, it became apparent that there was additional work not only in other parts of Texas but also throughout the United States that merited documentation.

Greg Smith, director of National Register Programs for the Texas Historical Commission, encouraged us to broaden our investigations. As a result, fifteen of Rodríguez's projects in Texas are now listed on the National Register of Historic Places. Encouragement for recording this information in a book came from many sources, and in January 2004, with Maria's blessings, I began to put it all together. To my knowledge, this book is the first comprehensive documentation of this artist as well as the first book about faux bois in the United States.

During his lifetime, Rodríguez was rarely recognized publicly. Only four media references to his work while he was working have been discovered (as of 2007): *Popular Mechanics,* October 1927, referred to "Dionicio Rodríguez of Mexico City . . . the artist who is making concrete wood"; articles in Little Rock's *Arkansas Democrat* of August 6 and 8, 1933, described the dedication of Pugh's Old Mill and included his photograph and a quote from Rodríguez's speech; an article by Eldon Roarck in the June 20, 1935, *Commercial Appeal* of Memphis, Tennessee, featured a description of Rodríguez's "naturalistic" work at Memphis Memorial Park Cemetery and a photograph of the artisan; and a feature, "Holding the Mirror up to Nature," in the gravure section of the July 26, 1936, *Washington Star* that pictured Rodríguez and his hollow tree sculpture along with an article about "Mexico's famous naturalistic sculptor" and his work at Cedar Hill Cemetery.

Although the San Antonio Conservation Society's interest in the preservation of Rodríguez's work in the city had sparked local interest and attracted San Antonio media attention in the 1980s, national recognition of his work began in 1986 when historian Julie Vosmik Langan wrote National Register of Historic Places nominations for his projects at five sites in Arkansas (1986) and at the Memorial Park Cemetery in Memphis, Tennessee (1991). Numerous magazine and newspaper articles soon followed and continue to appear. Historian William Rutter's Inventory for St. Joseph's Church and Shrine for the Michigan Bureau of History (1990) provided us with valuable information and bibliographic source material.

One of the most important of Vosmik's sources was a series of letters between Rodríguez and Clovis Hinds, owner of Memorial Park Cemetery, spanning a period of nine years from 1933 to 1942. Copies of this correspondence, which were given to us by Hinds's granddaughter, Katherine Hinds Smythe, yielded important insight into the personality of both men and afforded a record of Rodríguez's work and travels during this period.

We were fortunate to have the opportunity to record oral histories of individuals who knew Rodríguez. Through the aid of Johanna Phelan, whose grandfather had hired the artisan in the 1930s to work on sculptures at his residence in Beaumont, Texas, the author located and interviewed Manuela Vargas Theall, Rodríguez's niece, who had come from Mexico to accompany Rodríguez to his various jobs throughout the United States during 1937 and 1938. She loaned us her personal collection of archival photographs, many of which appear in this book. Previously unpublished information also came from interviews with faux bois artisan Sam Murray, who shared recollections of his association and work with Rodríguez, and with Mrs. Guadalupe Del Toro, who traveled with her husband, Mauro, and others to jobs in Port Arthur and Beaumont. It is probable that other unknown projects exist; readers who know of sites not mentioned in this book are encouraged to contact the author in care of the editorial department of Texas A&M University Press.

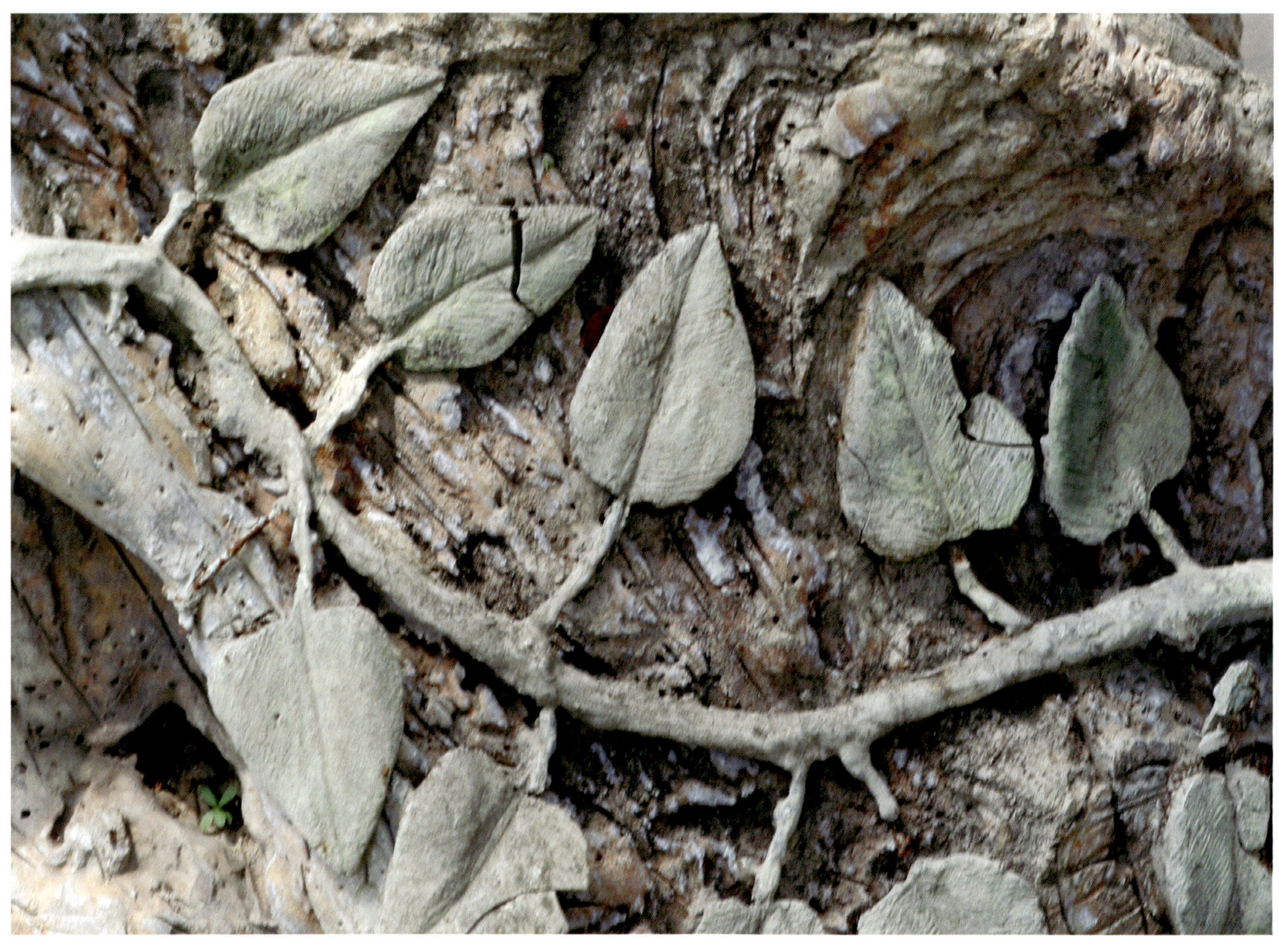

*Oak bark texture with vine, planter, private collection,
Austin, Texas. Photo: Bob Parvin.*

Acknowledgments

I owe many debts to people who have helped with this manuscript. In addition to those named in the preface, several individuals who have been interested in Rodríguez's life and his work generously shared information and their personal files: William Green, Ph.D., curator of history at the Panhandle-Plains Museum in Canyon, Texas; Mrs. Ruth Aubey of Beaumont, Texas; and San Antonians Stanley Schmidt and faux bois artisan Carlos Cortés, great-nephew of Rodríguez, who continues the tradition introduced to Texas by his uncle. Schmidt and Cortés also granted us interviews and allowed us to copy important documents and photographs. Tom Shelton, photo archivist at the Institute of Texan Cultures, University of Texas at San Antonio, was very helpful in locating archival photographs.

Valuable assistance came from San Antonio Central Library librarians Frank Faulkner and Matt DeWaelsche, volunteer Ira Lott in Texana/Genealogy, Angel Posadas in Inter-Library Loan, and Michael Kaminski and Wilson Plunkett in Government Documents; Beth Standifird, San Antonio Conservation Society Library; Martha Utterback and staff, Daughters of the Republic of Texas Library; Will Howard, Ron Lee, and Andy Hempe, Metropolitan Research Center at the Houston Public Library; Jonathan Gerland, Tyrrell Historical Library; Susan Arceneaux, Beaumont Historical Library; Director Maurine Gray and Archivist Penny Clark, Beaumont Public Library; Ray Cline and volunteer Yvonne Sutherlin, Port Arthur Public Library; Anne Prichard, Special Collections, University of Arkansas Libraries; and Houston historian Stephen Fox, Fellow of the Anchorage Foundation of Texas. Additional interviews and conversations with many individuals, site visits, and photography by the author and others further augmented our documentation.

My gratitude goes to the San Antonio Conservation Society for unwavering moral and continued financial support; Cappy and Suzy Lawton and Meta and Boo Hausser for their generous assistance in fundraising; Maria Pfeiffer for holding my hand throughout the years of work; my friend Laura Cadwallader for accompanying me on some of my travels; Gregory Smith, who continually urged us to delve deeper into our research and who allowed me to use some of his revisions to our National Register nominations; Dr. A. A. Urrutia for memories of his grandfather; Shelley Hendry, who assisted in keeping my house together while I was writing; my computer guru, San Antonian Helen Skeldon, who unselfishly provided her expertise and was teacher, editor, and advisor; photographer Bob Parvin, who caught the fanciful spirit of the artisan's genius; Mary Lenn Dixon, my Texas A&M University Press editor, who encouraged me through the actual publishing of the book; Sally E. Antrobus, my copy editor, whose expertise and helpful attitude polished my words; Diana Vance, editorial assistant, who patiently answered my incessant questions; Jennifer Ann Hobson, project editor, who guided my book to publication; and Barbara Mathews Whitehead, book designer, whose imagination captured the essence of the story and put it in visual form.

Hundreds of others deserve my thanks for helping me unravel the story of the elusive Rodríguez. If I have not listed your name, know that you are appreciated. Many generous friends and organizations shared their financial resources with Texas A&M University Press to assist with publishing costs (see Acknowledgment of Donors).

Special thanks go to my husband, Scotty Light; our family, Laurie Light Saunders and Bill, Myssie Light Acomb and Barry, and Walter Light; and our grandsons, William and Forrest Saunders. They not only helped measure, document, and photograph the works but also patiently endured my obsession with the "thrill of the chase," to borrow a phrase from historian James E. Crisp, Ph.D.

Many other individuals also contributed to this research, in countless ways. This extensive listing evidences the wide support received from individuals not recognized in Notes or elsewhere in the text:

Beulah Ahysen, *one of the owners of Eddingston Court*

Claire Alexander, *President, San Antonio Botanical Society*

Kellis Almond, *FAIA*

Candace Andrews, *Managing Director, San Antonio Botanical Society*

Ramon Aureliano, Armando Marcial, and Oscar Rubio, *Museum of Natural History, Mexico City*

Elise Barenblat, *great-granddaughter of Dr. Aureliano Urrutia*

Rick Barongi, Brian Hill, Hannah Bailey, William "Trey" Todd, Jerry Caraviotis, Ed Santos, and Joe Williams, *all of Houston Zoo*

Eugene Bean, *San Antonio River Authority cartographer*

Bryan Beadles, *Tennessee Historical Commission*

Denise Blackson, *Fort Lincoln Cemetery*

D. Ray Blakely

Adrienne Atwell Bogaerts

Michael Casey, *attorney*

Betty Cavender

Berta Cea-Echenique, *United States Embassy, Mexico City*

Robert Christiansen, *National Register of Historic Places and Michigan Historical Commission*

Mark Cooper, *Restland Cemetery*

Ranessa L. Cooper, Ph.D., *Director, Slayton Arboretum, Hillsdale College*

Jessie Cox

Andy Crews

Rick Dewees, *City of Houston*

Sister Mary Ann Domagalski, *Missionary Servants of St. Anthony*

Nina Eckstein, Lena Le Moal, and Francine Rowden, *French translators*

Elizabeth Elizandro, *North Little Rock Visitors Bureau*

Patty Elizondo and Dora Guerra, *research assistance*

Glen Evans

Ellen Engelke

Jo Lois Fuqua Ewing

Heather Ferguson, *Librarian, McNay Art Museum*

Rodolfo Flores, *River City Silver*

Linda Follis, *Moye Retreat Center Director*

William Cruse Fuqua, M.D.

W. Eugene George, *FAIA*

Deborah Gust, *Curt Teich Postcard Archives*

Kent Gutschke

Wayne Guthrie

Dennis Hamilton and Chad Blount, *Memorial Park Cemetery*

Katherine Lateer Hamison

Linda Hardberger, *Director, Tobin Theatre Arts Collection, McNay Art Museum*

V. J. Harper, *Eddingston Court information*

Michael Haynes, *Curator, Witte Museum*

Sister Dianne Heinrich, *C.D.P., Sisters of Divine Providence*

Kay Hindes, *Staff Archeologist, City of San Antonio*

Rebecca Huffstutler, *Director of Collections, Witte Museum*

Cecilia Hunter, *Archivist, Texas A&M University at Kingsville*

Frances James

Charles Jarrell, *Office of Cultural Affairs, City of San Antonio*

Barbara Johnson, Ron Bauml, and Roland Flores, *San Antonio Conservation Society*

Kevin Keim, *Charles Moore House*

Janelle Kleberg, *faux bois photograph*

Patrick Lamalle, *Institute of Texan Cultures, University of Texas at San Antonio*

Angela Lashaway, *Publications Design Coordinator, External Affairs, Hillsdale College*

Annie MacDonald, *Southeast Tennessee Development Office*

Frank Manaco, *Pyramid Stone Company*

Sandra and Curtis Maricle

Pinkie Martin, *former president, San Antonio Conservation Society*

Walter Nold Mathis, *Preservationist*

Ann Benson McGlone, *Historic Preservation Officer, City of San Antonio*

Char Miller, Ph.D., *history professor and Director, Urban Studies, Trinity University*

Dannielle Nelson, *graphic artist*

Michael Nye

Susan Oakes, *basket artisan*

Marion Oettinger Jr., Ph.D., *Director, San Antonio Museum of Art*

George Parish Sr.; Tom Parish; Wilson Parish Sr.; and Wilson Parish Jr.; *Alamo Photo Labs*

James Pearson, *Director, St. Elizabeth's Hospital*

Kelli Peters, *Registrar, Arkansas Historic Preservation Program*

Carmen Pfeinninger, *owner of faux bois gas station palapa by Basilio Aguilar*

Dianne Powell

Barbara Ras, *Director, Trinity University Press*

Tate Roberts, *photographs of Pugh's Mill*

San Antonio City Parks and Recreation Staff: Rodney Dzuik, *Park Design Superintendent;* Steven Coussoulis, *Parks Operations Supervisor, and his staff member* Benny Obledo; Scott Stover, *Parks Project Manager;* Richard Thompson, *Senior Horticulturist;* Nora Ward, *Spanish Governor's Palace Curator;* and Jamaal Moreno, *Brackenridge Park Rehabilitation Project Assistant Curator.*

John Sellers, Ph.D.

Helen Sherwood, *volunteer, Washingtonian Division of D.C. Public Library*

Kate Singleton

Sandra Keiler Smith and Cary Bradburn, *North Little Rock History Commission*

Claudette Stager, *Tennessee Historical Commission*

David Stallworth, *San Antonio City Planner Two*

Jack Stansbury, *AIA*

Jim Steely, *former director of National Register Programs in Texas*

Kwana Stephens and Dan Jones, *Elmwood Cemetery*

Ken Sullivan, *Executive Director, Lakewood Property Owners Association*

Sister Patrice Sullivan

Erin Teare, *Mrs. Henry Phelan's secretary*

Joe Thompson

Donna Vaughan, *Secretary, Alamo Heights Terrell Hills Garden Club*

Jill Vexler, Ph.D., *cultural anthropologist and exhibitions curator*

Carmelita Walker, Jesse Walker, and Wayne Latney, *Cedar Hill Cemetery*

Roger Wallace, *formerly Minister Counselor for Commercial Affairs, United States Embassy, Mexico City*

Ray Washington, *Old Calvary Hill Cemetery*

Dixie Watkins, III, *landscape architect, loan of Alamo Cement Company archival photos*

Don Weber, *antique car advisor*

Diane White, Kelly Sheftall, Sadie Allen, and Machelle Baird, *Haven River Inn—Lamb's Tale Ministries*

Ralph Wilcox, *National Register of Historic Places, and Survey Coordinator for Arkansas Historic Preservation Program*

Harold Williams, *Oakland Cemetery*

Lee Young, *AdTech Photographic Laboratories, Inc.*

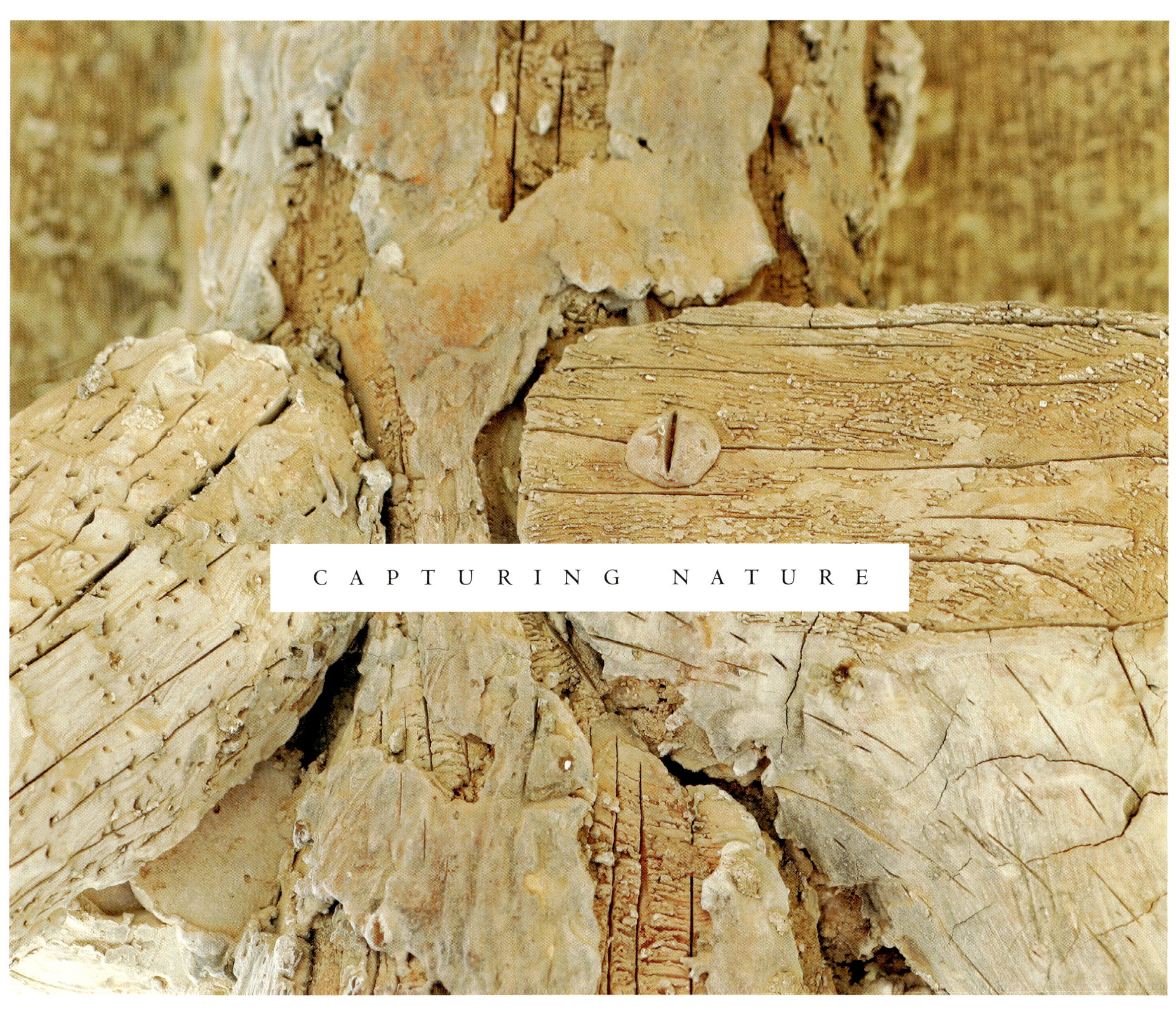

CAPTURING NATURE

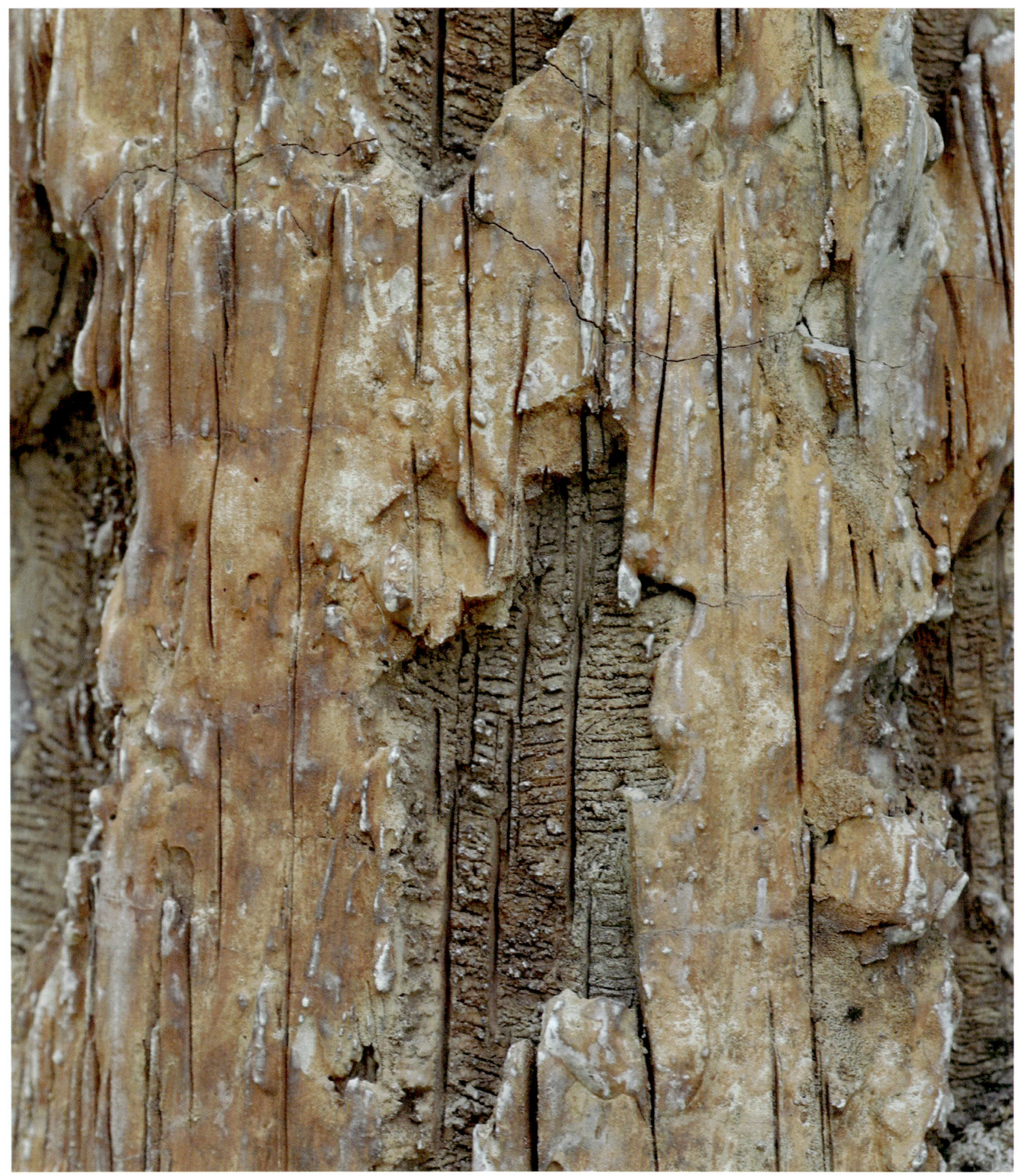

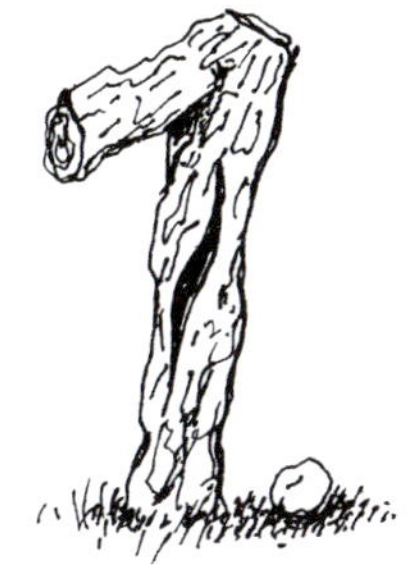

The Rustic Tradition

Mexican artisan Dionicio Rodríguez was a skilled practitioner of the technique variously described as *rustic, trabajo rústico* (rustic work), or *faux bois* (imitation wood).[1] Though he and his work were largely unrecognized for many years, individuals, conservation groups, and folk art historians have begun to realize their importance.[2] There is increased public interest in the genre, as evidenced by imports of older European (mostly French) pieces by antique dealers throughout the United States and in the emergence of contemporary artisans who are producing new works using Rodríguez's technique.[3]

Opposite: *Pine bark, Albert Steves gazebo, Comfort, Texas. Photo: Bob Parvin.*
Below: *Pagoda and bridge commissioned by the Duke d'Uzes at Bonnelles, France, ca. 1780 (not extant). Engraving by Georges-Louis Le Rouge. Courtesy of Bibliothèque nationale de France.*

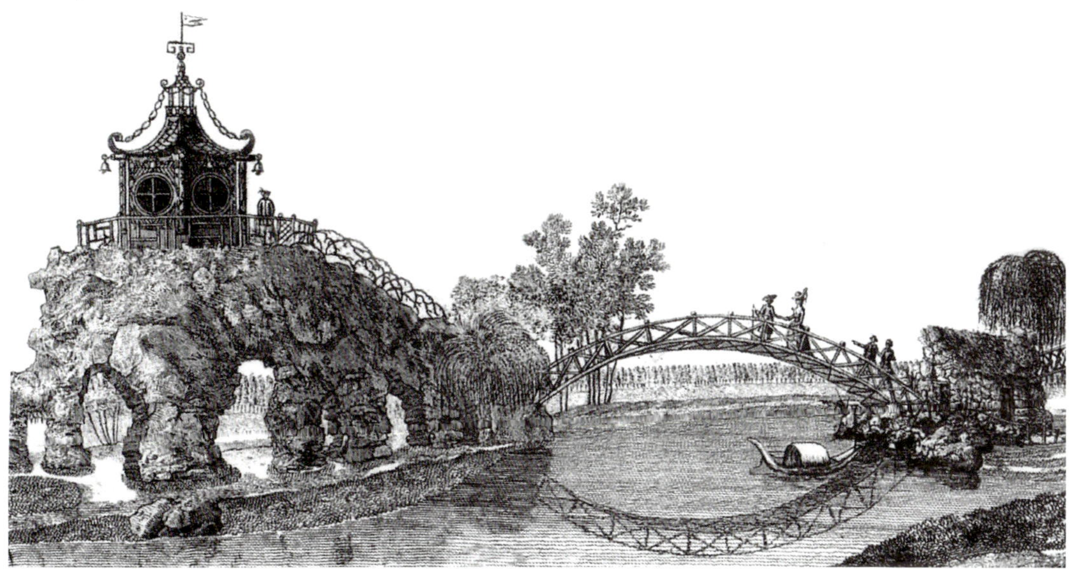

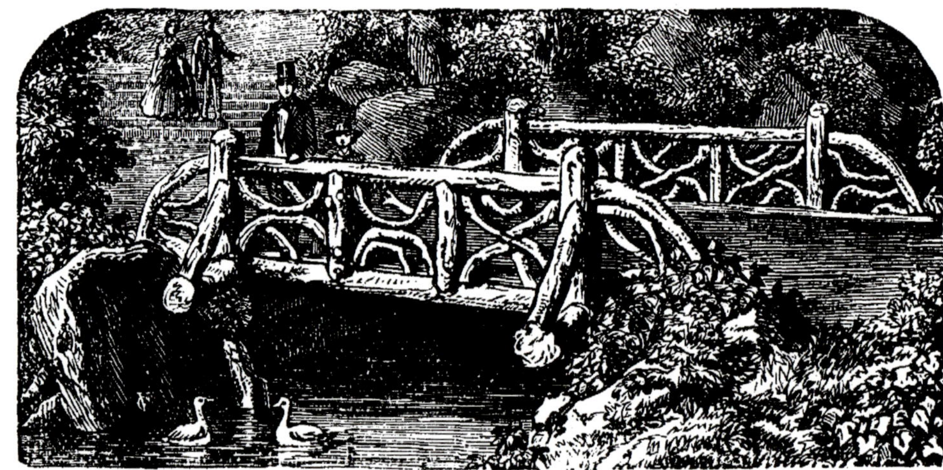

Drawing by Calvert Vaux for Central Park Bridge, from his Villas and Cottages: A Series of Designs Prepared for Execution in the United States.

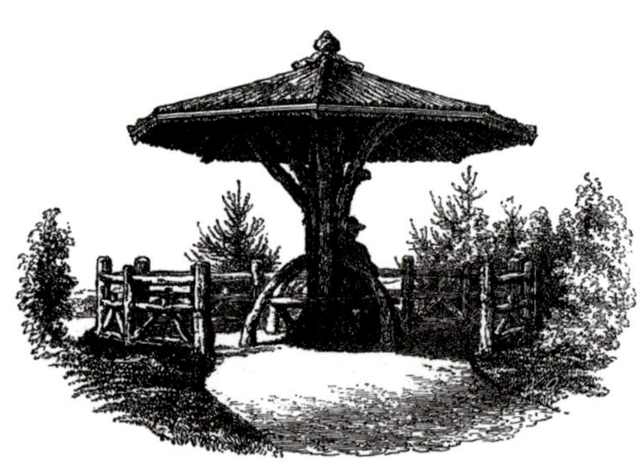

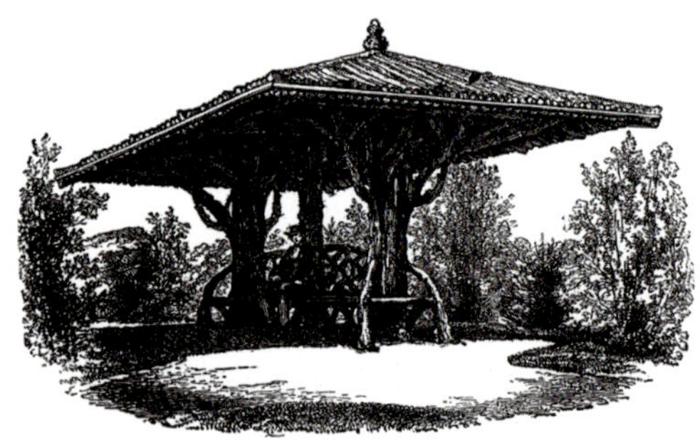

Illustrations by Calvert Vaux for Central Park, from his Villas and Cottages.

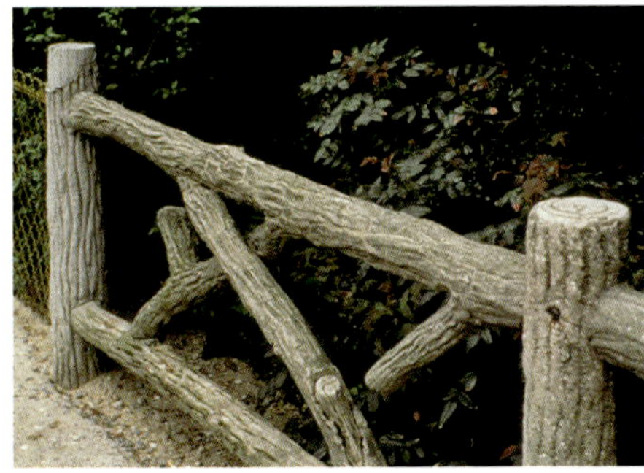

Branch railing, Parc Buttes-Chaumont, Paris, France. Courtesy of Elizabeth Barlow Rogers.

Over a period of more than twenty years, from 1924 to the early 1950s, Dionicio Rodríguez traveled through eight states creating reinforced concrete sculptural works that imitated the natural forms and textures of rocks and wood. His great-nephew by marriage, Carlos Cortés, who continues to practice this art form today, describes Rodríguez's naturalistic style as "organic."[4] Rodríguez's designs include gates, fences, bridges, steps, grottos, fountains, baskets, hollow tree shelters, fallen tree and thatched roof benches, tables, and building façades.

Antecedents

Dionicio Rodríguez's use of the rustic theme in garden design has documented antecedents in Europe, Asia, Central and South America, and the United States that span several centuries. Many early rustic garden designs executed in wood were associated with whimsical themes and known as follies, as exemplified by Marie Antoinette's folly, the Petit Trianon at Versailles. A less well known example was the fanciful pagoda and bridge at Bonnelles, France, commissioned by the Duke d'Uzes, ca. 1780.[5] The tiny structure on an artificial rockwork island in a lake was reached by a series of arched wooden bridges that are amazingly similar to chinoiserie-style cement bridges built by Rodríguez 150 years later.

In the United States A. J. Downing designed naturalistic landscapes in the 1840s, and landscape engineer George Woodward's drawings of rustic wooden seats were published in 1869 in Woodward's *Architecture and Rural Art*.[6] Architect Calvert Vaux, who, with Frederick Law Olmsted, was responsible for much of the early design of Central Park, published

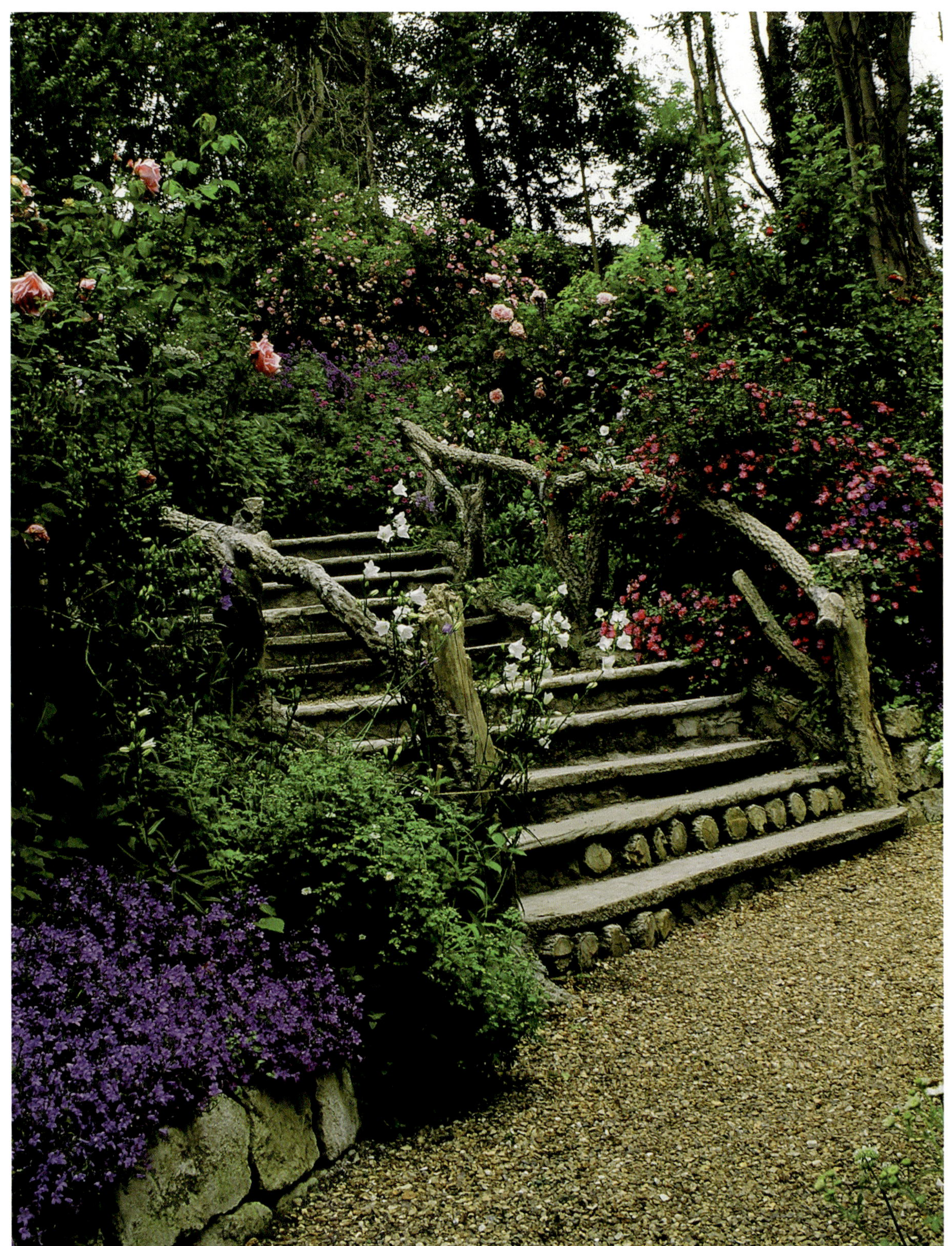

One of two log stairways in the garden of the Musée Hotel Baudy, Giverny, France. The garden is noted for its two thousand old rose bushes. Photo: © Elizabeth Murray.

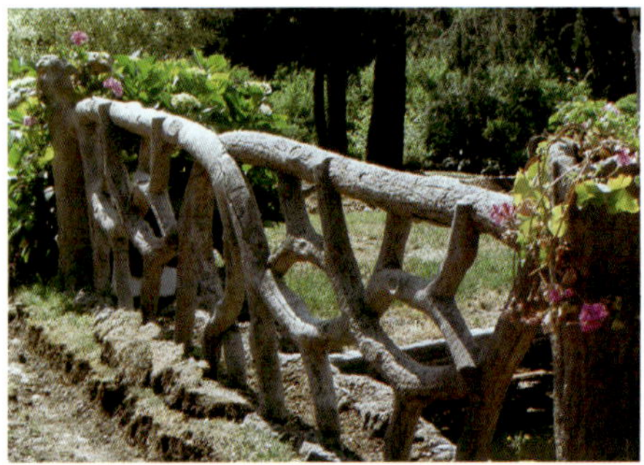

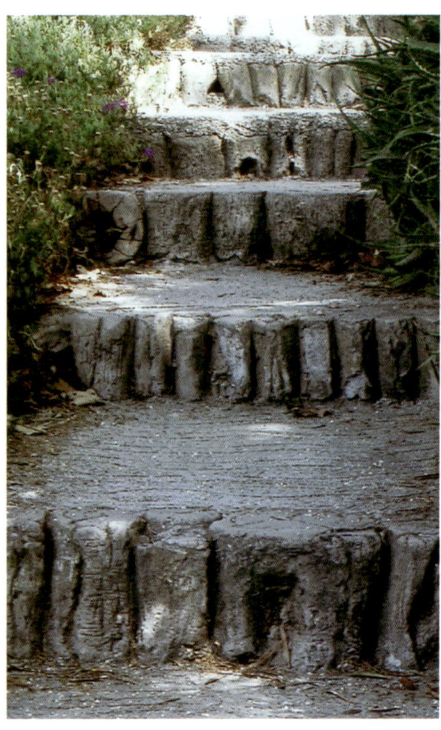

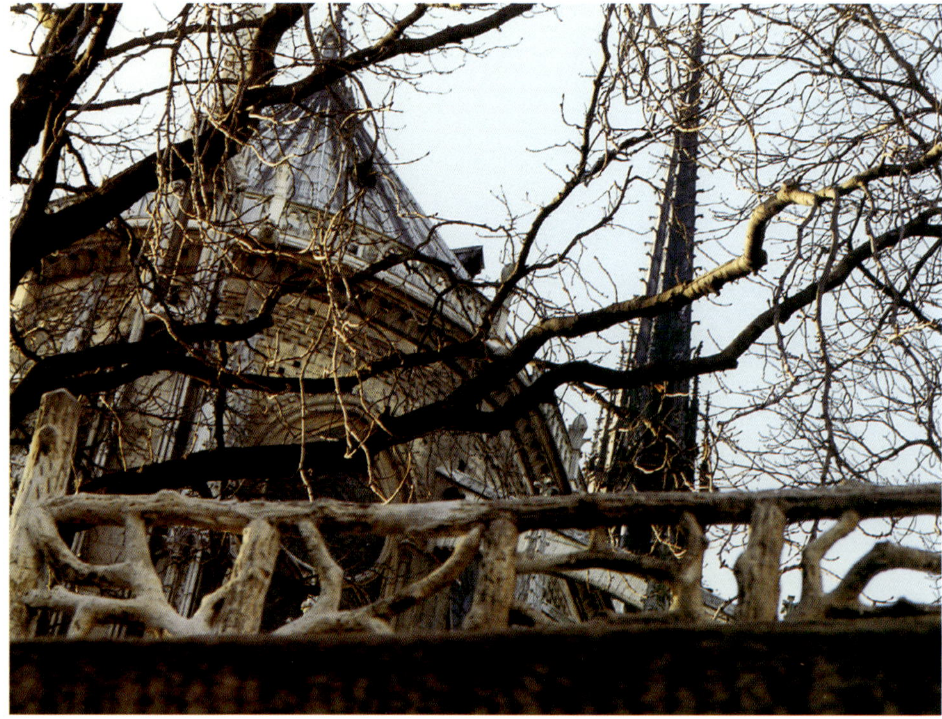

Top: *Fence at Yidliz Park, Istanbul, Turkey, built in 1877. Photo: Kathleen and Curtis Gunn.*
Above: *Steps in the garden of Villa Ephrussi de Rothschild, Saint-Jean-Cap-Ferrat, France. Photo: Curtis Gunn.*
Above right: *Log detail, outbuilding behind Notre Dame Cathedral, Paris, France. Photo: Bill Saunders.*

drawings of a rustic wooden bridge and shelters for the park in 1854.[7] Several of these structures have been reconstructed using the original drawings.[8] Rustic wooden gazebos, seats, and shelters perched on overlooks at Lake Mohonk Mountain House west of New Paltz, New York, serve as retreats for city dwellers during the heat of summer.

It is not surprising to find examples of cement sculpture in nineteenth-century Europe when we read that the earliest exponent of the use of reinforced concrete for garden decoration was a French gardener, Joseph Monier. In about 1850 he developed the technique of using wire to reinforce concrete and created garden containers for plants: tubs, garden pots, and tanks.[9] He patented his invention in 1867 and exhibited at the Paris Exhibition that year.[10] Numerous faux bois artisans, many of whom did not sign their work, followed. Hilaire Muzard and his son Charles, of Avon, France, have been identified for their work in the genre for clients in the late 1800s; their home was embellished with rustic cement ornamentation.[11]

Landscape scholar John Beardsley wrote that faux bois pieces were "incorporated into the landscape of public parks in nineteenth-century Europe."[12] Concrete wooden stairways and railings can be seen in two parks in the environs of Paris—Parc Buttes-Chaumont and Parc Montouris—and there are two stairways at the Musée Hotel Baudy in Giverny,

France.[13] A small building behind Notre Dame Cathedral in Paris has a wood-textured façade and roof and bears a plaque reading "Ciment Arme, Travaux Rustiques" (reinforced concrete, rustic works) and identifying the artisan as J. Dunaigre. There are several examples of faux bois in the Villa Ephrussi de Rothschild at Saint-Jean-Cap-Ferrat on the French coast, including a series of steps.

In Turkey the entrance road and gardens of the Sale Kiosk built by Sultan Abdulhamid in Yidliz Park outside Istanbul have faux wood bridges built in 1877, and a bridge is in the city of Tekidag, west of Istanbul.[14] Faux wood cement work is also found in Japan, where it is called *giboku*.[15] Other examples exist in Italy, Belgium, Buenos Aires in Argentina, and in several cities in Mexico—Monterrey, Toluca, Mexico City, and Zacatecas.[16]

Overview of Rodríguez's Work

Difficult economic times and the revolution in Mexico brought a wave of Mexican immigrants to San Antonio, and "new genres of folk art appeared: cement sculpture, jail art and murals." Folklorists differentiate between folk art objects that have an aesthetic function (those which give decorative pleasure) and folk craft (those which are utilitarian).[17] With some exceptions, Rodríguez's work falls within both categories.

This influx of Mexican artisans, musicians, and performers has a long history. In the mid- to late sixteenth century, a training school for artisans was established in Mexico City. Records from the five San Antonio missions reveal that this school provided individuals for their construction. It is also documented that others from throughout Mexico contributed their talents.[18] In 1748 two men were recruited from San Luis Potosí to work on the construction of the San Fernando Cathedral: "*maestro* Geranimo de Ibarra, a builder-stonemason (*abañil*) and Felipe de Santiago, a stone-cutter (*cantero*)." Ibarra remained for the completion of the cathedral and later joined Santiago, who had left to work on Mission Concepción.[19]

Rodríguez's story parallels those of many talented and creative individuals who came north during the years from the 1920s to the 1940s. In South Texas, because of proximity to the Mexican border, people with special skills came to settle. Don Emiliano Garcia, a sixth-generation weaver from Mexico, wove saddle blankets for the King Ranch near Kingsville, and bootmaker Leopoldo Torres worked his craft in Raymondville.[20]

San Antonio proved to be a magnet for a series of Hispanic artisans. Stone carver and master mason Reymundo Rodríguez worked with the Hunts, a noted stonemason family. Decorative cement tile maker Larry Peña made tile for the McNay residence (now an art museum) and Mi Tierra Restaurant's Mariachi Bar in Market Square. Ceramic tile designer Fernando Ramos and Angel Rendón, a rope and palm leaf weaver, tile setter, and

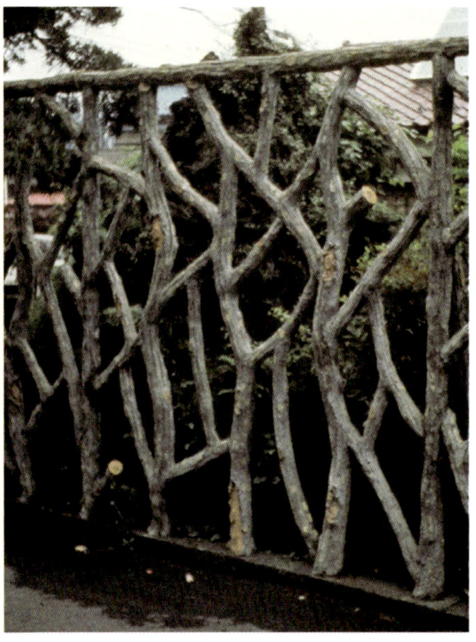

Giboku fence, Honshu, Japan. The photographer studied the technique while living there. Photo: Sharon Crutchfield.

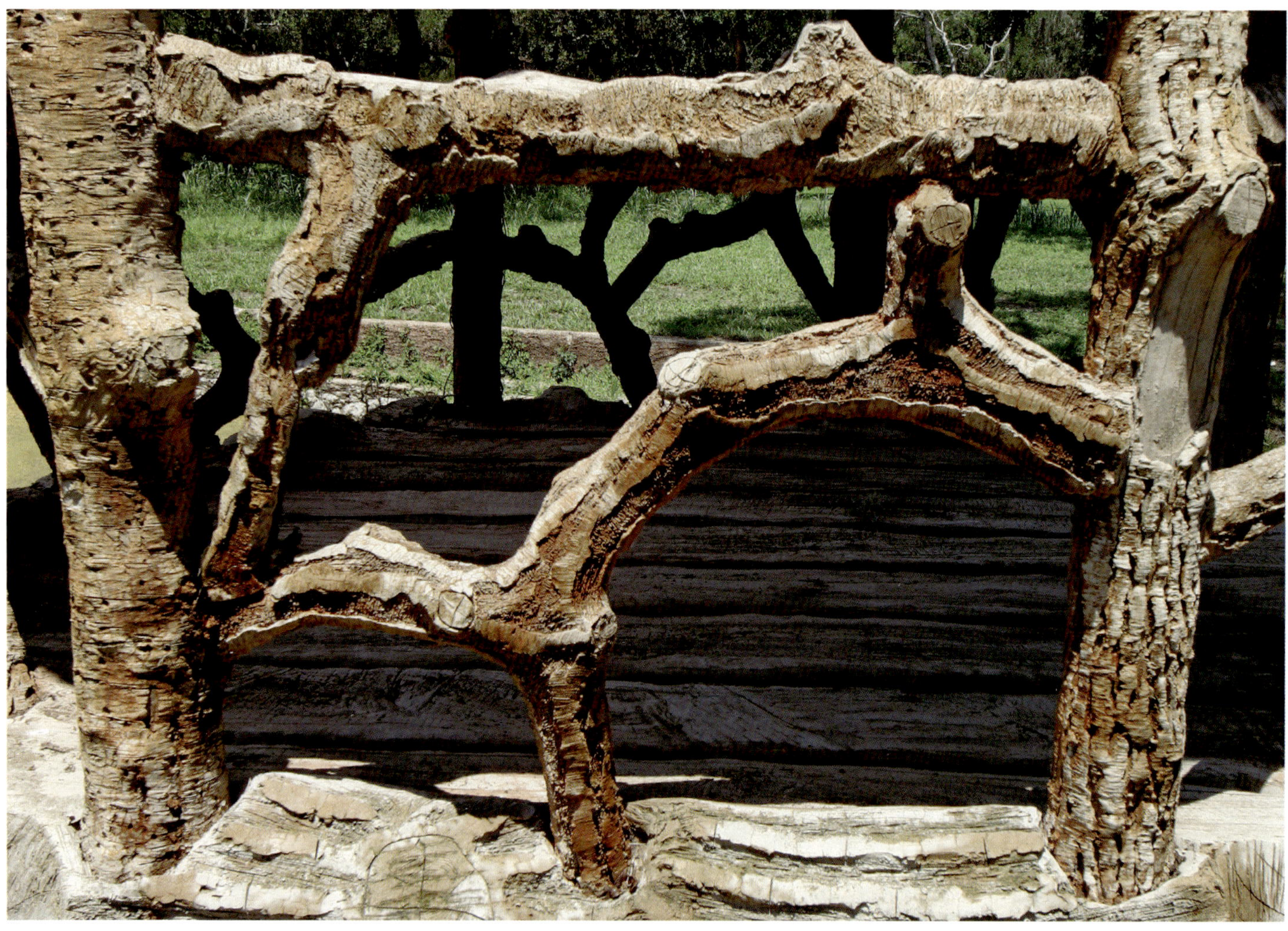

Detail, branch rail of James Richard Marmion's gazebo, private property, Brazoria County, Texas. Photo: Bob Parvin.

all-around craftsman, both worked at the Mexican Arts and Crafts workshop organized by preservationist Ethel Wilson Harris on the downtown banks of the San Antonio River; it was later moved to Mission San José and renamed Mission Crafts. Ceramic sculptor José Varela worked at the D'Hanis Brick and Tile Company (near San Antonio), where he fired his clay figures along with the brick in the kilns. Metal forgers Helario and Jesús Gonzales worked for Theo Voss Artistic Metalworks. And the classical music composer and noted violin soloist Silvestre Revueltas was concert master of the Aztec and Majestic movie theater orchestras.[21]

When Rodríguez was working in Texas and throughout the United States, there were other artisans practicing the trabajo rústico genre. It can be assumed that several of them

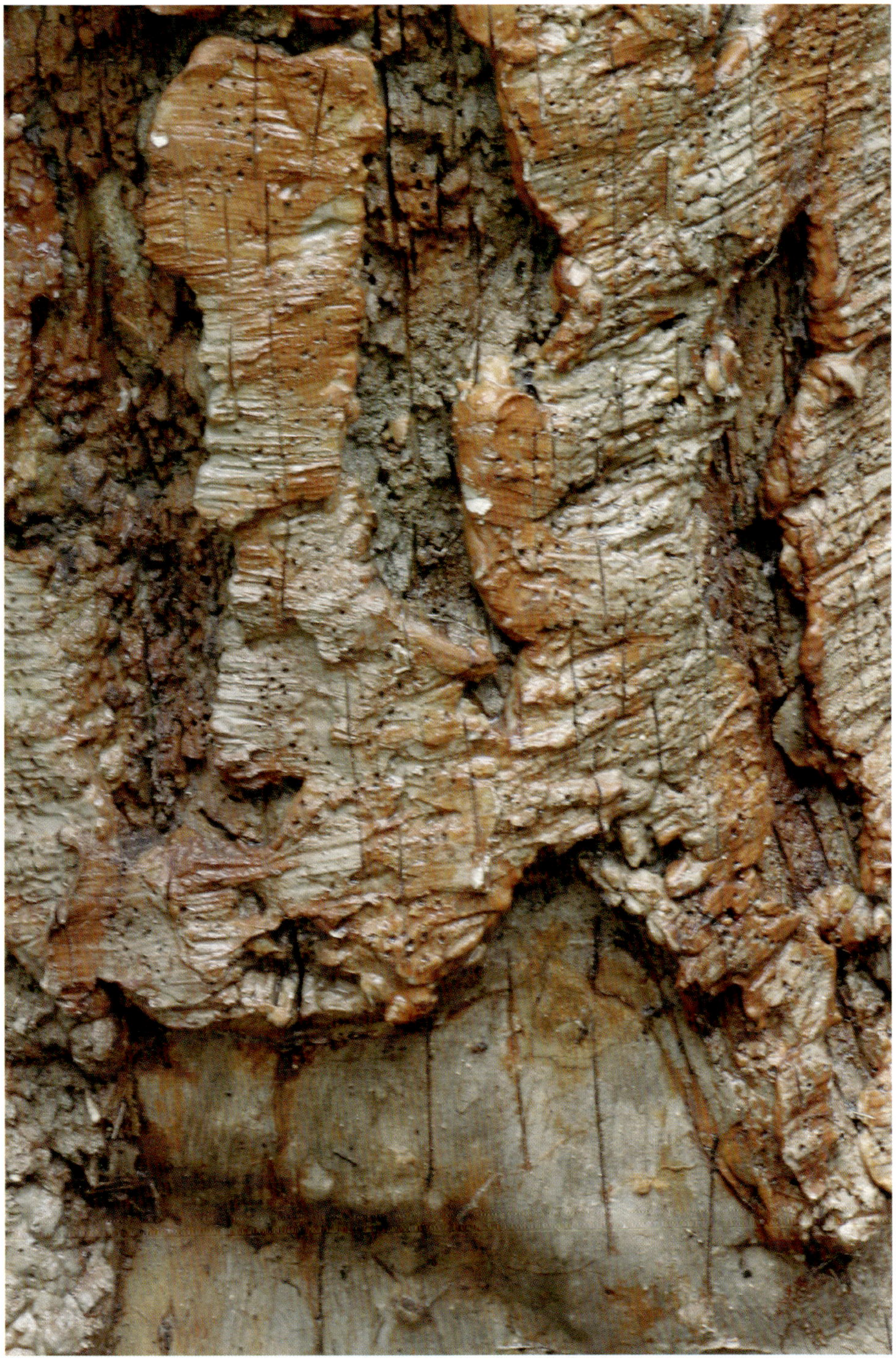

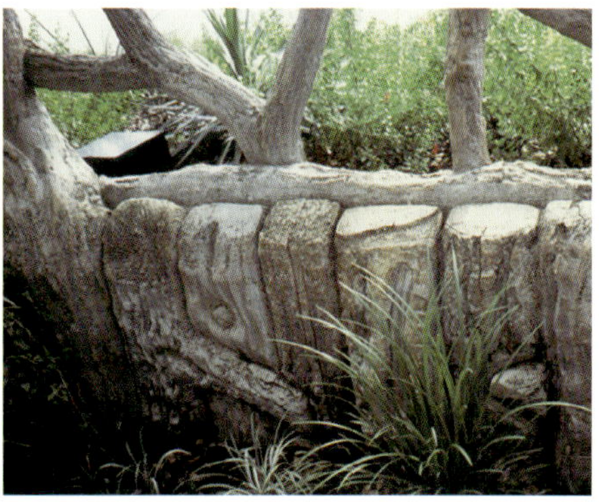

Left: *Detail, base of James Richard Marmion's gazebo, private property, Brazoria County, Texas. Photo: Bob Parvin.*
Above: *Fence detail, Alamo Cement Company office, San Antonio. Photo: Patsy Light.*

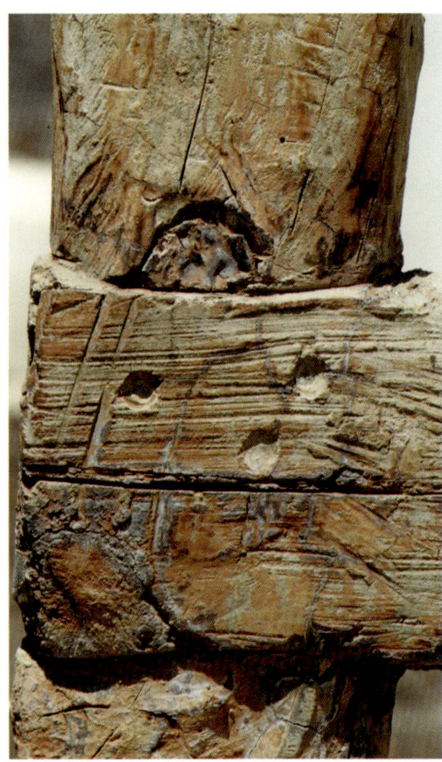

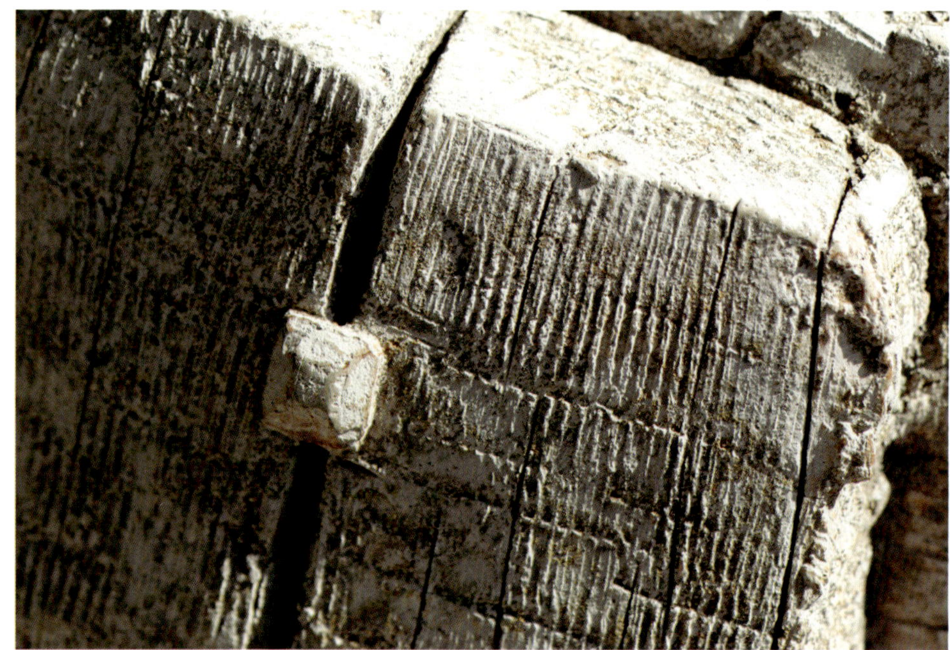

Right: *Pyramid-headed bolt, Brackenridge Park,*
San Antonio. Photo: Bob Parvin.
Above: *Countersunk screws, Spanish Governor's Palace,*
San Antonio. Photo: Bob Parvin.

learned the technique by working with him, among them Maximo Cortés and his brothers, Ruben and Carlos; Julius Tober (father-in-law of Maximo); Mauro Del Toro; Rafael (Ralph) Corona; and George Cardosa.[22] Sam Murray, who began working in concrete with Southern Cement Products, fabricators of precast "stone" for the Milam Building, later joined the ranks of faux bois artisans and taught Pedro Ximénez.[23] Maximo Cortés and Murray opened their own businesses, and examples of their sculpture are seen in and around San Antonio.

Additional cement artisans included Basilio Aguilar, Modesto Dena, Dionicio Rosales, Tony Lopez, J. M. Martínez, C. Ramírez, and Eliseo Alvarado.[24] Julian Sandoval produced works and was also a mold maker for others, including Sam Murray.[25] Genaro Briones, an Austin bricklayer and plasterer, worked with Rodríguez in Memphis, Tennessee, probably at Memorial Park Cemetery. In 1947 Briones built his own house in Austin using brightly colored low relief designs and faux wood and stone cement surfaces. Rodríguez visited the house during the construction.[26]

Although there are fine extant works by the sculptors mentioned (and others whose identities are unknown), it is generally agreed that Rodríguez was the most skilled practitioner of the genre. Examples of other artisans' work in San Antonio are in the Friedrich family burial plot in the City Cemetery No. 1 by an unidentified sculptor; a *palapa* shelter over gas pumps by Basilio Aguilar at 3011 North St. Mary's Street; animal enclosures at

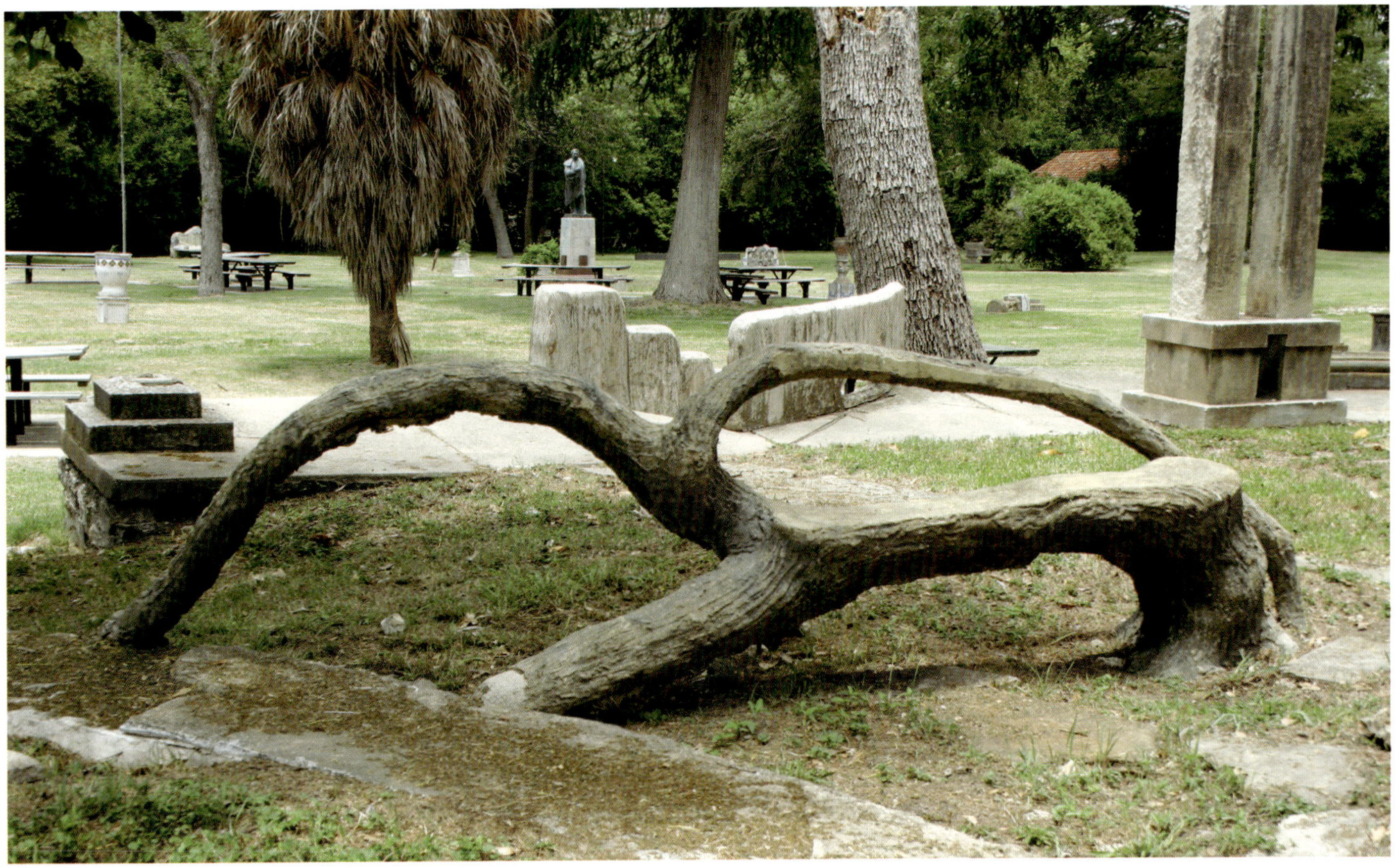

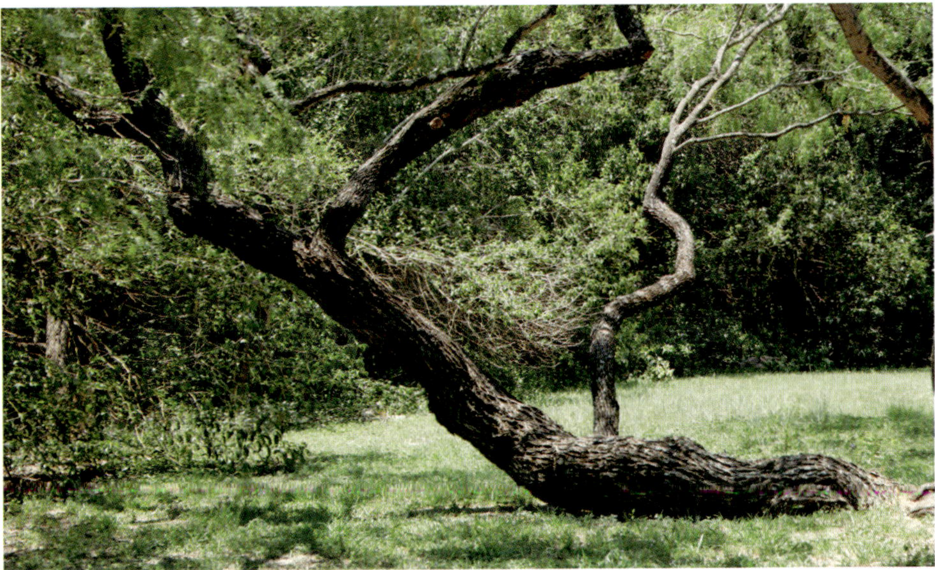

Above: *Fallen tree bench, Miraflores, San Antonio. This bench was possibly the first of this style made by Rodríguez in the United States. Photo: Bob Parvin.*
Left: *Mesquite tree trunk, San Antonio.*
Photo: Bob Parvin.

the San Antonio Zoo by Tony Lopez; a tree trunk gate by Maximo Cortés (originally for the Henry Guerra house, now at the Witte Museum); and a house façade by Mauro Del Toro. The rustic cement *canales* (roof drains) on the reconstructed granary and mill at Mission San José de Aguayo in San Antonio have all the characteristics of Rodríguez's style; however, no documents have been found to substantiate this claim. The work could have been executed by one of his contemporaries or made of cast concrete.

Close inspection of Rodríguez's work reveals attention to details and sensitive treatment of materials not always found in the work of his peers. His careful molding of bark textures, with worm holes, peeling sections, and lichen, and his sensitively formed drooping and twisted branches and heavily grooved tree trunks challenge the onlooker to separate the real from the art form. His work, in comparison with that of others, possesses a fanciful spirit; his sensuous forms appear almost like graceful dancing figures, while his treatment of "rock" surfaces imitates the cragged textures and massive naturalistic forms of boulders and ledges.

Despite the high quality of his sculpture, it is sometimes difficult to distinguish his pieces from those of others because he did not always sign his work. Positive identification is further complicated by the scarcity of both primary and secondary source material.

A majority of Rodríguez's sculpted pieces can be categorized into three groups with distinctive characteristics: faux wood, faux stone, and natural stone works. The bridges and fences have bark-covered branch handrails, intertwined horizontal and diagonal branches for their guardrails, and planed and crosscut logs for their footpaths. Birdbaths were a combination of faux wood and stone. Two gate entries are styled with crossed tree trunks at the apex. His hollow tree houses are strikingly similar in design to hermit's huts or hermitages, follies that decorated the landscaped gardens of wealthy landowners, particularly during the romantic age of the nineteenth century. These small structures housed "paid hermits" and/or true religious people who chose to live a solitary life. The artisan's tree houses are modeled with heavily textured bark surfaces; one is faced and lined with conch shells. All have openings for doors and/or windows that accommodate standing adults. One of the tree houses is utilized as an entry gate; others have carved interior seats. Archival photographs reveal that Rodríguez built scaffolding to facilitate construction of the houses. Unfortunately, the tree house that he built for himself as his home in San Antonio has been demolished.

Fallen tree benches copy the growth pattern of the live oak and mesquite trees that are found in Rodríguez's native Mexico and in South Texas. Occasionally, entire trees or single branches bend at a 90-degree angle and continue to grow parallel with the ground. His benches have smooth planed surfaces on the seats and backrests and rough bark on the exterior.

Many of Rodríguez's works depict wooden shade structures with bundled straw roofs, known in Mexico as *palapas*. Using cement, he reproduced the technique in minute detail. The straw is bound into neat bundles and positioned on the log trusses in parallel rows. The roofs are of various styles, hipped, gabled, and "mushroom." Included in this group are a tree trunk bus stop, slat benches, tables of crosscut planks with log benches, a log shelter enclosing a fountain, gazebos, and two oriental-style portals reminiscent of Torii gates. These gates mark entrances to Shinto shrines as seen in Japan, where they indicate the division between physical and spiritual worlds; they possess three basic architectural elements, "two pillars with a straight crosspiece at the top and a lintel above it, usually curving upward."[27]

One-of-a-kind sculpted works include a ten-thousand-pound working mill wheel, a barbeque pit shaped as a tree trunk (not extant), and a cave lined with crystals from the Ozarks. Conch shells are the most unusual material found in Rodríguez's sculptures. In Port Arthur, Texas, he used the conch shells to face the surface of a fence and to line the walls of a hollow tree house.

Two known building façades are of different simulated materials. One in San Antonio appears to be a structure clad with horizontal boards; the other, in Memphis, is faced with cut stone. Pyramid-headed steel bolts are present in many of the pieces, and counter-sunk screws are sometimes evident.

During his early work in Mexico, Rodríguez became proficient at creating artificial rocks and stone. He is credited with creating artificial cut stone facings, boulders, pathways, canals, chairs, and fountains of layered cement rock throughout the United States.

Several projects of natural honeycomb limestone were constructed during the early 1940s. Three were in the San Antonio area, a Stations of the Cross site and two grottos, and two in Houston, a fountain and a planter. His niece Manuela Vargas Theall said that during the World War II years it was difficult for Rodríguez to acquire materials, which may account for his use of readily available local rock.[28]

Several Rodríguez projects were monumental undertakings of a kind attempted by few of his peers: the planned landscape environments, including seven cemeteries and the Old Mill at T. R. Pugh Memorial Park in North Little Rock, Arkansas; Eddingston Court in Port Arthur, Texas; and the Phelan residence in Beaumont, Texas (not extant). Only the McCourtie Park work by two of his associates, Corona and Cardosa, rivals these large-scale Rodríguez installations. These projects were mostly commissioned through word-of-mouth recommendations by wealthy men, who hired Rodríguez to embellish their personal gardens and commercial properties. His rustic sculptures were appropriate embellishments for the new cemeteries with flat burial markers that were being developed during this period.

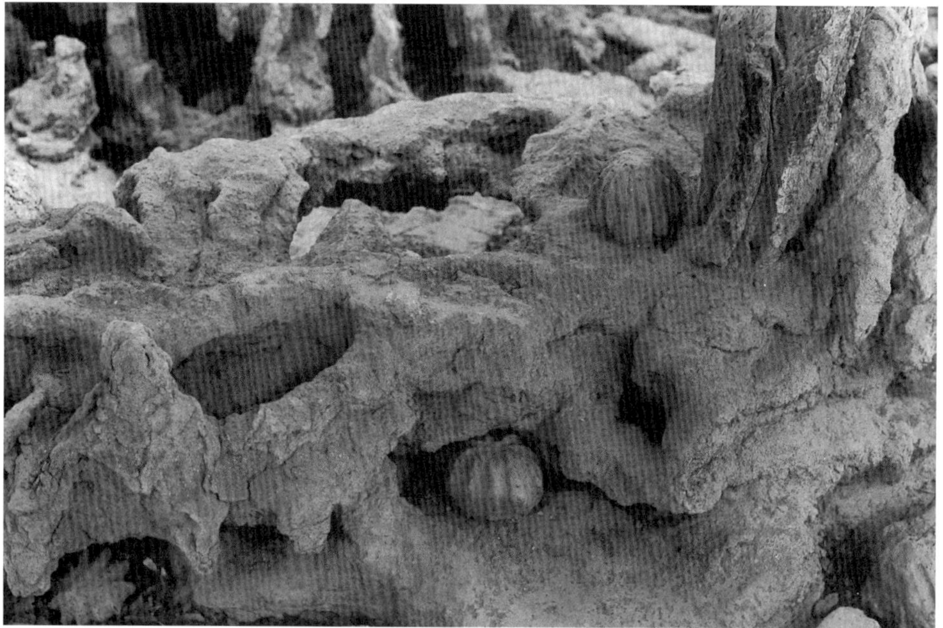

Right: *Cacti nestled in the crevices of Alamo Cement Company palapa fountain. Photo: Patsy Light.*
Below: *Cactus at Alamo Cement Company palapa fountain. Photo: Bob Parvin.*

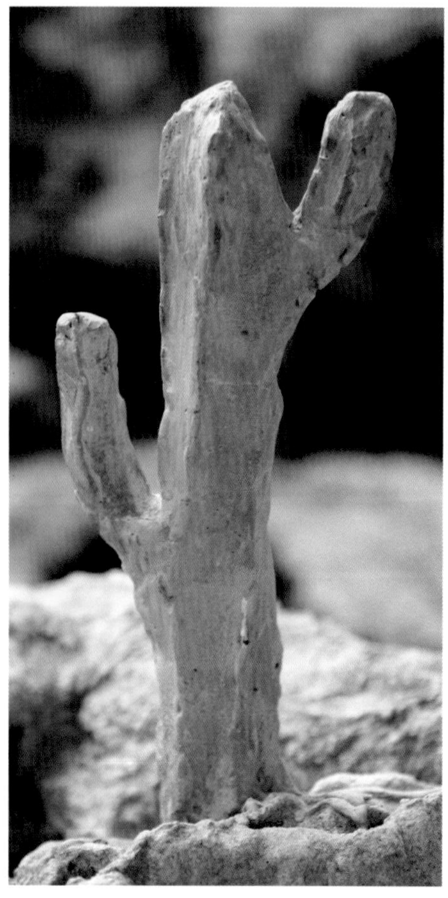

Examples of theme-oriented environments include a cave, a tomb, and a pool at Memorial Park Cemetery in Memphis; the Stations of the Cross and grotto at the Shrine of St. Anthony of Padua in San Antonio; and the Old Mill in North Little Rock. A close viewing of Rodríguez's work reveals bits of whimsy that suggest a keen sense of humor:

- two entwined snakes on supporting posts and small cactus plants nestled in crevices on the edge of the fish pond at the Alamo Cement Company in San Antonio
- the glass-eyed owl in a knothole in the steps at Couchwood
- an owl that once sat perched on the hollow tree house gate in Miraflores
- cactus plants on the bridge at Pugh's Old Mill and along the stream at the Houston Zoo aviary
- a diving board, conch shell grotto, and cacti at Eddingston Court
- the tree trunk water fountain at Lakewood Park and the fountain in the Pool of Hebron at Memorial Park Cemetery, both embellished with human faces
- the tree trunk barbeque pit at Little Switzerland
- mushrooms at Pugh's Old Mill and Memorial Park Cemetery

- hollow tree houses, one with a bird house at Lakewood Park
- two hearts applied to branches on the bridge in Brackenridge Park

All attest to a playful yet subtle aspect of this man, who was described by some as having a very sober temperament.

The extent of Rodríguez's travels is evidenced by known remaining examples of his artistry that are found in Texas, Arkansas, Maryland, Michigan, Illinois, Tennessee, Alabama, and New Mexico. His work is listed on the National Register of Historic Places at fifteen sites in Texas, five in Arkansas, and one in Tennessee.[29] In addition, the sculpture created by Corona, with Rodríguez's assistance, at St. Joseph's Church and Shrine in Cambridge Township, Lenawee County, Michigan, was listed by the Bureau of History, Michigan Department of State, in 1990.

It is interesting to note that a large body of his work was done during the lean years of the Great Depression. His labor was cheap and the materials were inexpensive. Rodríguez wrote of his work, "It doesn't take much material or time and gives wonderful results."[30]

Rodríguez left few commentaries about his work, and if he made preliminary drawings or sketches, they have not been found. Many of his pieces, like the fallen tree benches, hollow tree houses, and palapa-roofed tables and benches, which he repeated at several sites, were obviously his original designs, but others, including the Annie Laurie Chair and the Cave of Machpelah, appear to have been dictated by his clients. Manuela Theall recalled only one event when her uncle sketched a design. On that occasion, the manager of Cedar Hill in Suitland, Maryland, showed him a magazine photo or picture of an Egyptian bench, requesting one about eleven feet long, and Rodríguez responded with a drawing of a dragon and a flower for the bench ornamentation.[31]

Rodríguez's work did not afford him the same recognition achieved by other Mexican artists and creative individuals who became famous in the United States during the period of intense nationalism following the revolution in Mexico: Diego Rivera, for his mural for the Detroit Institute of Art, commissioned by Henry Ford, and for the ill-fated mural in the Rockefeller Center in New York, commissioned by the Rockefellers; José Clemente Orozco, for his murals at three U.S. colleges; Rufino Tamayo, for the distinct painting style that found a large audience in New York; the composer, conductor, and educator Carlos Chavez, who conducted major symphony orchestras throughout the United States, including the San Antonio Symphony before World War II; and photographer Manuel Alvarez Bravo, who exhibited with Henri Cartier Bresson.[32]

However, his clients recognized Rodríguez's talent, and they promoted his prestige as

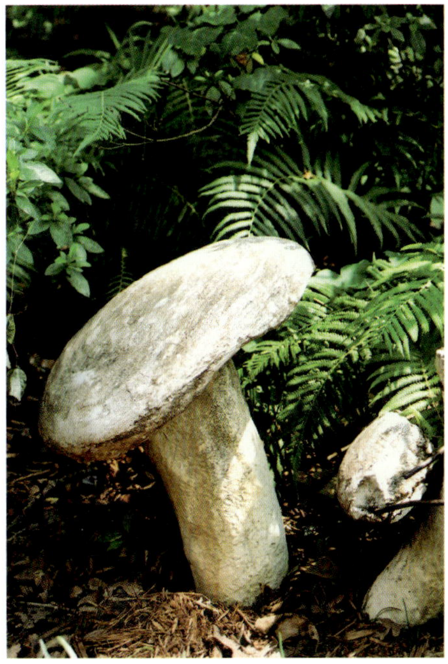

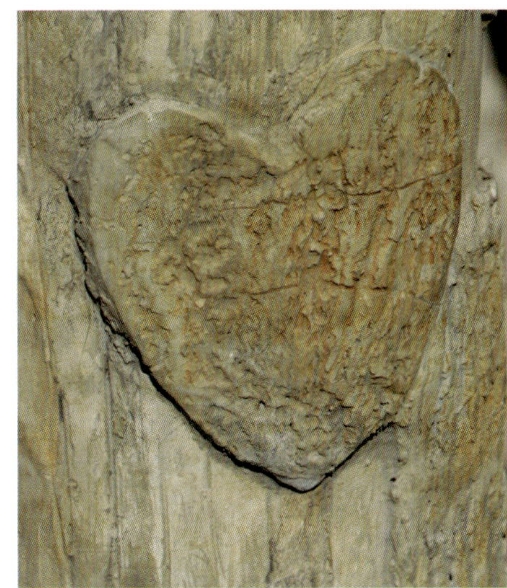

Top: *Mushroom, Old Mill, North Little Rock, Arkansas. Photo: Myssie Light Acomb.*
Above: *Heart detail on log bridge in Brackenridge Park, San Antonio. Photo: Bob Parvin.*

a Mexican artist. Evidence that they regarded him as more than a mere laborer is illustrated in their references to him. He was introduced as "the famous Mexican artist who made so many beautiful motifs in Cedar Hill" in a letter from Manager J. R. Clevlen to Mr. George Magher of Whitemarsh Memorial Park in Philadelphia.[33] Dr. Aureliano Urrutia wrote to the San Antonio Parks commissioner, Ray Lambert: "This man is an expert."[34] In Memorial Park Cemetery, Clovis Hinds erected several plaques, including one beside Abraham's Oak that is inscribed:

Abraham's Oak

1935

The Field of Machpelah, the trees and the cave at the end of the field were purchased by Abraham on the death of his wife Sarah as a family burial place nearly 4,000 years ago (Genesis 23). Near the Cave of Machpelah stood an old stump named for the founder of the Hebrew nation, Abraham's Oak. Sr. Dionicio Rodríguez, a descendant of the artistic Aztec race, founders of the Mexican Empire, has reproduced this historic stump entirely of concrete, reinforced with steel and copper bar so as to ensure its existence for many centuries to come.

Perhaps to explain Rodríguez's unusual technique or maybe to add romance to his sculptures, cemetery owners often placed bronze plaques beside the works. The following inscription is from Cedar Park Cemetery, at Calumet Park, a suburb of Chicago:

Shady Rest

This shelter, made entirely of stone, is the work of Dionicio Rodríguez, Mexican sculptor. Note the natural appearance of bark, grain, coloring and weathering.

Another plaque describes a lost but enduring love:

The Thatched Old Oak Legend

There is a tradition that, long before the coming of the white man, an Indian maiden, whose young brave met a heroic death on the field of battle, caused his remains to be interred beneath the spreading branches of a sturdy young oak tree. There beneath its cool, protecting shade, she found solace and comfort as she communed with the spirit of her departed lover. The oak grew strong and

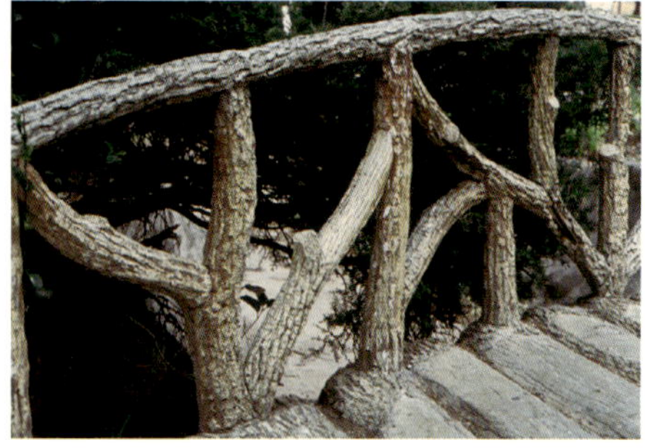

Log railing of bridge in Zacatecas, Mexico. Photo: Laurie Light Saunders.

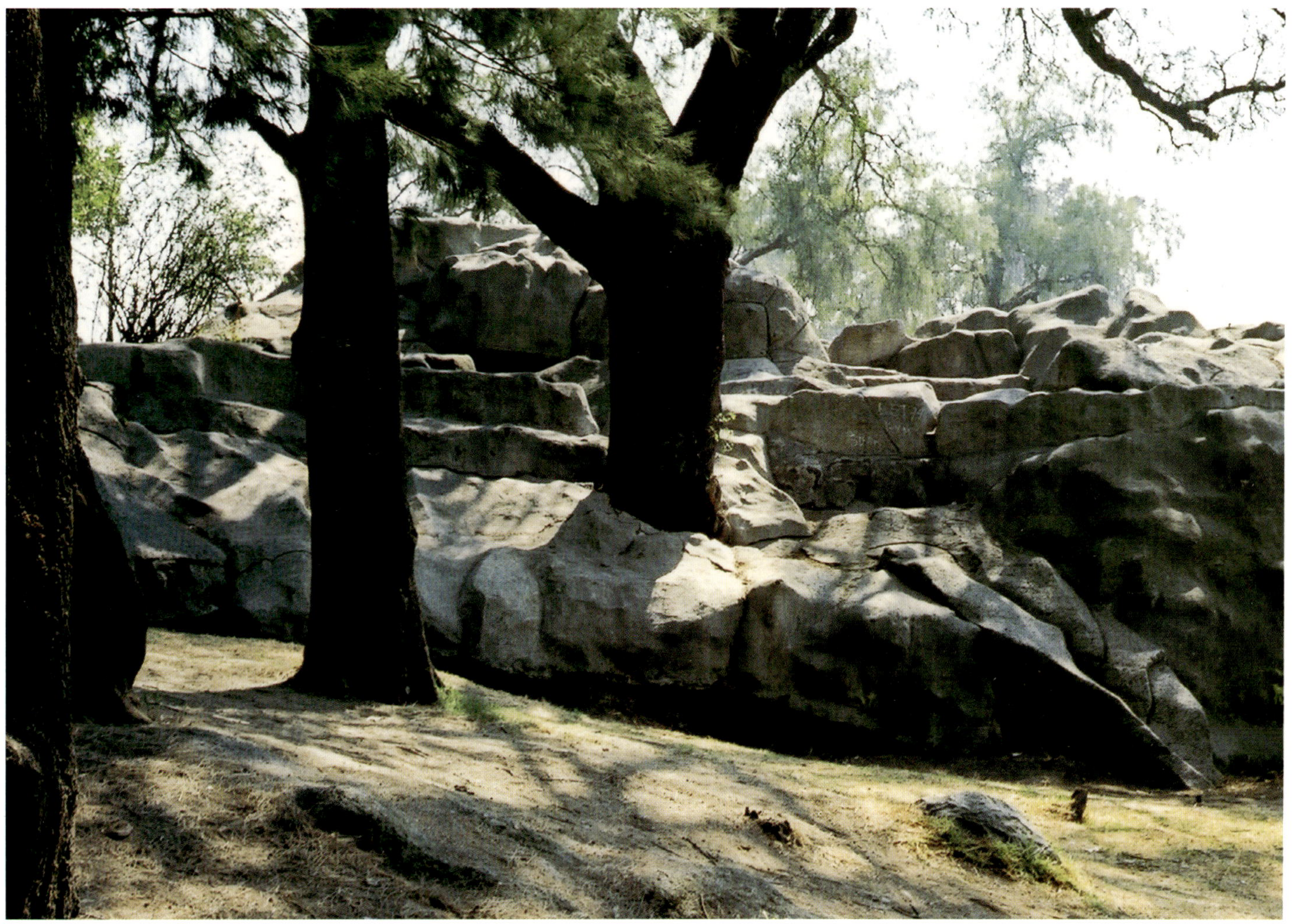

Rock around Lagos de Chapúltepec, Castillo de Chapúltepec, Mexico City, D.F. Photo: Patsy Light.

venerable. From its leafy bower, friendly birds chirp their happy song have, in token of their esteem, thatched it over to provide her with added protections. Mother Nature in commemoration of the maiden's enduring love preserved the oak that it might stand as a symbol of everlasting affection and loyalty. This memorial, which shall stand eternally, is erected as an exemplification of our reverence for the loved ones who have here found peace and rest.

Artist: Senor Dionicio Rodríguez
Material: Reinforced Concrete

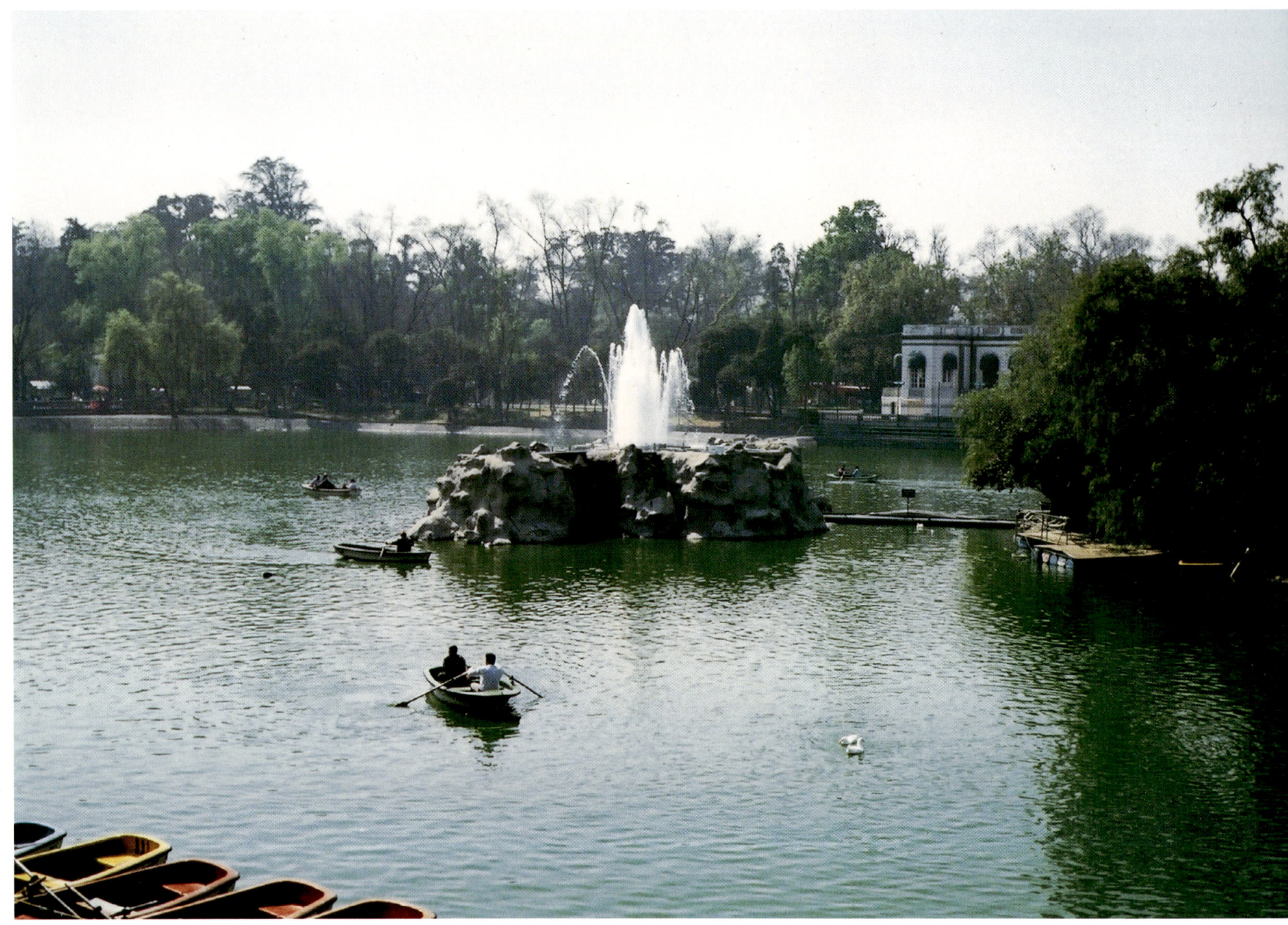

Fountain at Lagos de Chapúltepec, Castillo de Chapúltepec, Mexico City, D.F. Photo: Patsy Light.

This book is an attempt to celebrate Rodríguez's known work in the United States, including projects no longer extant; it is probable that additional work continues to exist at yet undiscovered sites, some in private collections.

Rodríguez's Personal Life

Much of what is known about the life and work of Dionicio Rodríguez is based on interviews—with his niece, Manuela Vargas Theall, who traveled with him to work on projects outside Texas from May 1937 to March 1938; fellow artisan Sam Murray; Mrs. Guadalupe Del Toro, the wife of Mauro Del Toro, who worked with Rodríguez; and Carlos Cortés, Rodríguez's great-nephew by marriage.[35]

Dionicio Rodríguez, born in Toluca on the outskirts of Mexico City on April 11, 1891, was the son of Luz Alegría and Catarino Rodríguez. His family moved to Mexico City, where, as a young man, he assisted his father and his brother in building brick houses. He and his brother would compete to see who could lay bricks the faster.[36] Later he was employed by Luis Robles Gil, a civil engineer and contractor who specialized in works of reinforced concrete that imitated wood or rock. It is possible that Gil was familiar with faux bois antecedents in Europe. Oral tradition reveals that Gil had come to Mexico from Spain, which could possibly account for the kinship between the themes of Rodríguez and Gaudi. Rodríguez also worked for J. W. Douglas, another concrete contractor, making concrete objects. Discussing Rodríguez's work on the artificial rocks and the fountain in Lagos de Chapúltepec, near the presidential palace in Chapúltepec Park in Mexico City, Manuela Theall said: "They made everything that looked like rock."[37] Although they are not documented as his work, some one hundred faux bois palapa benches and a fountain in Parque de Mexico in the La Condessa district of Mexico City may be attributable to Rodríguez, as they are similar to benches he created in the United States.

In the early 1920s, armed with letters of recommendation from Gil and Douglas, Rodríguez left Mexico City and lived for a short time in Monterrey.[38] There he joined Maximo Cortés's father, who worked near a cemetery, where he made *piedra prensada* (ornamental cast stone). While Rodríguez was in Monterrey, he crafted two faux bois benches for the grounds of a brewery complex, the Cervecería Cuauhtémoc.[39] The elder Cortés suggested that Rodríguez go to Laredo, Texas, and there he found work with Maximo Cortés, who was casting cement embellishments for a school. After a short period, Rodríguez left Laredo and moved to San Antonio, arriving in about 1924 during the city's pre-Depression building boom.[40]

The 1924–25 *San Antonio City Directory* lists "D. Rodríguez," an employee of Alamo Cement Company, living at 1919 W. Commerce.[41] This area of San Antonio, on the western edge of the central downtown area, was home to many of the Mexican immigrants who settled in the city following the revolution. Soon after moving to San Antonio, Rodríguez encountered Maximo Cortés at the corner of Santa Rosa and Commerce streets, near the Nacional Theater, and informed him that there were employment opportunities. Rodríguez told Cortés: "I'm going to return the favor, and you can work with me." The two later collaborated on numerous projects.[42]

According to photographs, Dionicio Rodríguez was small in stature with a dark com-

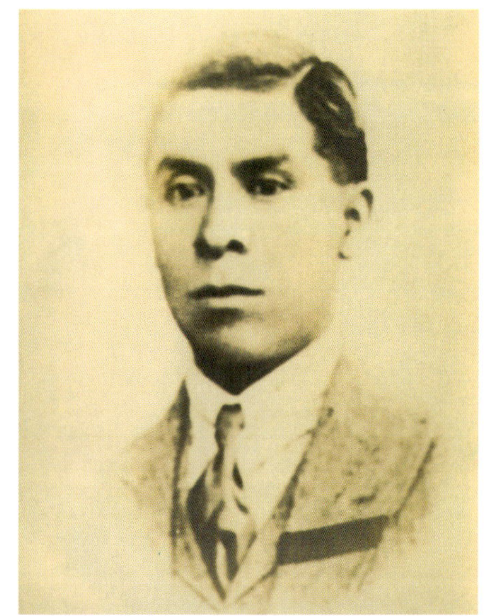

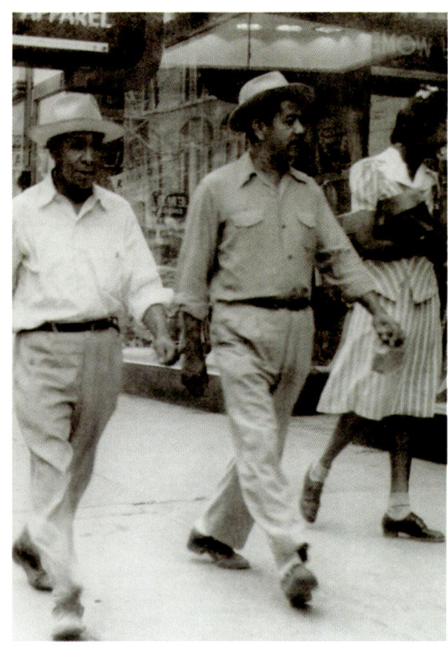

Top: *Dionicio Rodríguez, ca. 1916. Courtesy of Manuela Vargas Theall.*
Above: *Dionicio Rodríguez (left) with Maximo Cortés on Houston Street, San Antonio, ca. 1940. Courtesy of Carlos Cortés.*

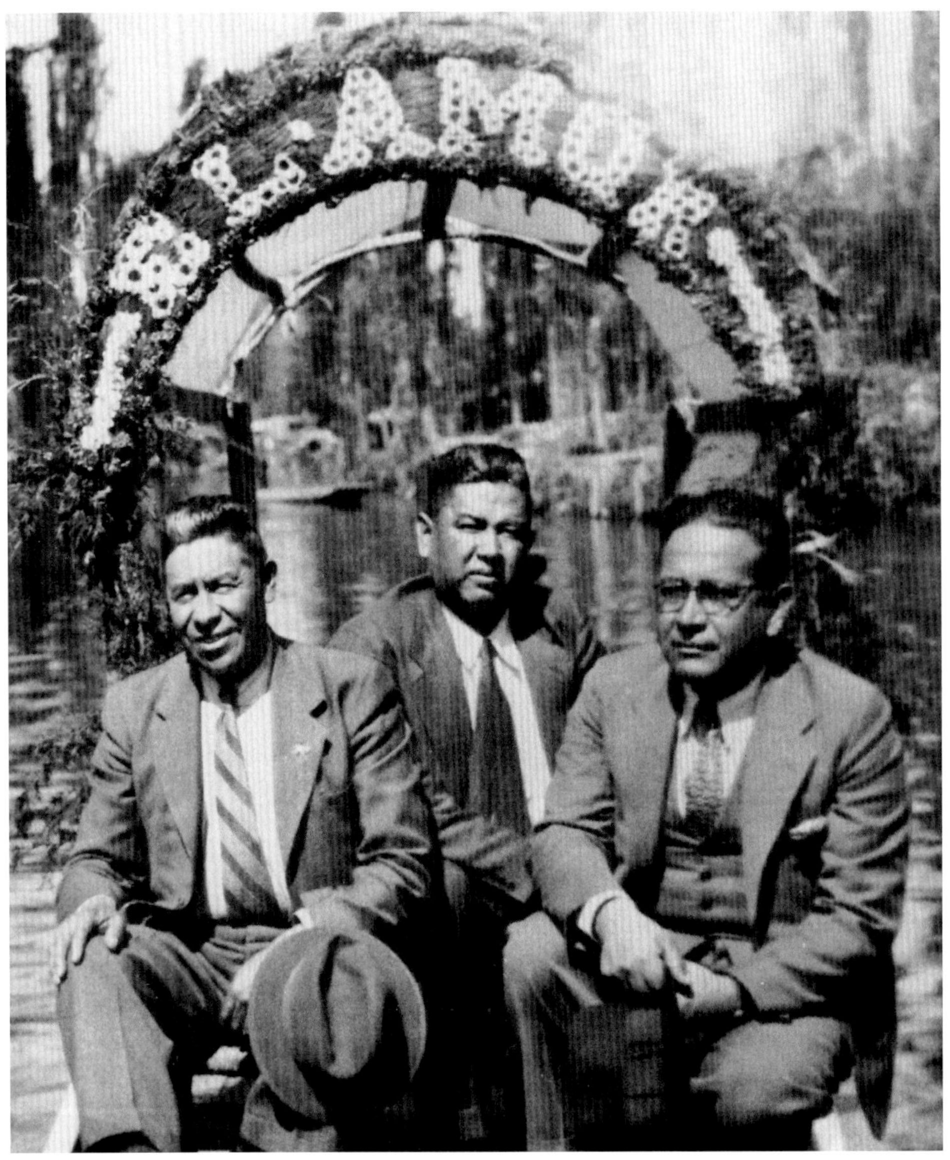

Dionicio Rodríguez (left), Maximo Cortés (center), and unidentified man at the floating gardens of Xochimilco, Mexico, D.F., ca. 1928. Courtesy of William Green, Ph.D., copied from a photo loaned by Maximo Cortés.

plexion. In a 1935 newspaper article he was described as "a stumpy little brown man from Mexico City."[43] He suffered throughout his adult life with diabetes, which eventually caused him to lose his sight. Apparently his diabetic condition was not treated until he exhibited extreme fatigue and loss of weight, along with suffering from excessive thirst. Two of his clients, E. Clovis Hinds and Justin Matthews, arranged for him to seek medical help in Arkansas in 1935.[44] They arranged an appointment with Dr. McCrae in Little Rock, who would see Dionicio on Sunday afternoons after the doctor played his Sunday morning golf games. He began administering twice daily insulin injections, which were later given to the artisan by his niece Manuela, who had previously worked in a clinic in Mexico. After she went home to Mexico, Rodríguez learned to administer his own injections.[45]

His personality has been described as "muy aparte y muy serio" (very distant and serious).[46] Manuela Theall said: "He didn't have many friends because he was always going—he didn't stay in one place too many days." According to Theall, Rodríguez always "dressed up, wearing a coat, vest, nice shoes and dress shirt with cuff links and tie." She said he told her, "I want you to look nice when you are with me," and he bought her "nice" clothes. She said that when he started a job, "he took off his coat, put on a pair of long pants (over his good pants) and his galoshes, and rolled up his sleeves and went to work" to apply the details and color to the forms that had been constructed by laborers under his supervision.[47]

In spite of his extensive travels and many commissions, Rodríguez did not learn to speak or write English. By the time he arrived in the United States, he was thirty-three years old and spent many long hours at his work. It appears that learning English was not a priority with him; he was able to communicate with his clients through interpreters or by using sign language. Manuela Theall relates that sometimes Dionicio's words were not interpreted correctly.[48] Letters from Rodríguez to one of his clients, Clovis Hinds, were written for him by others.[49] He worked intermittently for Hinds at Memorial Park Cemetery in Memphis from the early 1930s through the early 1940s, and his correspondence indicates that he was a conscientious worker. He wrote to Hinds in 1939: "I always try to do the best of my ability."[50]

Rodríguez purchased a new car each year for his travels across the United States. Theall said he did not know anything about cars, and he usually would not let anyone else drive, although occasionally she was permitted to drive on country roads. Traveling companions were friends or family members, including Julius Tober, father-in-law of Maximo Cortés, who accompanied Dionicio to work on projects in Little Rock, Memphis, Birmingham, and Detroit and served as an interpreter. Tober preferred tying the rebar frames, attaching the metal lath, and infilling the form with cement and rubble in preparation for the finish work.[51] The group would rent rooms in boarding houses, hotels, or YMCAs, and occasionally they would cook their meals, but often they would go out to eat.

Throughout the years, Hinds treated Rodríguez with a paternalistic attitude, providing him with advice and handling his finances. On one occasion, he sent Rodríguez fifty dollars to pay for his niece's tonsillectomy.[52] It appears that Rodríguez's hourly wage ranged from $1.00 to $2.25. In 1940, the U.S. average wage for all industries was just under $0.51 per hour.[53] Some retail prices for food from the 1940s may illustrate the cost of living and put these wages in perspective: a loaf of white bread was eight cents, milk was twelve cents

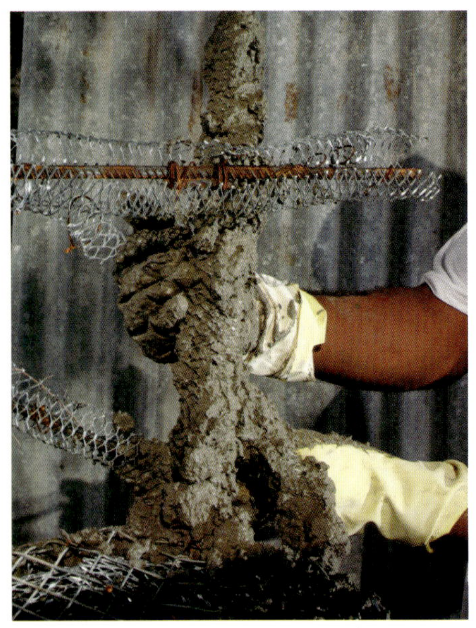

Above: *Covering rebar and metal lath frame with first coat of cement, Studio Cortés, San Antonio. Photo: Bob Parvin.*
Below: *Application of scratch coat of cement, Studio Cortés, San Antonio. Photo: Bob Parvin.*

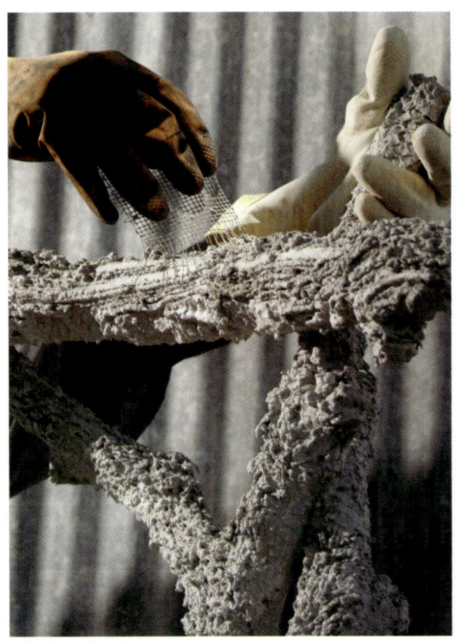

a quart—delivered fresh daily, and a dozen eggs were thirty-three cents.[54] In comparison with other less prosperous artists of the period, Rodríguez was able to support himself and other members of his entourage rather well. For many families during the Depression years, purchasing a new car each year would have been a real luxury.

Indicating the racial prejudice that existed during the period, Clovis Hinds advised Rodríguez before the sculptor left to work in Washington in 1935: "Be sure not to eat, drink or associate with negroes in Washington as your social equal—as such conduct will not elevate you as a great artist in the estimate of the Washington people."[55] Manuela remembers that she and her uncle were never subjected to any prejudicial attitudes and that they used "white" drinking fountains and ate in restaurants of their choosing.[56] According to the 1930 U.S. Census, there were very few Mexicans in Arkansas, Memphis, Birmingham, or Washington, D.C.[57]

Asked about contacts with other people of Mexican descent, Manuela recounted that they visited the Little Rock home of Mr. Rocha, an assistant to Rodríguez on some of the jobs; they shared a "pork and bean" supper, heated on a pot-bellied iron stove, with the Rochas and their six children. She had never eaten this dish before, and she looked questioningly at her uncle, who told her: "Don't say anything, just eat it." In Memphis, they frequented a restaurant owned by a Mexican couple, where the owners' daughter entertained them with Mexican songs, including *El Rancho Grande* and *La Cucaracha*. She said that on many occasions they were tired in the evenings and did not have time for social life.[58]

Rodríguez hired local laborers as his assistants at the various job sites. At times, when he was under pressure to finish a job and his workers were reluctant to work late, he would purchase a bottle of wine for them, and the work would continue. Between projects, when weather conditions were not right for working in concrete, during cold weather, or when he was not feeling well, Rodríguez would travel to Mexico or San Antonio. United States Immigration Service records document several of his trips to Mexico, including his return on 26 February 1937, when he was readmitted as a "Legal U.S. Resident, Laredo, Texas."[59] He was married and divorced twice and had no children.[60]

Rodríguez's Technique

Rodríguez's work is on a human scale, and the tints he used mimic the colors of the natural surfaces that he emulated: surfaces of crosscut and hewn logs, tree trunks, logs and branches with heavily textured and peeling bark, knotholes, stalactites, insect borings, and patches of lichen. With assistance from his helpers he formed the armatures of the sculptural works from steel reinforcing rods. He then bound the rebar together with wire, wrapped the form with metal lath, infilled the lath with cement—adding rubble for large pieces—and applied a coat of rough cement. In at least two instances, at the Pugh's Old Mill project in Arkansas and at Memorial Park in Memphis, he used copper rebar in order to ensure longevity of the work. For larger pieces, he poured a concrete footing.[61] He then applied a final coat of "neat" (pure) Portland cement to the armature directly from the bag. In the text descriptions of his work, the terms *cement* and *concrete* are used interchangeably as his work incorporates both materials. According to Stanley Schmidt, "He just sat down on the ground with a sack of cement, and started working."[62]

Rodríguez initially used homemade tools, combs, and ordinary tableware, although he later acquired some professional tools. He was able to reproduce such realistic textures of rock, thatch, and wooden surfaces that it is often impossible to distinguish the cement imitation. He was secretive about his work, especially the final step involving the application of color when the cement was slightly damp. Theall attributes this secrecy to the fact that he did not want anyone to copy his work. Hosing the sculpture with water was the last step in the process.[63]

According to John Kagay, the chemist at the Alamo Portland Cement Company who supplied him with these colorants when he was in San Antonio, to create various tints Rodríguez used a mixture of water and chemicals—sulfuric acid, muriatic acid, iron oxide, saltpeter, and some lampblack to darken the colors.[64] Theall recalled a later source for his chemicals. He purchased blue, green, red, brown, and black "little stones" from the San Pedro Drug and Laboratory in San Antonio, owned by María and Alberto J. Paparelli, the daughter and son-in-law of Rodríguez's client, Dr. Aureliano Urrutia.[65] Manuela said Rodríguez boiled the "stones" in water to make his dyes and then bottled them. He would sometimes share some of the mixed formula with other artisans—"just enough to do their work."[66]

John Richmond, who worked with Rodríguez in Memphis, recalled that the artisan always wore rubber gloves when he was applying "acid," a solution that "smelled like bananas," which he heated over a fire. Richmond believed that this mixture served as a bonding agent between the layers of cement.[67] At times Rodríguez would keep the colorants in the trunk of his car, and if anyone came too close, he would immediately shut the trunk lid. Sometimes he would mix them in a tent adjacent to his work site. Richmond recalls that Rodríguez would break the bottles of chemicals when they were empty in order to keep anyone from learning their ingredients.[68]

Referring to Rodríguez's secrecy about his colorants, the artisan Sam Murray recalled that "Rodríguez was dodging people all the time." Murray said it did not take him "long to pick it up," as his earlier cast stone work in the 1920s for the embellishments for the Milam Building and the City Hall in San Antonio had provided him with a good background in mixing colors.[69]

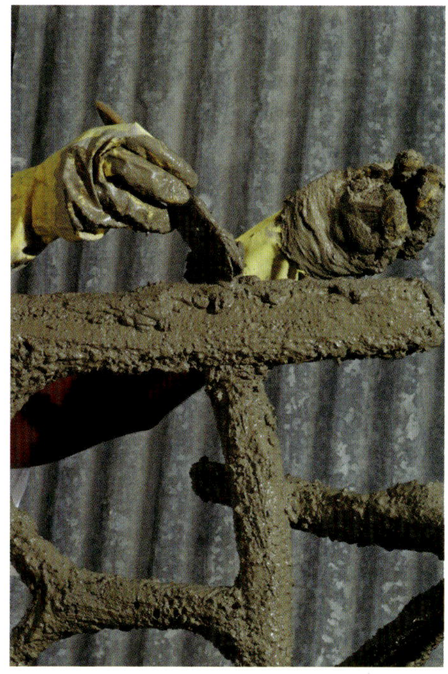

Adding texture coat of cement, Studio Cortés, San Antonio. Photo: Bob Parvin.

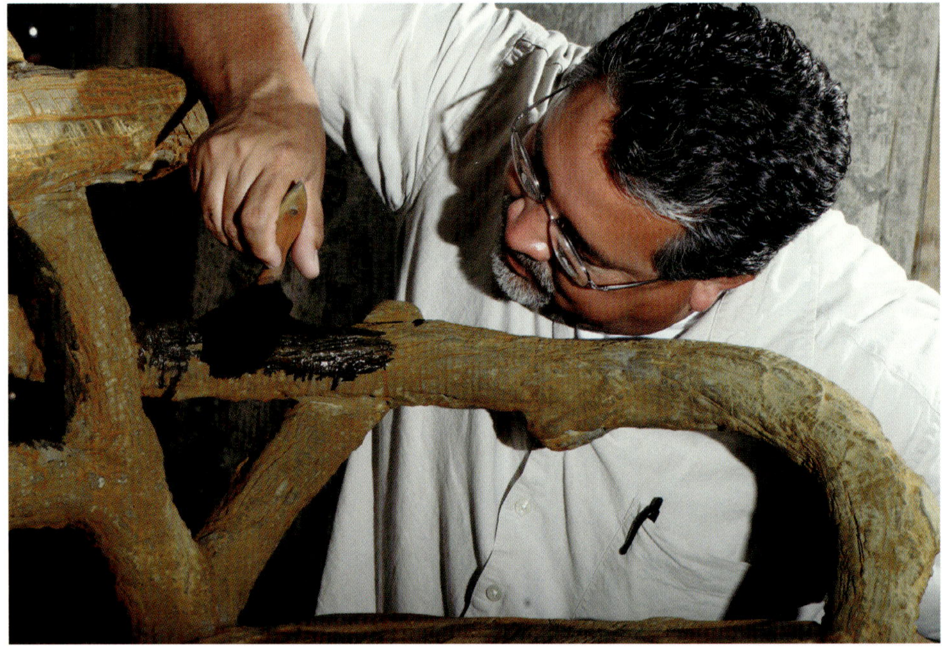

*Final application of stain by Carlos Cortés, Studio Cortés,
San Antonio. Photo: Bob Parvin.*

Dionicio Rodríguez's itinerant lifestyle makes it difficult to catalogue his work precisely by place and year. His first jobs after he arrived from Mexico were in San Antonio, and the largest concentration of his work in Texas can be found there. The second phase of his work was primarily in other parts of Texas, and he then began securing commissions elsewhere in the United States. As some of his jobs were under way simultaneously, their timing overlaps.[70]

Dionicio Rodríguez overcame illness and language barriers to build a successful career from a technique he learned in Mexico that had European origins. He left a significant body of work that includes benches emulating fallen trees, carefully crafted thatch, hollow trees, shell-encrusted walls, and cacti in a string of U.S. cities, with the heart of it showcased in San Antonio.

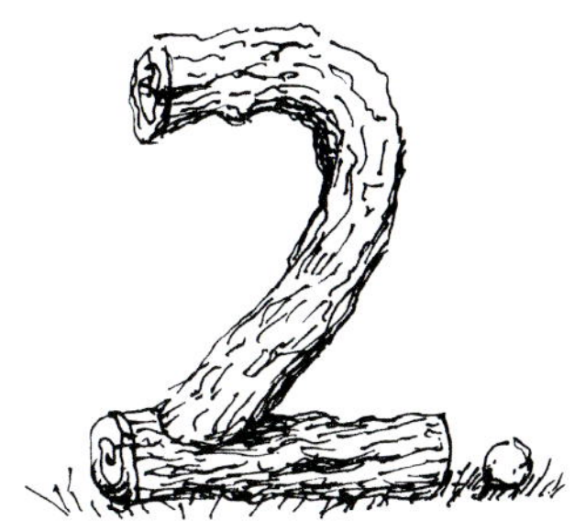

Rodríguez in San Antonio

Among the distinguished citizens of San Antonio in the early twentieth century was the Mexican surgeon Aureliano Urrutia, who had been exiled from his country during the 1910 revolution. Arrested by General Frederick Funston, Urrutia was deported from Mexico, arrived by ship at Galveston, and settled in San Antonio in 1914. He had owned an established clinic in Mexico where he performed surgeries and taught medical students. In San Antonio Dr. Urrutia became a respected member of the medical community, performing many difficult surgeries, including the separation of Siamese twins at Santa Rosa Hospital in 1917. In recognition of this and other operations, he was elected to the American College of Surgeons.

Aureliano Urrutia built an elaborate residence, Quinta Urrutia, in the 3300 block of Broadway north of downtown San Antonio, "a self-designed blend of Moorish and Spanish architecture."[1] Architectural historian Mary Carolyn George deemed Quinta Urrutia "the city's most famous example of exuberant eclecticism."[2] The residence was demolished in 1962, but a portion of Urrutia's fifteen-acre garden, Miraflores, remains. A tangible reminder of the man who became such a prominent citizen, it is "an idiosyncratic personal playground, full of vitality in its juxtapositions and eccentricities," sited approximately half a mile from his home at the intersection of Broadway and Hildebrand Avenue.[3]

THE WORK OF DIONICIO RODRÍGUEZ IN SAN ANTONIO

Brackenridge Park

1. **Japanese Tea Garden Gate**
   (with Maximo Cortés)

2. **Bridge**

3. **Hollow Tree House**

4. **Palapa Bench**

5. **Palapa Table and Benches**

Other locations

6. **Building Façade**
   2702 N. St. Mary's St.
   Front board façade, window,
   door trim, and portico

7. **Alamo Heights Trolley Stop**
   Broadway and Patterson

8. **Buckeye Park Gate**
   1600 West Wildwood

9. **Urrutia Gate**
   San Antonio Museum of Art
   200 West Jones Avenue
   Faux rock facing

10. **Spanish Governor's Palace**
    105 Plaza de Armas
    Benches and light poles (patio)

11. **Stone Werks Café**
    7300 Jones Maltsberger
    Fence, gate, palapa,
    fountain/fish pond

12. **Miraflores Park**
    800 Hildebrand
    Hollow tree entry gate;
    nine additional works within
    the park (no public access)

13. **Shrine of St. Anthony
    of Padua**
    100 Peter Baque Road
    Grotto and Stations of
    the Cross

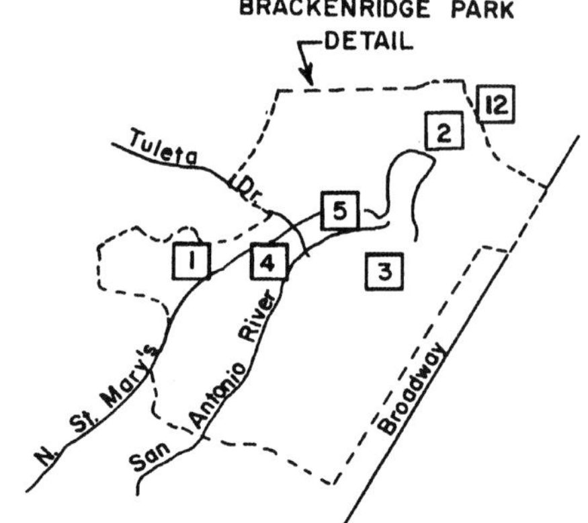

David Lopez, cartographer

Designs for Dr. Aureliano Urrutia and Miraflores

It is assumed that Rodríguez's first work in San Antonio was for Dr. Urrutia. There is strong evidence that Urrutia had known Rodríguez in Mexico, and in June of 1924 the doctor wrote a letter to San Antonio's commissioner of parks, Ray Lambert, recommending the artisan and inviting the director to see some work. Urrutia told Lambert: "He came from Mexico City to make for my residence some very artistic things in which line, this man is an expert. He made for Chapúltepec, in Mexico City, 'Las Rocas Fuentes' [the faux rock fountain in the lake in Chapúltepec Park]. . . . I want you to see the work in the gate, and also some additional ornaments."[4]

The land where Miraflores lies was originally part of a 1733–34 grant to the City of San Antonio from the king of Spain, and the Acequia Madre, the first *acequia,* was built in 1718 just to the south to supply water to Mission San Antonio de Valero (the Alamo). Dr. Urrutia purchased the property in 1921, and in 1962 he sold the garden to United Services Automobile Association.[5] The company built an eight-story office building and a parking lot, leaving 4.5 acres of Miraflores next to the San Antonio River.

In 1974 the United Services Automobile Association sold the property (including Miraflores) to the Southwestern Bell Company (later SBC, now AT&T). One of the original gates that provided an entrance from Broadway was moved to the western portion of the remaining garden on Hildebrand. This gate, with pillars faced with faux terra cotta–colored stones that are attributed to Dionicio Rodríguez, is an elaborate structure embellished with polychrome Talavera tile in fanciful repetitive designs of peacocks, tigers, plants, flowers, and an image of the Virgin of Guadalupe.[6] A split scroll cap of bronze is inscribed "Dr. Urrutia." Moved to the San Antonio Museum of Art in 1998, it is part of the Nelson Rockefeller Latin American Collection. A small log bench made by Rodríguez was given to the Witte Museum in 1974. An additional gate, designed by the architect Marcelo Izaguirre, remains on the northern boundary of the garden.[7] Four pillars embellished with Talavera tiles frame a large opening spanned by a decorative iron gate.

In 2001 SBC deeded Miraflores to the University of Incarnate Word (UIW). During this period, a large fountain resembling others that Rodríguez would later build at other sites was demolished. It was composed of a series of flat rocks progressing from larger at the base to smaller at the apex. Water flowed downward, dripping on each successive level into a series of canals, which flowed southward to fill the now nonexistent oval pool where Dr. Urrutia swam year round at five o'clock in the morning.[8] A grandson, Dr. A. A. Urrutia, recalls that his grandfather taught him to swim in this pool by tying a belt around the youngster's waist and pulling him through the water.[9] Based on land records, the City of

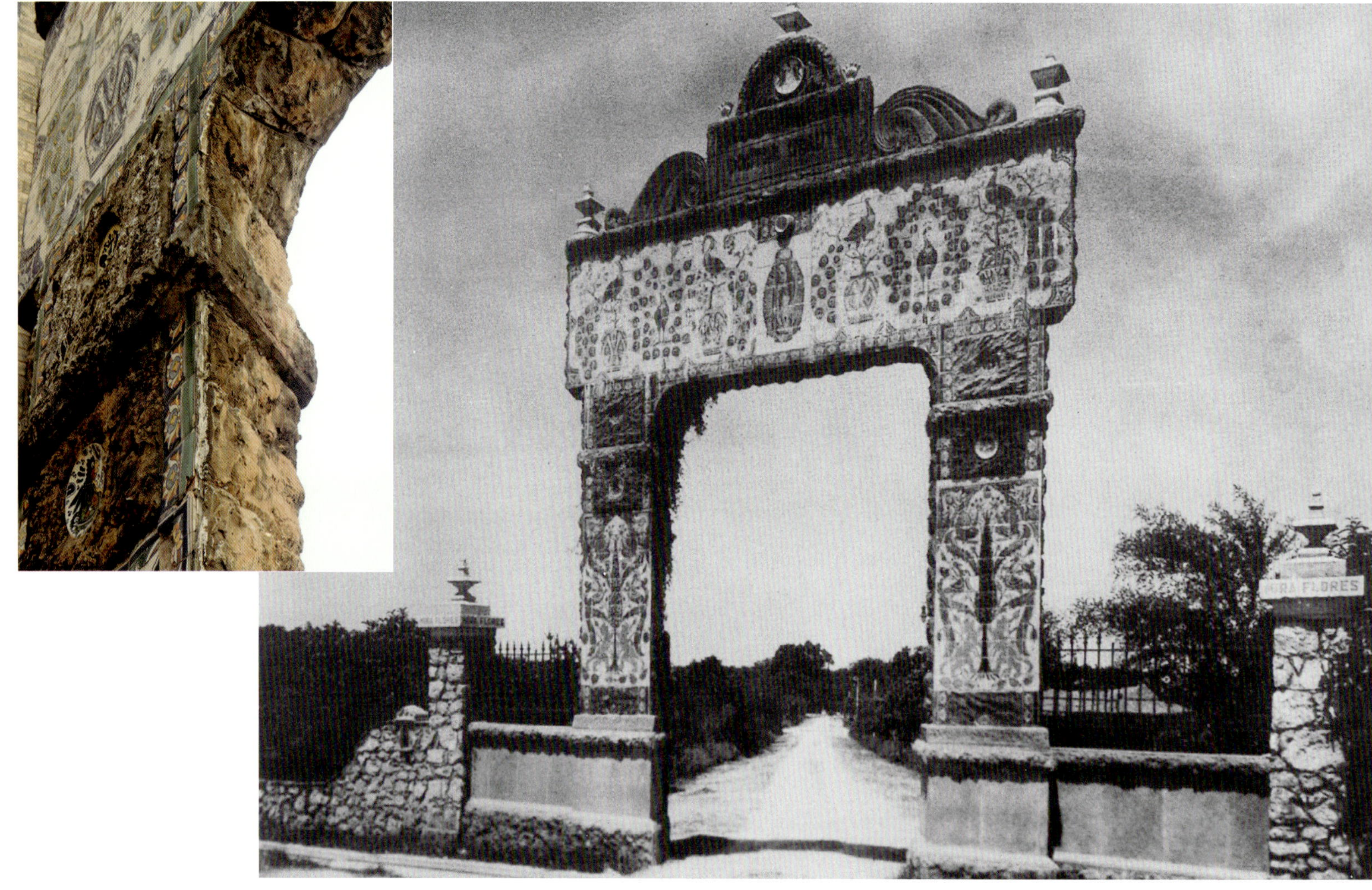

Top: *Detail of rock facing credited to Rodríguez,*
Miraflores gate, San Antonio Museum of Art.
Photo: Bob Parvin.
Right: *Talavera tile and bronze gate to Miraflores,*
San Antonio, in original siting with road leading from
Broadway into the park. The stone facing is credited to
Rodríguez. Photo from Dr. A. A Urrutia's Pinacoteca
(n.d.). Courtesy of Chris Amberson.

San Antonio sued the university for ownership in 2003.[10] A settlement was negotiated in 2005, whereby UIW acquired city-owned land adjoining its campus and the City became the owner of Miraflores, which has become an addition to Brackenridge Park.

Thirty-six objects adorned the gardens, including nine reinforced cement works by Rodríguez. When Dr. Urrutia left Mexico, many of his possessions were confiscated, although he later related that he had "managed to get two railroad boxcars across the border, stuffed with booty from the National Palace, to help him furnish his new home and other ventures."[11] It is possible that some of the statuary, Talavera tiles, and whole glazed ceramic plates used as decoration on benches, walls, and entrance gates in the garden were included in this shipment.

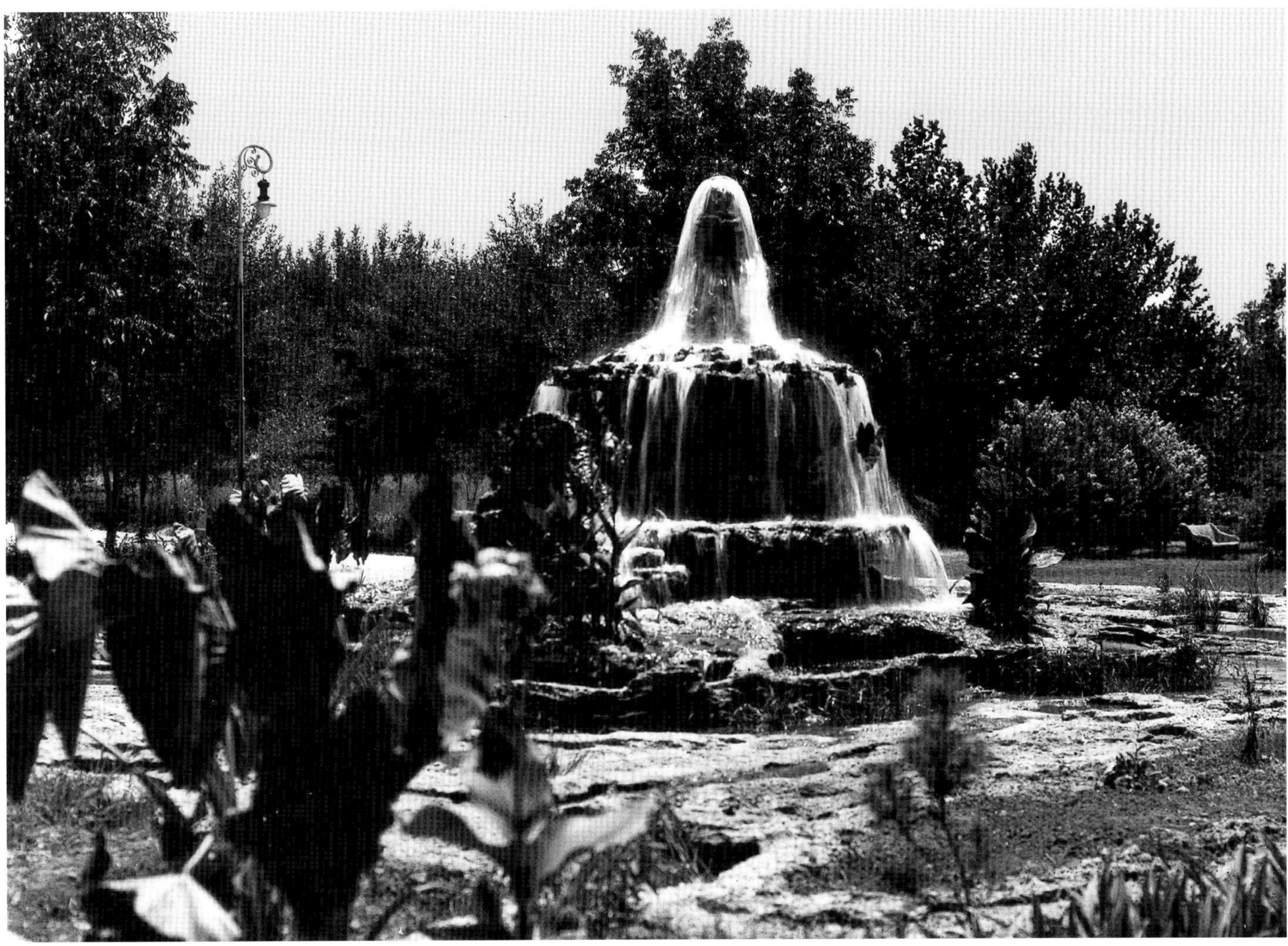

Extant works by Rodríguez in the garden include:

• A wooden bench, which originally stood on the grounds of Quinta Urrutia before Urrutia sold his home in 1962. A side-gabled palapa roof, supported by massive, heavily textured tree trunks, covers a seat made of a crosscut slab. "Dionicio Rodríguez" is incised into the rear of the bench.

• A small grotto made of amazingly realistic stalactites and stalagmites. An opening near the center houses two figures resembling cherubs without wings, probably sculpted by another artisan, as there are no existing representational sculptures of human figures attributed to Rodríguez. "Ana Maria, 1925" is

Rock fountain, Miraflores, San Antonio (not extant). Photo: Atlee Ayers, Atlee B. Ayers Collection, Institute of Texan Cultures, University of Texas at San Antonio.

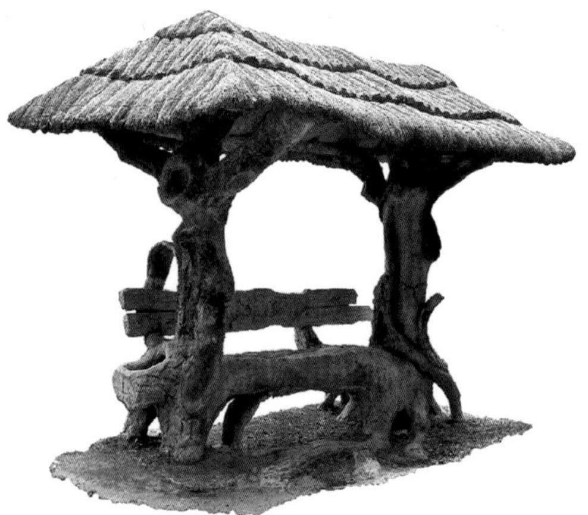

Above: *Palapa bench in Miraflores, San Antonio.*
Photo: Bob Parvin.

Opposite: *Grotto, Miraflores, San Antonio. The plaque*
reads "Ana Maria, 1925." She was the daughter of
Dr. Urrutia and his second wife, Catalina Tazzer.
Photo: Bob Parvin.

inscribed on the sculpture. Ana Maria was born in 1925 to Urrutia and his second wife, Catalina Tazzer.[12]

• A set of faux wood steps by Rodríguez, which serves as one of the transitions between upper and lower garden levels. Crosscut log steps curve downward onto a landing and are bordered with row of vertical planks that serve as handrails. The stairway is unique; it appears that no similar pieces by the artisan exist in the United States.

• Two matching pools, now filled with soil, encircled with well-detailed hewn logs bound with a concrete cable; water originally sprayed from central pedestals.

• A hollow log with well-defined bark texture housed electrical equipment on a metal pole inside the structure and probably provided power for the park's illumination.

• A fallen tree bench sited near cement rocks that delineate the edge of the pool. One of Rodríguez's oft-repeated designs, this early version of the design has a single backrest of a textured bark log that tapers to the ground and a crosscut section of a tree trunk that serves as a seat. In later years, Rodríguez would duplicate this bench in exaggerated lengths, one as long as forty-three feet.

• One of the three original gates to the property, the hollow tree sculpture by Rodríguez provided access to the guesthouse, Quinta Maria, as well as an entrance for foot traffic from Hildebrand Avenue. The gate exhibits heavily textured and deeply colored areas and is similar in design to his later tree shelters (at Alamo Plaza in San Antonio; Memorial Park in Memphis; Lakewood Park in North Little Rock, Arkansas; Suitland, Maryland; and Clayton, New Mexico). A half-gate of sawn planks is trimmed with Rodríguez's trademark, pyramid-headed steel bolts, and opens onto a series of twelve crosscut log steps that curve downward to the garden level. A single log handrail with an inset planter curves along the edge of the steps.

• A ten-foot-tall, two-branched saguaro cactus, several feet east of the stairway, capped by electrical wiring. Unusual in its shape and tinting (although there are large cacti at Eddingston Court in Port Arthur), this is the only extant solid green tinted work found by the author as of 2007.

Along with the Rodríguez pieces, decorated benches, urns, and monuments, there are additional sculptural works: two statues represent Indian figures, one of Cuahtémoc,

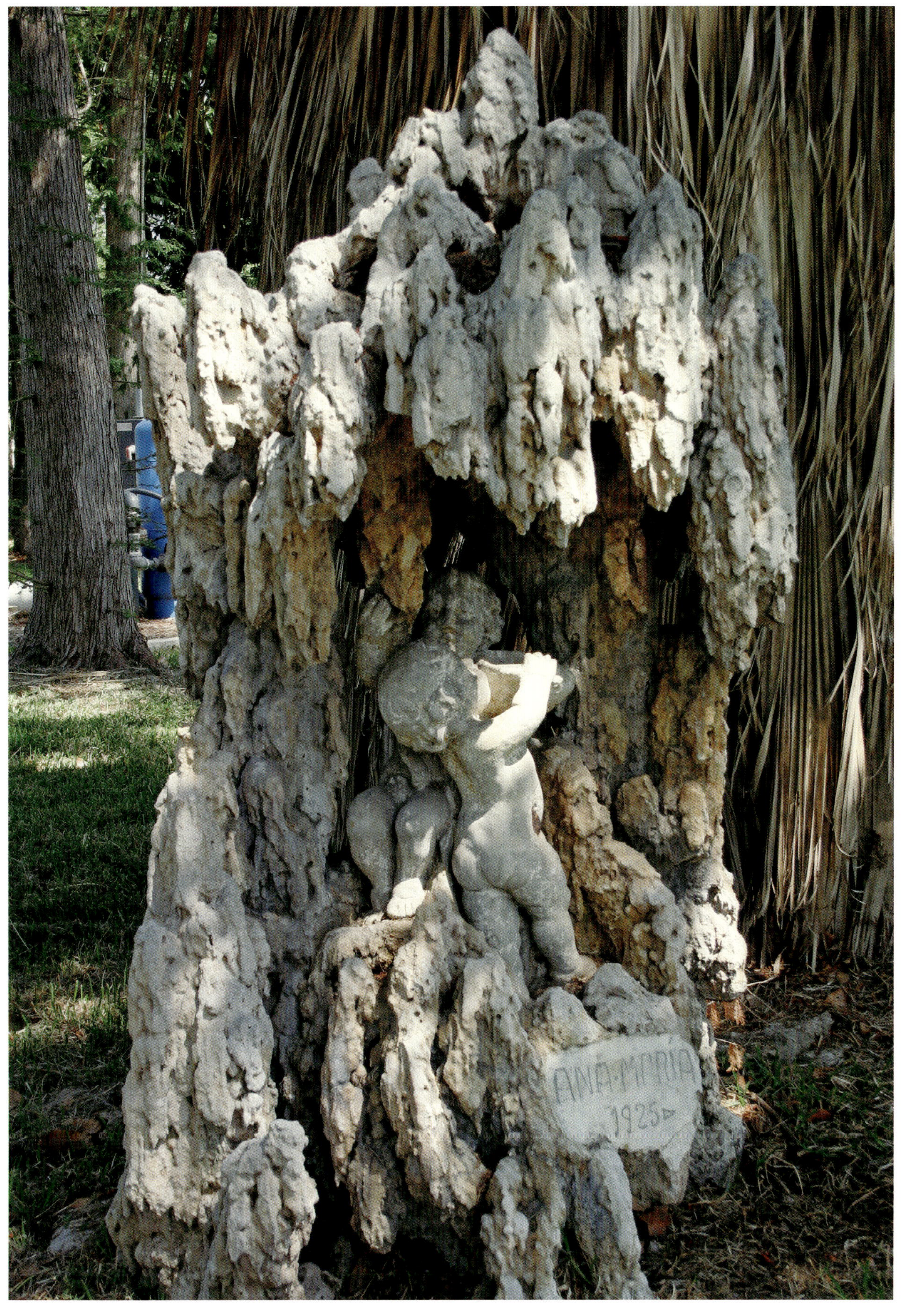

ANA·MARIA
1923

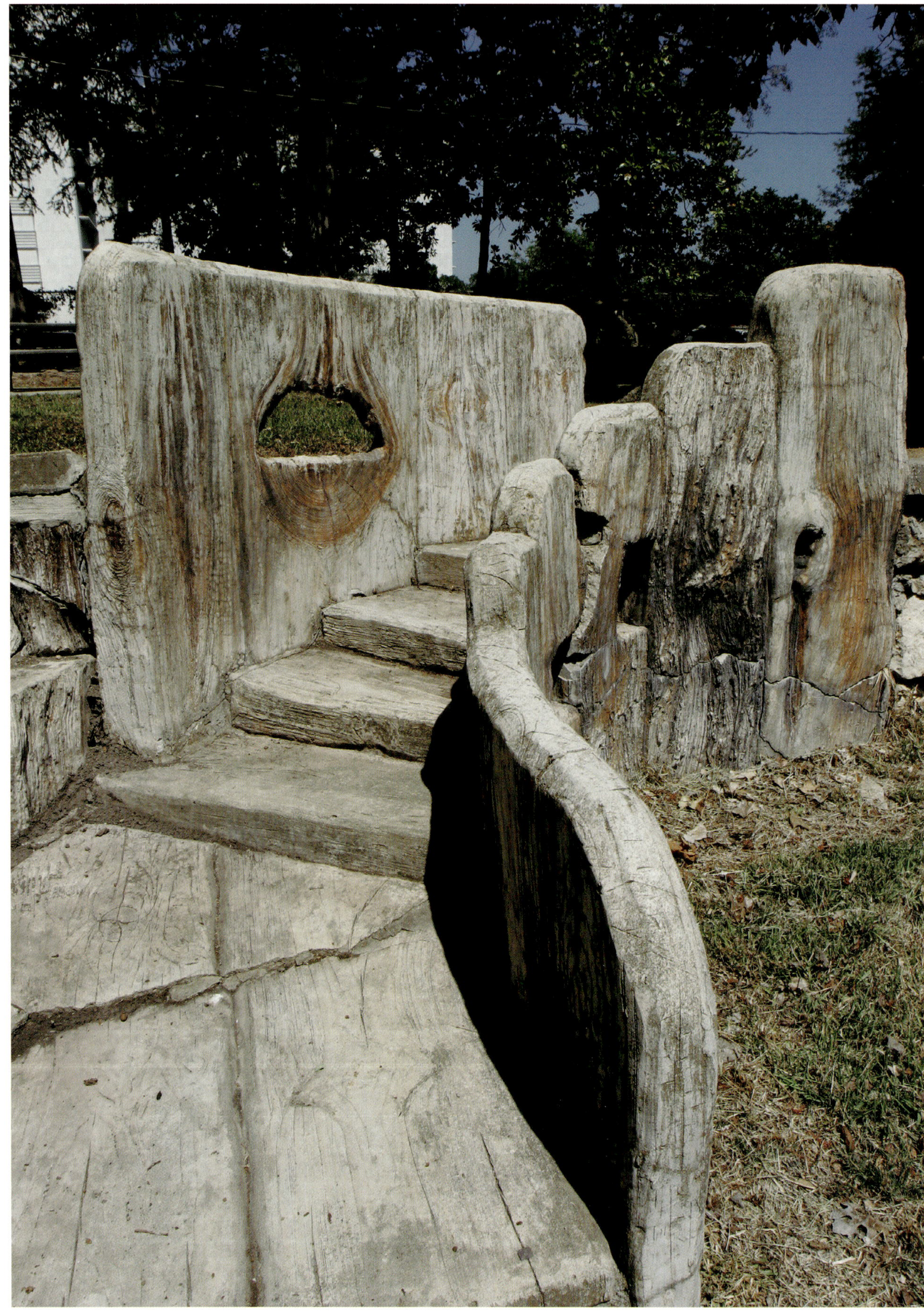

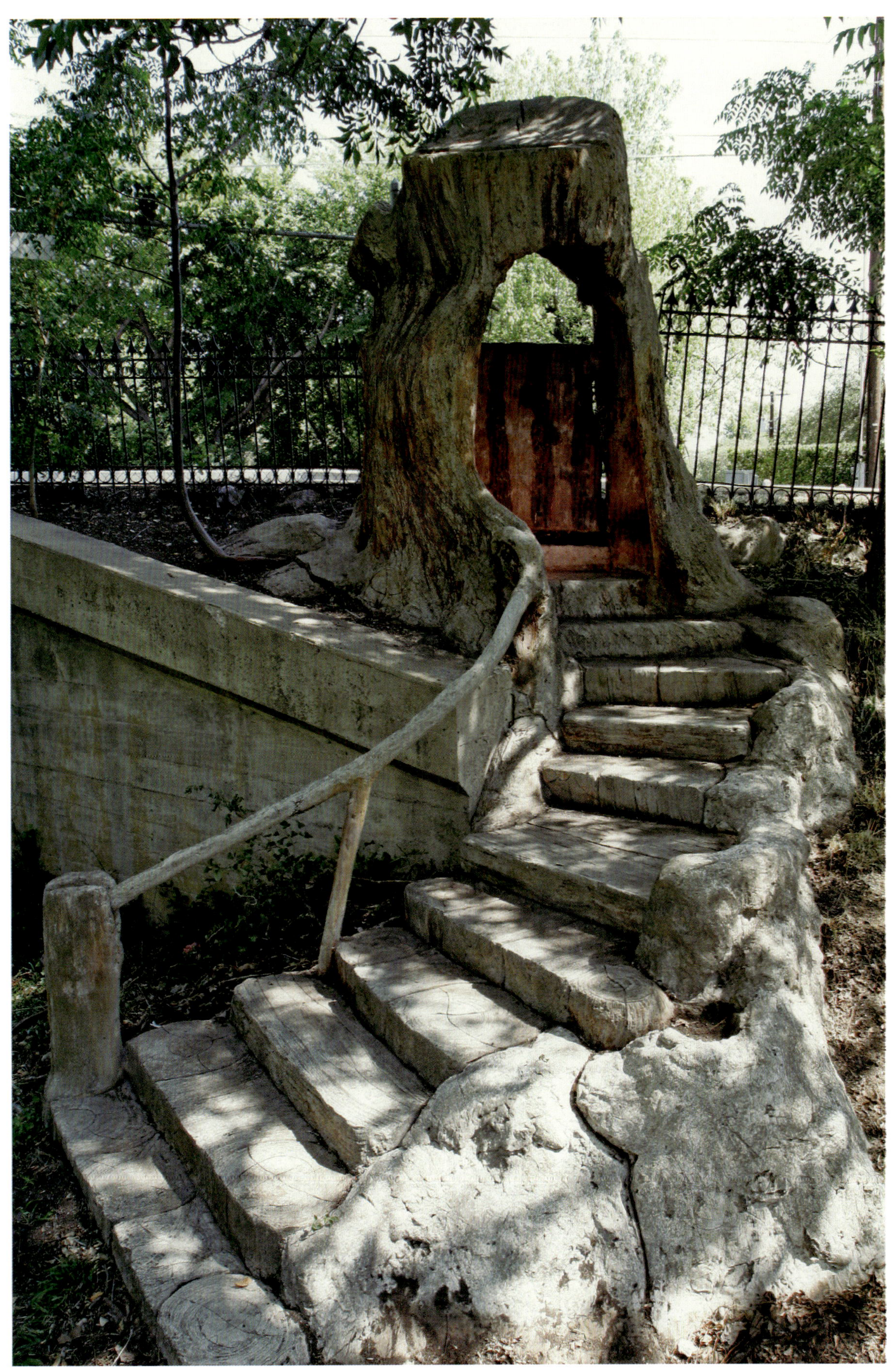

Opposite: *Wooden steps, Miraflores, San Antonio. Photo: Bob Parvin.*
Left: *Hollow tree entry gate and steps, Miraflores, San Antonio. Photo: Bob Parvin.*

33

the last Aztec leader, and the other, the Aztec moon goddess, Coyolxauhqui. A life-sized bronze sculpture of Dr. Urrutia in his black cape is sited in the now empty reflecting pool at the western end of the garden. Nearby is a concrete replica of the Nike of Samothrace, which originally stood on the roof of the Quinta Urrutia main house, centered above the front entrance. On either side of the sculpture are two lions, which originally guarded the entrance to the home. Urrutia liked to take early morning walks through Miraflores, usually barefoot but always wearing his long cape, stopping frequently to examine exotic plants and trees. He told his family that contact with nature was important for the spirit.[13] He cultivated healing and culinary herbs in the garden, often adding a pinch of one to season a pot cooking on the stove.[14]

Oral tradition reveals that Urrutia wanted to recreate the atmosphere not only of his hometown of Xochimilco, Mexico, known as the "floating gardens," but also of Chapúltepec Park in Mexico City. The site he chose, next to the San Antonio River and just downstream from the river's headwaters on the campus of the University of the Incarnate Word, provided him with several water sources. As in other locations where Rodríguez would later work, water served as a unifying element in Miraflores. Numerous springs on the property and an artesian water well that Urrutia had drilled afforded him an opportunity to plan the many water structures, canals, pools, and the large fountain.[15]

The garden of Miraflores, listed on the National Register of Historic Places in 2006, served as both a private retreat and a place where the doctor entertained his expansive family of fifteen children (he was married five times) and circle of friends. His grandson remembers large family parties on Sundays during good weather.[16] When the national convention of the Association of Architects was held in San Antonio in 1931, Dr. Urrutia entertained the group with a party at Miraflores.[17]

The relationship between Urrutia and Rodríguez continued for many years. During the last part of his life, Rodríguez was hospitalized with pneumonia. Manuela Theall recalled that her uncle in his eagerness to finish a job did not dress warmly enough in cold weather or otherwise take care of himself. Urrutia treated Rodríguez, advising him "to eat steak" and "drink a shot of whiskey" so he could "get strong."[18]

Charles Baumberger's Projects

It was apparently Dr. Urrutia who introduced Rodríguez to Charles Baumberger, founder of Alamo Portland Cement Company. It seems that this word-of-mouth recommendation from one client to another continued through the years and resulted in ongoing work for Rodríguez. Like Urrutia, Baumberger employed Rodríguez to complete multiple

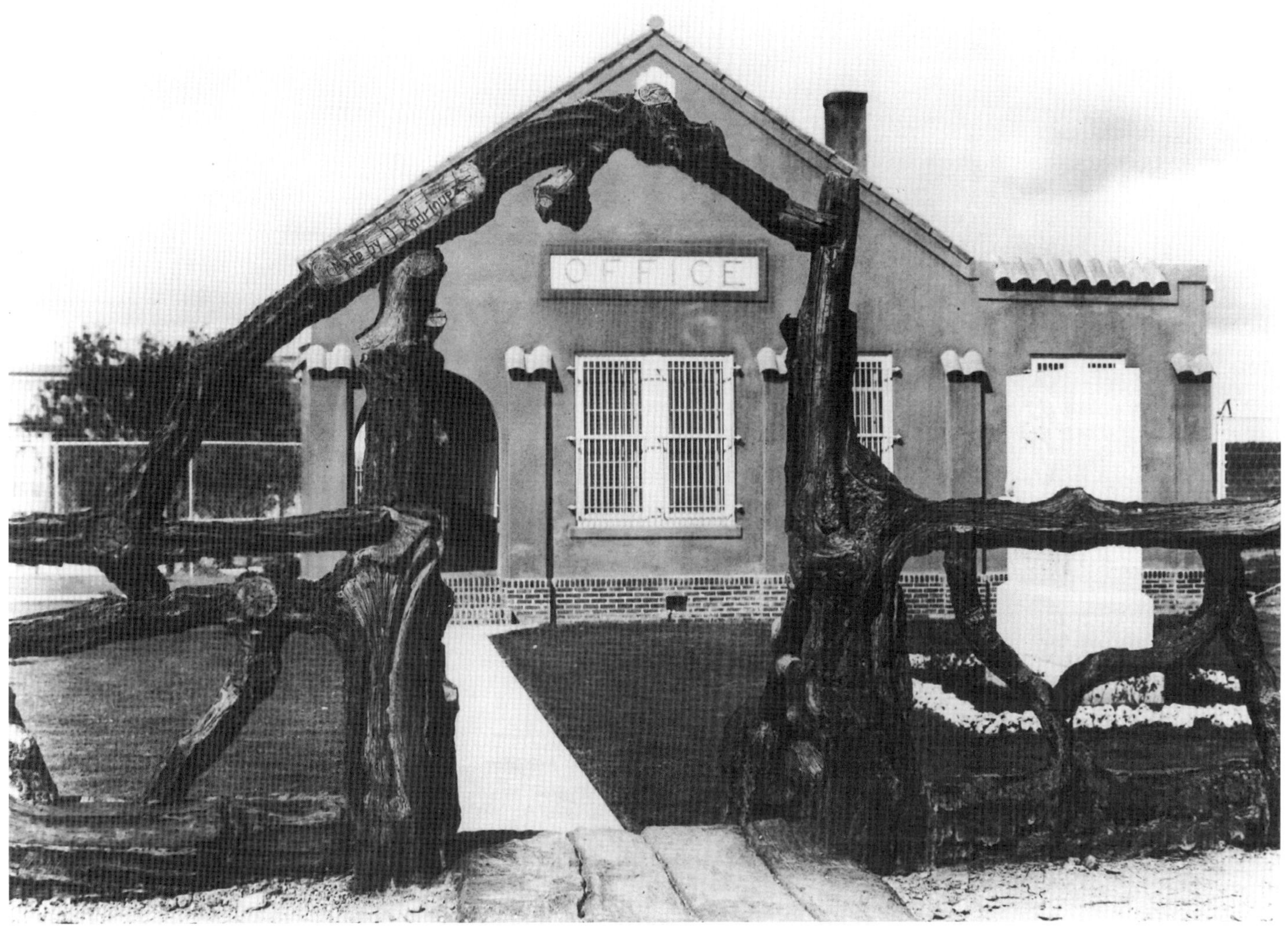

works for him, including pieces for the City of Alamo Heights, his company headquarters, and his personal residence.[19]

Alamo Portland and Roman Cement Company, later renamed Alamo Cement Company, began excavations at the City of San Antonio's quarry north of downtown in 1880. As the quarry operations grew and railroad connections were required, the company moved farther north in 1908, remaining at this new location for seventy-seven years. The old quarry was incorporated into Brackenridge Park, and in 1917, City Parks Commissioner Ray Lambert used prison laborers to transform the area into the Japanese Tea Garden,

Log gate and fence, Alamo Cement Company office, ca. 1926. Photo: Harvey Patterson. Courtesy of Stanley Schmidt.

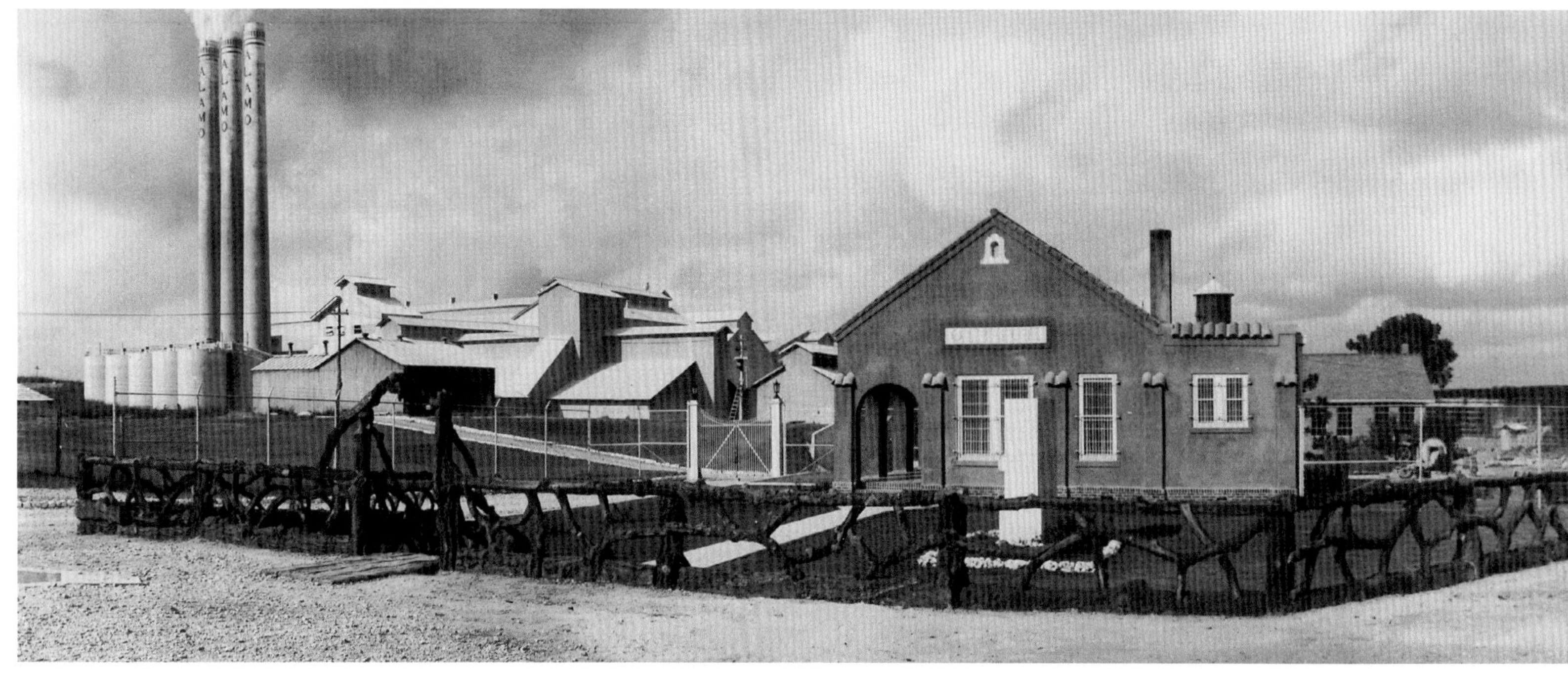

Log fence, Alamo Cement Company office. Courtesy of Dixie Watkins III.

which was recognized in 1979 as a Texas Historic Civil Engineering Landmark, and in 1991, as a Recorded Texas Historic Landmark. In 2004, the gate was listed on the National Register of Historic Places.

Baumberger hired Rodríguez to build two faux projects for the company's office complex at its second location. One was a 125-foot-long wooden fence surrounding the north, east, and west boundaries of the company office, centered with an elaborate arched entryway formed by two large interlocking tree trunks and a curved branch handrail. Fence rail branches imitate twenty species of tree bark, including eucalyptus, a species prevalent in the artisan's native Mexico. Because he did not always sign his work, the "Made by D. Rodríguez" signature etched into a smooth area of the west side of the archway is an important feature.

The second was a round fountain (not operating in 2007) covered by a palapa roof, encircled by a wooden fence, and situated between the company office and the laboratory. Vertical trunks serve as uprights for the fence of intertwined branches and as supports for the roof. The fountain, made of cement and a large honeycomb rock from the Texas Hill Country, tapers upward from its base and is topped by a mushroom-shaped cap. Cement cactus plants embellish crevices on the lower edge of the fountain. Stanley Schmidt notes that the cactus "may seem incongruous, but may have been something that he saw in his country." Twisting snakes encircle two of the vertical tree branch roof supports. No longer

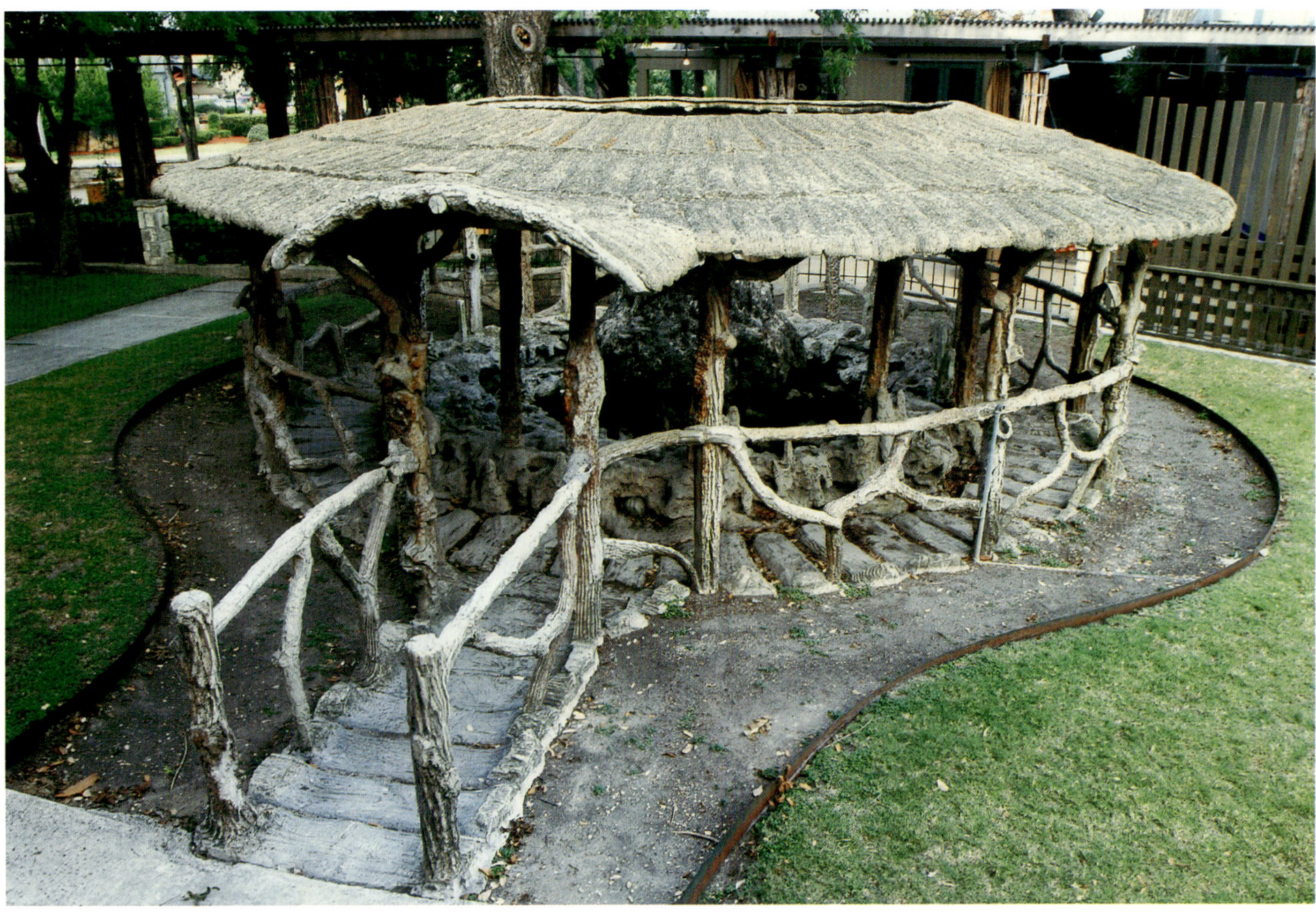

extant is a small concrete alligator that early observers remembered as resting near the pool. Schmidt recalls that when the fountain was in operation, "live goldfish were kept in the pond . . . lavished with live green fern."[20] Both the palapa and fountain were listed on the National Register of Historic Places in 2004.

A large hollow tree sculpture (similar to others by Rodríguez) was moved from Baumberger's home to the grounds of the cement company. According to Stanley Schmidt, it was equipped with electric lighting. This work was removed when the company sold the property, and its 2007 location is unknown.

When Alamo Cement Company moved in 1985, the 468-acre site was sold to investors for a mixed-use development including the Quarry Market. Some original industrial structures were demolished, while others, including three smokestacks, were integrated into

Palapa-covered fountain, Alamo Cement Company office (now Stone Werks), San Antonio. Photo: Bob Parvin.

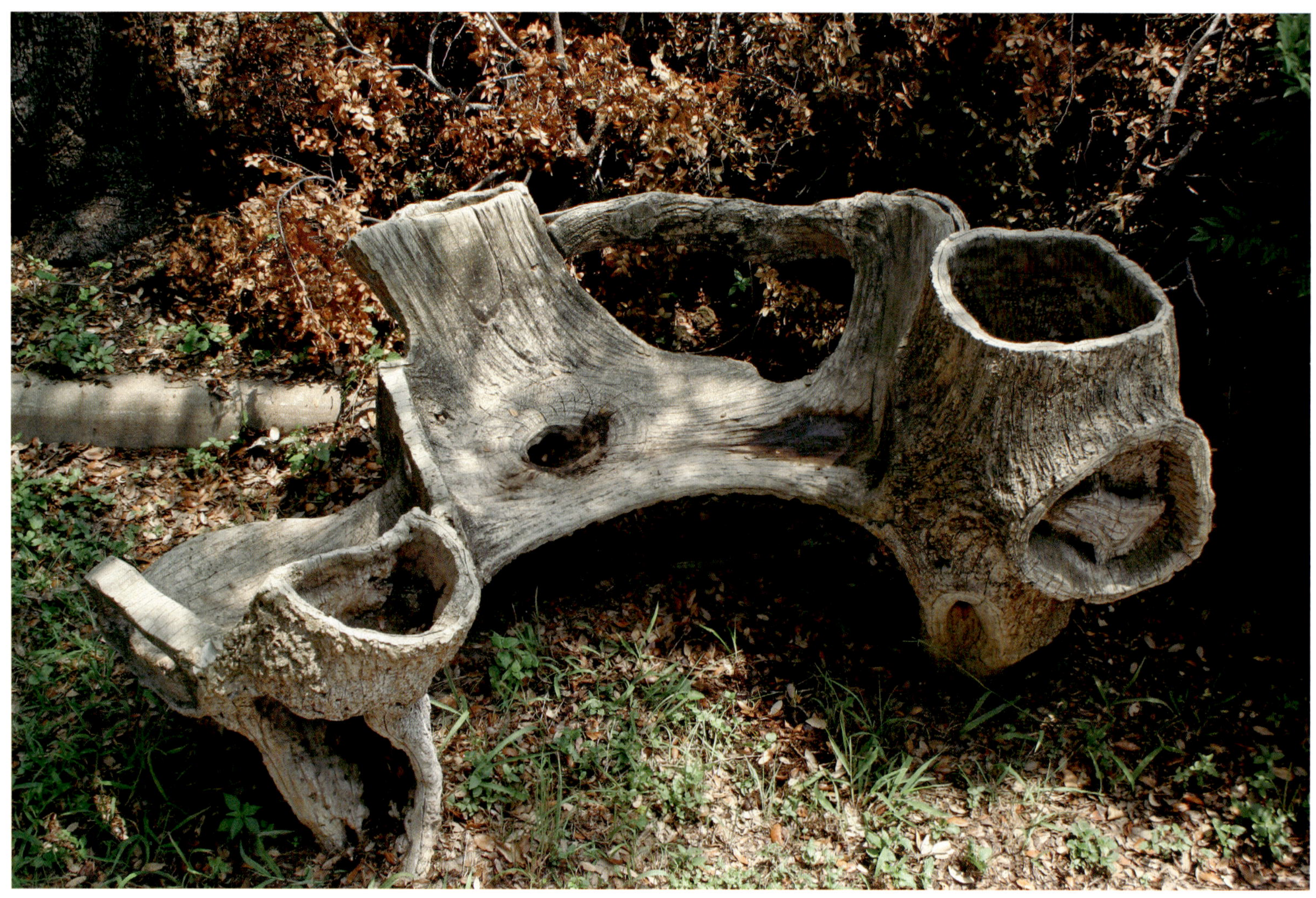

Wooden loveseat. Private collection, Jennifer Robuck. Photo: Bob Parvin.

the project. The company office and laboratory north of the shopping area were purchased separately in 1993, and Rodríguez's fence and fountain were preserved in place. Both the office and the former laboratory were remodeled as restaurants.[21]

Charles Baumberger's garden at his home at 325 West Lynwood (Monte Vista National Register Historic District, 1998) was filled with Rodríguez's concrete work, including the tree house, benches, and planters. When the house was sold in the 1990s, some pieces were sold to private collectors. These works illustrate some of Rodríguez's most inspired creations executed during the 1920s.

Charles Baumberger also engaged Rodríguez to construct a trabajo rústico streetcar stop as a gift to the City of Alamo Heights, an incorporated municipality north of San

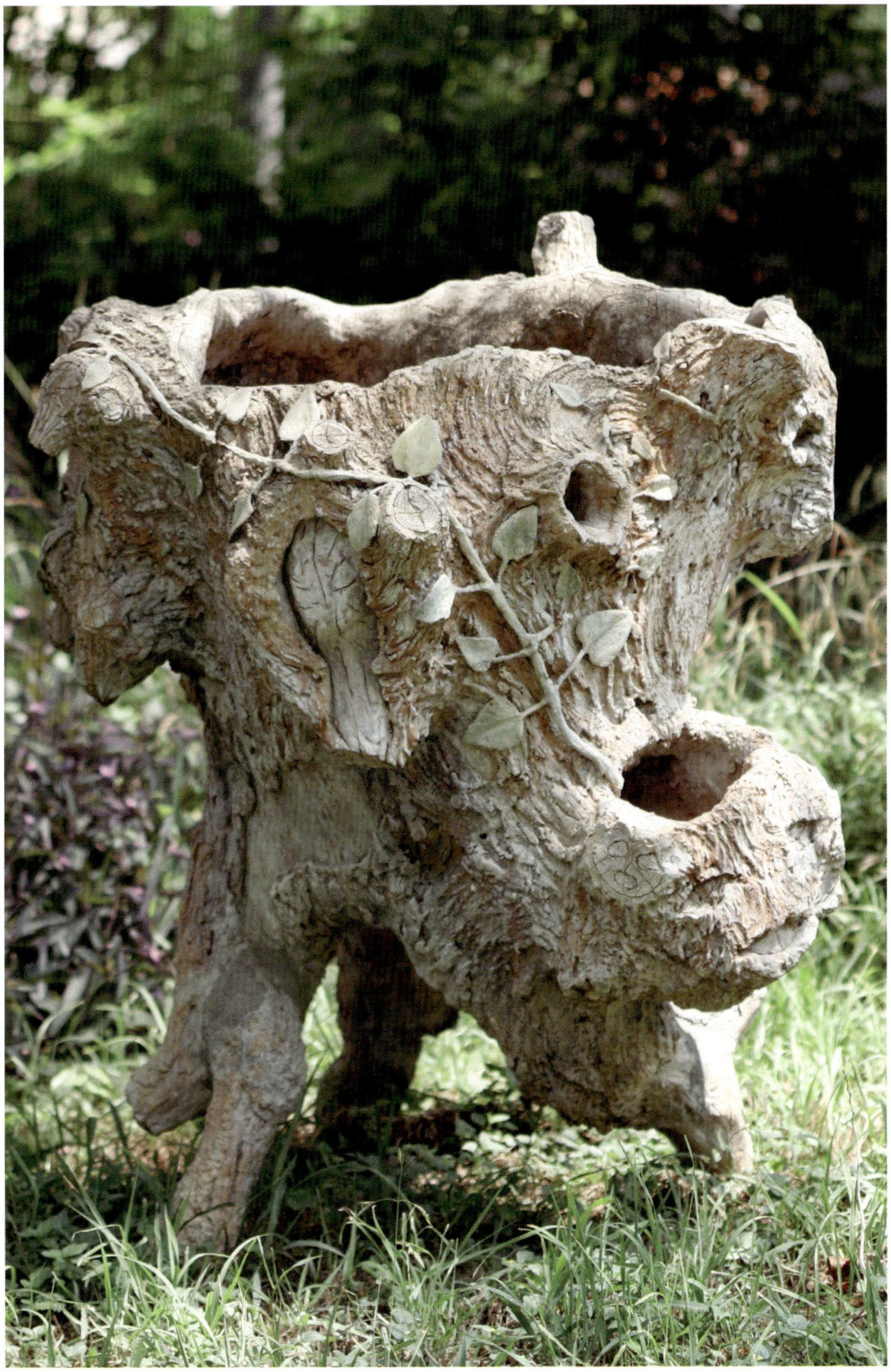

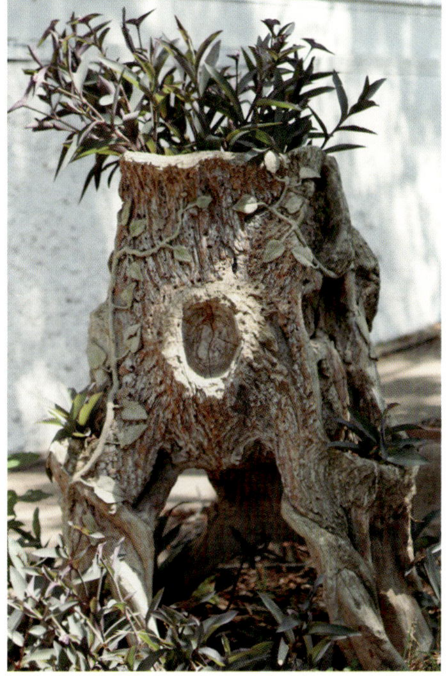

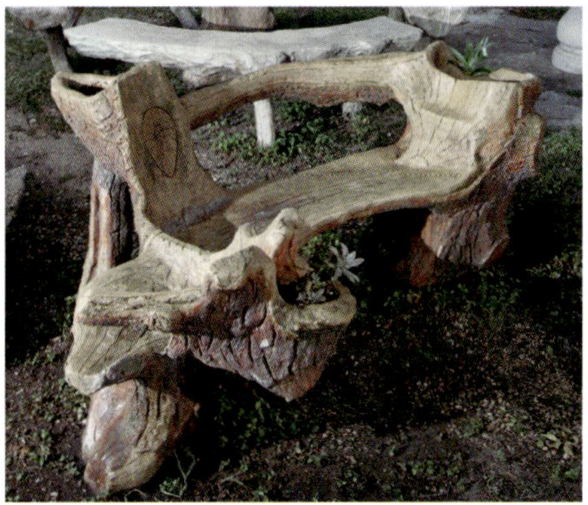

Left: *Footed wooden planter. Private collection, Jennifer Robuck. Photo: Bob Parvin.*
Top: *Footed wooden planter. Private collection, Jennifer Robuck. Photo: Bob Parvin.*
Above: *Wooden loveseat. Private collection, Carlos Cortés. Photo: Bob Parvin.*

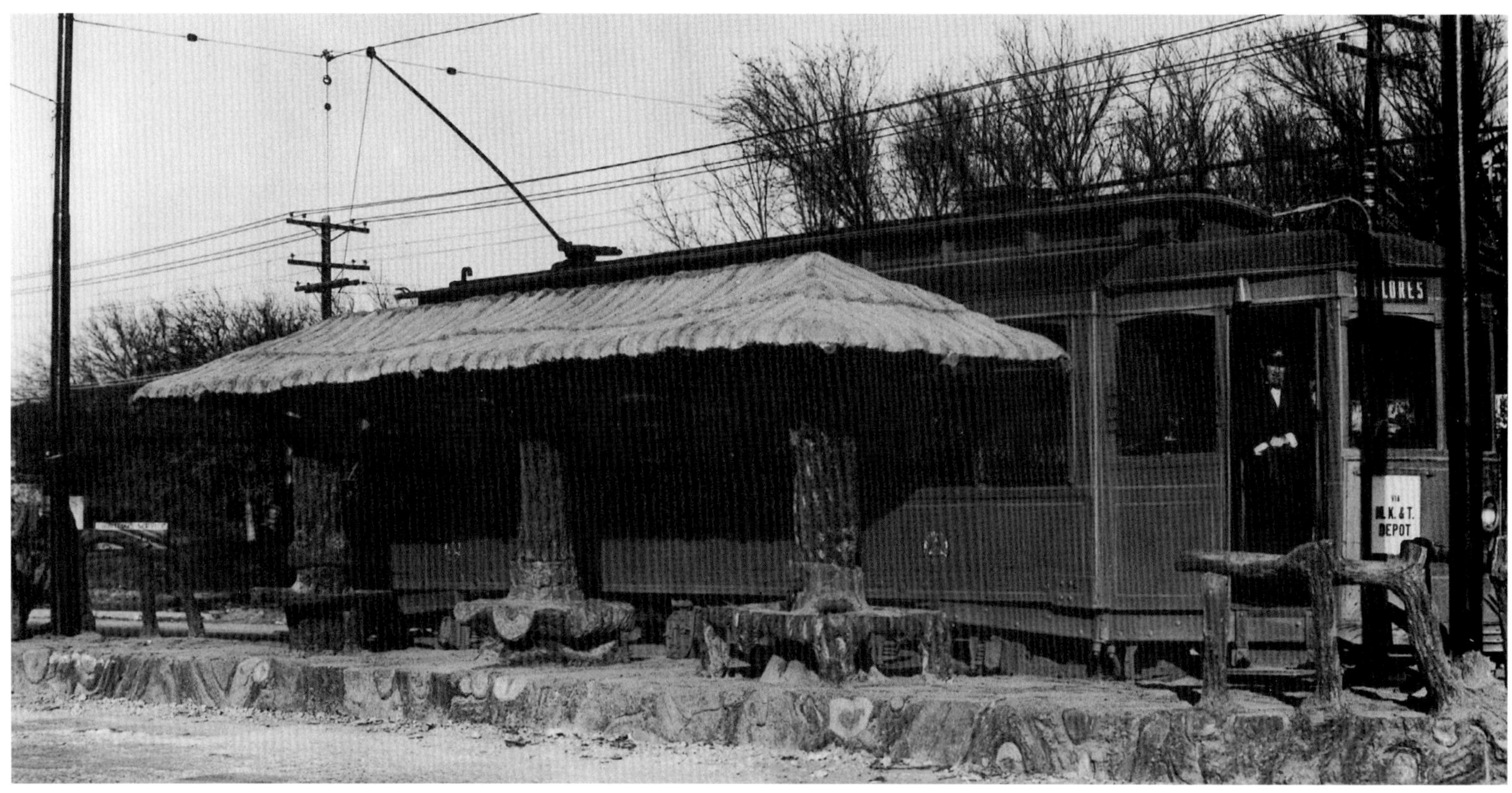

Palapa-roofed trolley stop, Alamo Heights, Bexar County, Texas, ca. 1927. Courtesy of Stanley Schmidt.

Antonio's city limits. John Kite, former plant engineer with the San Antonio Transit Company who documented the city's streetcar system, stated that the structure was so realistic "that I've even seen birds sit on it."[22] Three large tree trunks with branches serving as brackets support a gabled palapa roof and rest on a floor of heavily textured crosscut logs. The shelter, located at Broadway and Patterson Avenue, is still used as a bus stop and was placed on the National Register of Historic Places in 2004. A bronze plaque attached to the inside of the roof reads:

Presented to

City of

Alamo Heights

by

San Antonio Portland

Cement Company

Charles Baumberger, Pres.

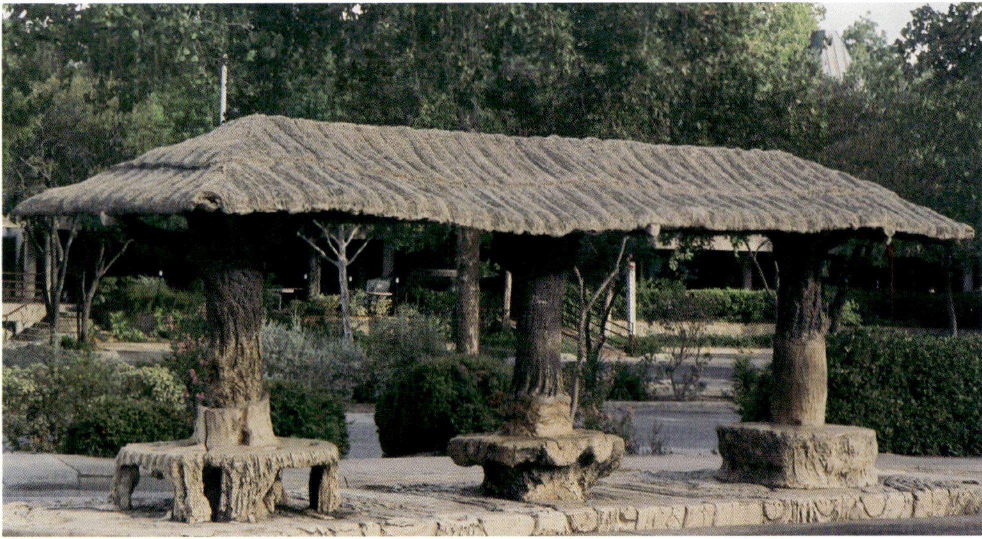

Works for San Antonio Parks and the City of San Antonio

Dionicio Rodríguez completed numerous works for the City of San Antonio and the San Antonio City Parks Department that were installed in Brackenridge, Pittman-Sullivan, and Buckeye parks, Alamo Plaza (National Register Historic District, 1977), and the garden of the Spanish Governor's Palace (National Register, 1970).[23] The designs of several of these municipal projects are unique, though others were replicated elsewhere in the United States during his thirty-year career.

Brackenridge Park

Five of his cement projects are located in Brackenridge Park, including two of his best known pieces—a footbridge and the entrance to the Japanese Tea Garden, both listed on the National Register of Historic Places in 2004. The park is named for philanthropist Col. George Brackenridge, who gave the city 199 acres of land for park use in 1899. It has expanded through the years and now covers 344 acres. Built around 1925, the wooden footbridge is a curved structure resembling an elongated arbor; it parallels a bend in the road and spans a flood channel of the San Antonio River. The design features thirty-three pairs of vertical tree trunks that support horizontal branches. Handrail branches are infilled with intertwined cross branches, similar to the fence at the Alamo Portland Cement Company office. Crosscut planks form the walkway. The realism of the structure's detailing (insect borings, knotholes, bark textures) was described in *Popular Mechanics* magazine in 1927: "stripped bark exposed the channel made by some wood borer, a spot where

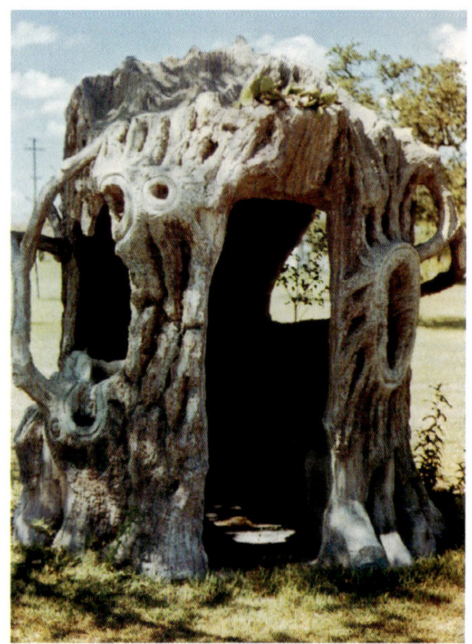

Left: *Palapa-roofed trolley stop, Alamo Heights, Bexar County, Texas, 2006. Photo: Laurie Light Saunders.* Below: *Hollow tree house originally located at Charles Bamberger's home and later moved to Alamo Cement Company. Present location unknown. Courtesy of Stanley Schmidt.*

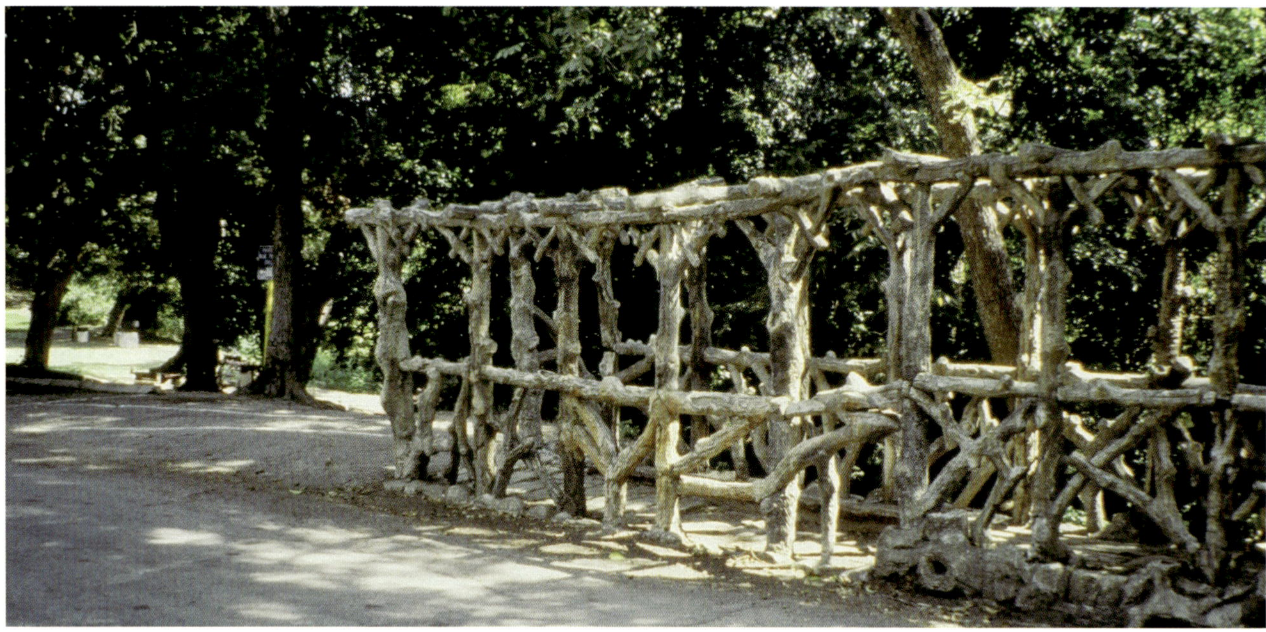

Wooden bridge, Brackenridge Park, San Antonio.
Photo: Patsy Light.

some industrious woodpecker sought a grub. Park attendants say this bridge even fools the woodpeckers."[24]

Although Rodríguez would later build many bridges, this design remains unique among known sites of his work. "D. Rodríguez" is incised in one of the horizontal branches and on a lower projecting support. Maximo Cortés, who was an assistant on the construction, was quoted in a newspaper interview in 1981: "Under the bridge . . . we made these figures. They're knocked down now. Not many people have seen them." He drew a sketch of the bridge illustrating "eerie figures . . . emerging from the structure but at the same time holding it up."[25] To small children, these gnome-like figures would have had a magical appearance with their bits of color and peaked hats.

In 1908, the Alamo Portland and Roman Cement Company moved their operations near the central city to a site farther north, abandoning their quarry and a group of rock huts where the laborers lived. Some of the workers and their families remained and operated little shops for tourists, where they sold pottery, baskets, embroidery, and food.[26] Later, in the 1940s, the small houses were used as artists' studios. The cavity, which had become a municipal trash dump, was transformed when City Parks Commissioner Ray Lambert began construction on the municipal lily pond and Japanese garden in the quarry in 1917 on land that was part of the city's original Spanish grant. Using prison labor, Lambert transformed the site into a garden with a pagoda with a palm thatch roof, lily ponds, waterfalls, and landscaped areas.[27] In exchange for his assistance in developing the

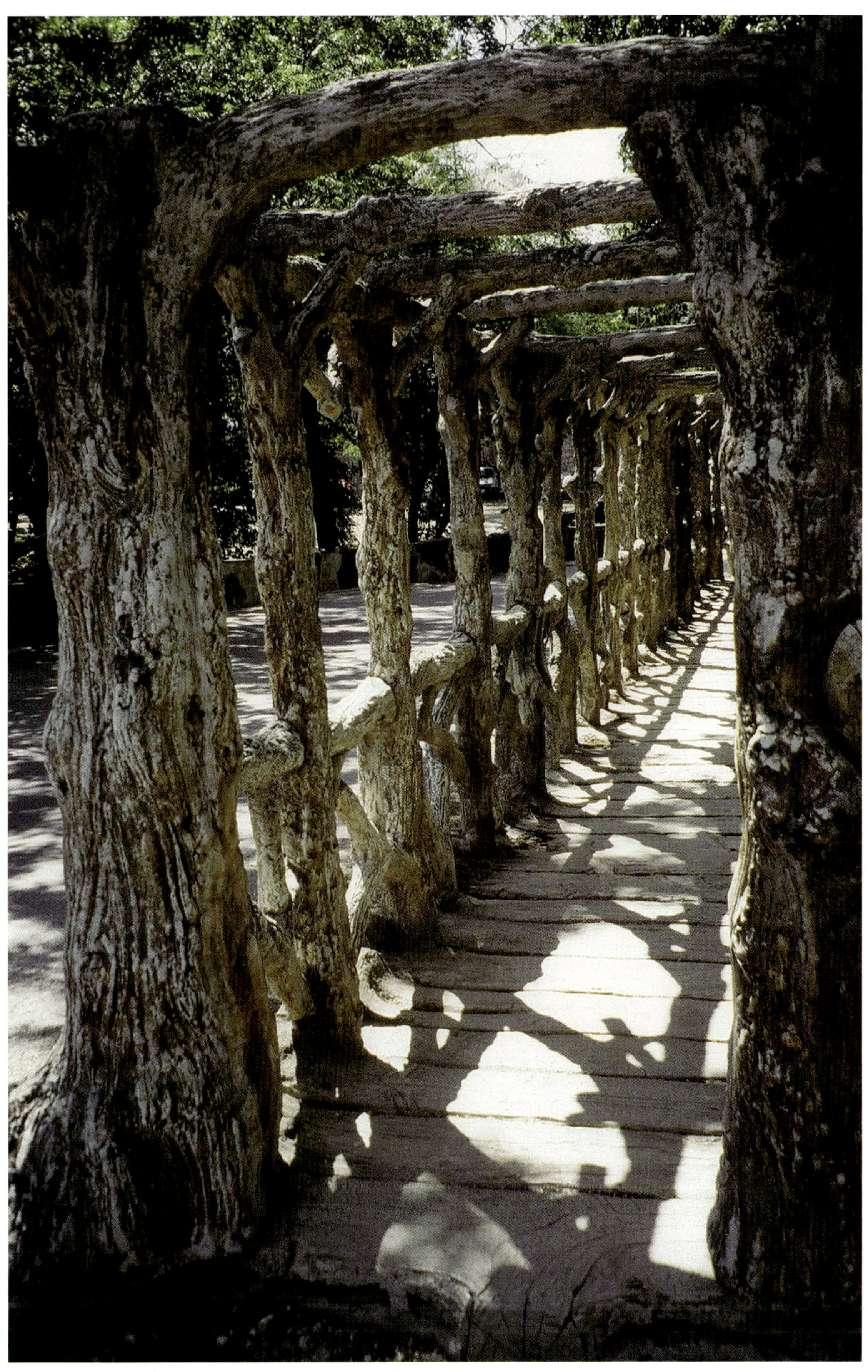

Wooden bridge, Brackenridge Park.
Photo: Patsy Light.

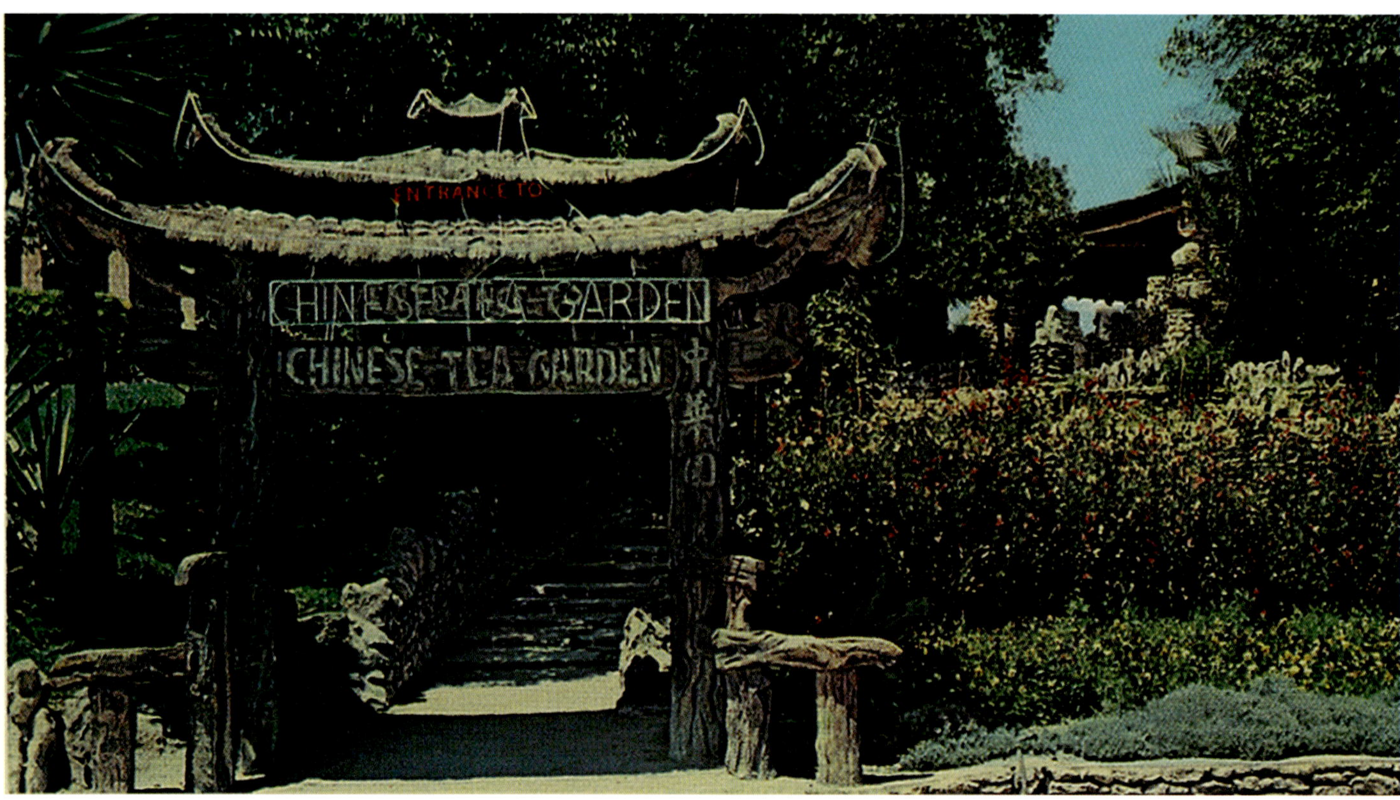

Chinese Tea Garden gate with neon signage, Brackenridge Park, ca. 1942. It is now called the Japanese Tea Garden. Postcard courtesy of Weiner Publishing Company and Tim McHugh.

garden, Lambert invited Japanese immigrant, artist, and tea importer Kimi Elizo Jingu and his wife, Miyoshi, to live there. The Jingus managed a concession, serving green tea and green tea ice cream. All but one of their eight children were born in the garden. In response to the anti-Japanese sentiment in World War II, the Jingus were told to leave. When they refused, their water was cut off, and the then widowed Mrs. Jingu (her husband died in 1938) and her family were evicted from their home. Forty-two years later, in 1984, the city officially renamed the garden the Japanese Tea Garden and invited surviving Jingu family members and their children to attend a special event honoring them.[28]

The garden—which has been known by several names, including Japanese Sunken Garden, when the adjacent Sunken Garden Theatre was built in the 1930s—was renamed the Chinese Tea Garden in 1942, and Dionicio Rodríguez was hired to build what is considered one of his most exuberant works: the entrance portal. A neon sign was attached to the gate, which, according to Carlos Cortés, was built as a collaborative effort by Rodríguez and his father, Maximo. The elder Cortés said their work was done "media y media," half done by Rodríguez and the other half by Cortés.[29] Rodríguez's signature is etched into the left handrail.

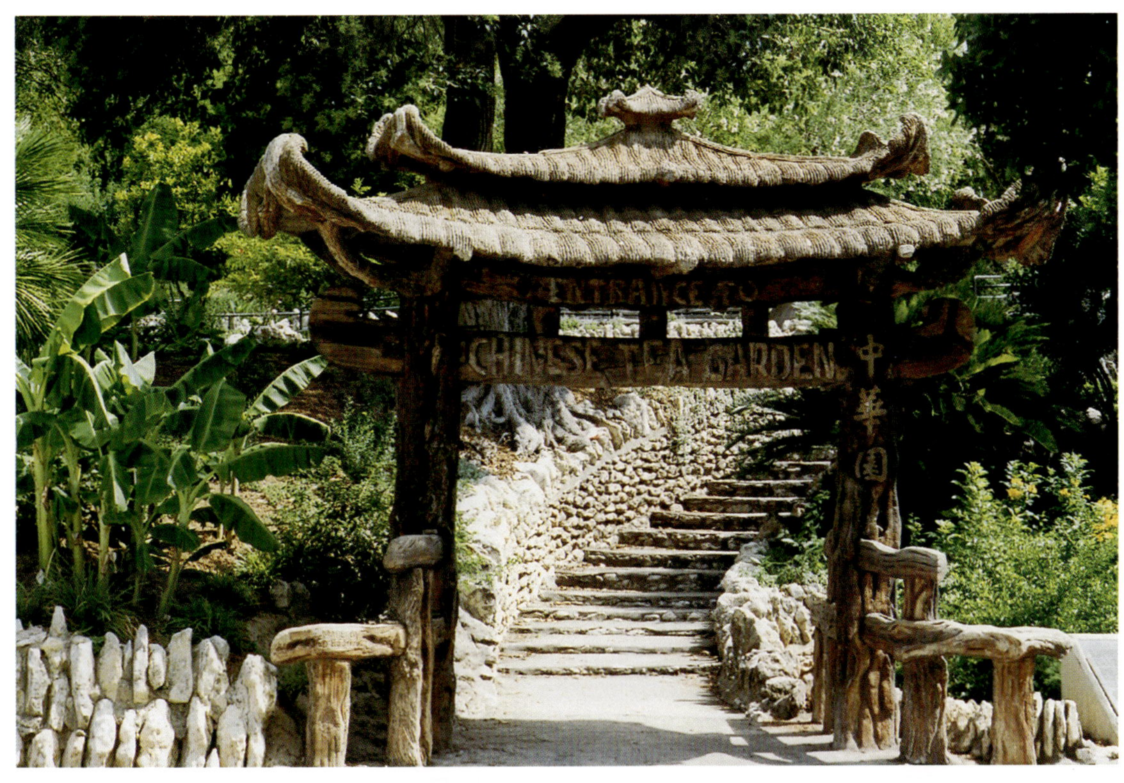

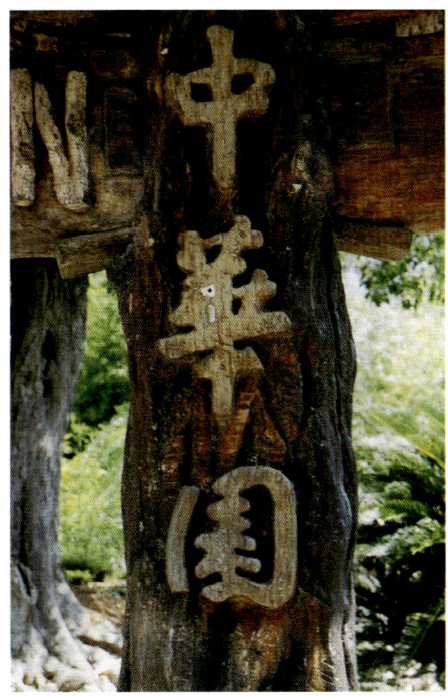

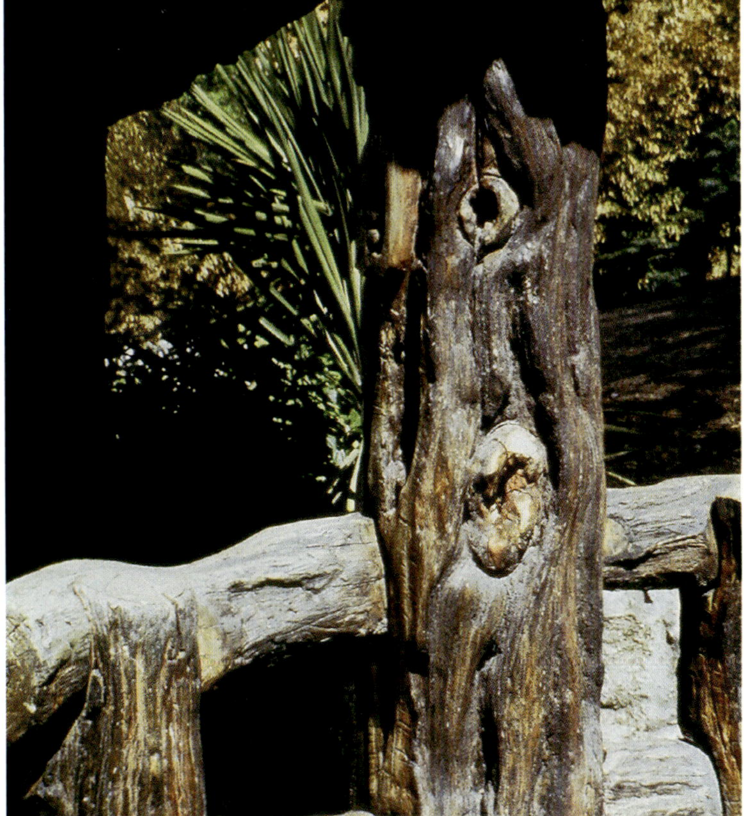

Above Left: *Japanese Tea Garden entrance, showing 1942 name. Photo: Laurie Light Saunders.*
Above: *Japanese Tea Garden. Calligraphy reads: "China Garden." Photo: Laurie Light Saunders.*
Left: *Detail of Japanese Tea Garden gate railing, Brackenridge Park, San Antonio. Photo: Patsy Light.*

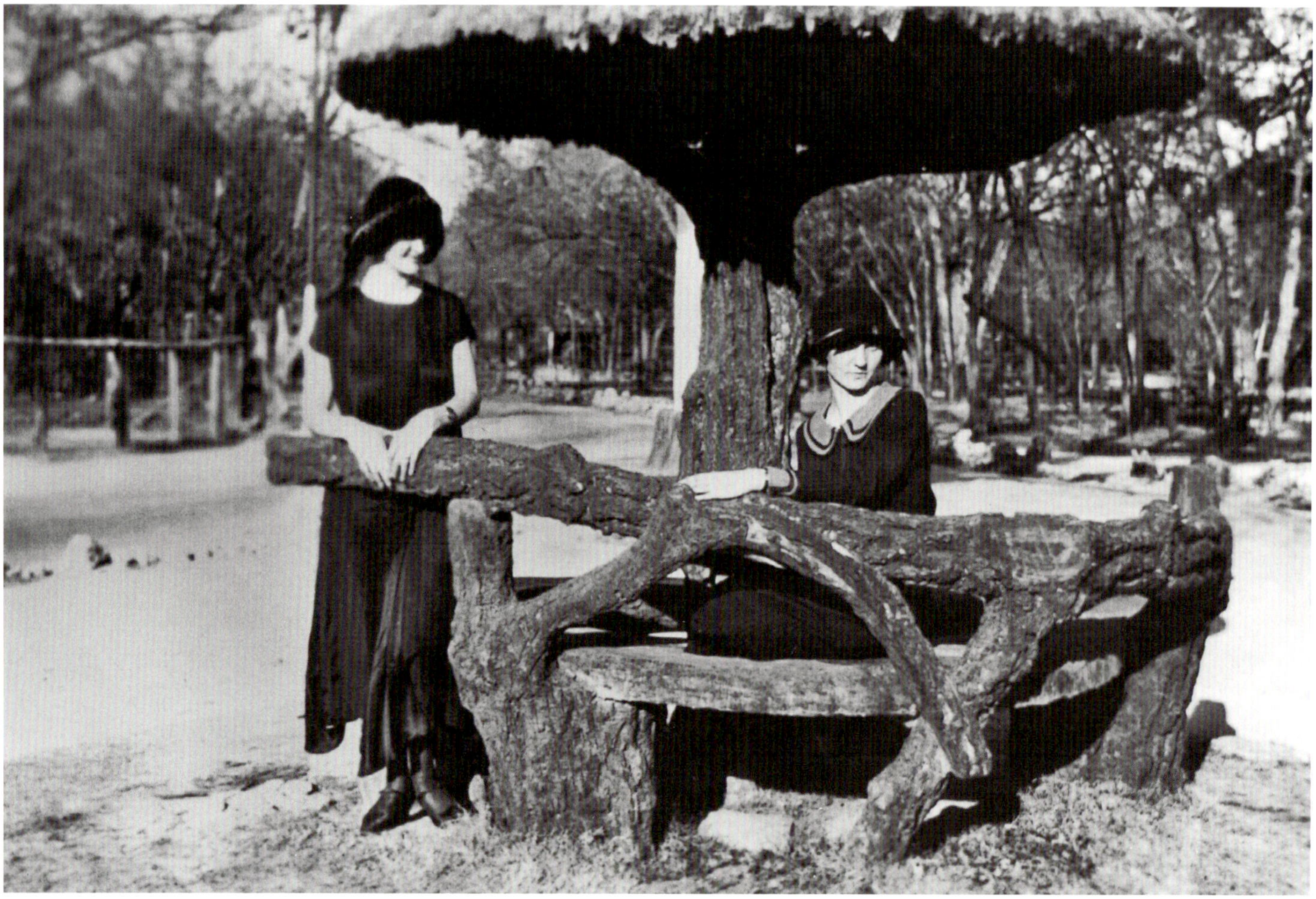

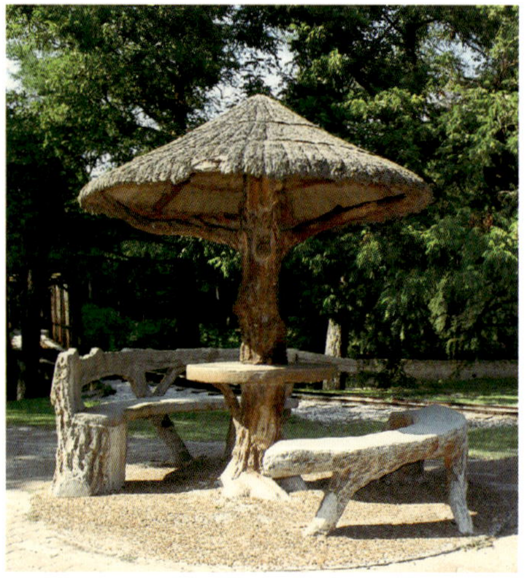

Four sturdy vertical tree trunk posts with branches as brackets support lintels and a thatched roof, with four upturned corners. A smaller palapa roof, also with the curved detail, is built on top of the main roof, and a third smaller roof of the same design caps it. At strategic joints, wooden shims are inserted. Two front lintels bear the inscription "Entrance Chinese Tea Garden." The vertical supporting logs and attached curved horizontal handrails have worm holes, crevices, patches of lichen, and exaggerated knotholes. At critical points Rodríguez applied his signature pyramid-headed bolts. Chinese calligraphy sculpted in relief adorns the right-hand post and the reverse side of the largest lintel. A translation of the writing is "China Garden."[30] It is interesting that in 1922 a Chinese school was established, which children attended for classes in calligraphy and philosophy after the regular school day. Areas of color—rich tans and yellows—remain very intense, in comparison with other pieces in the San Antonio area. Rodríguez sculpted a smaller

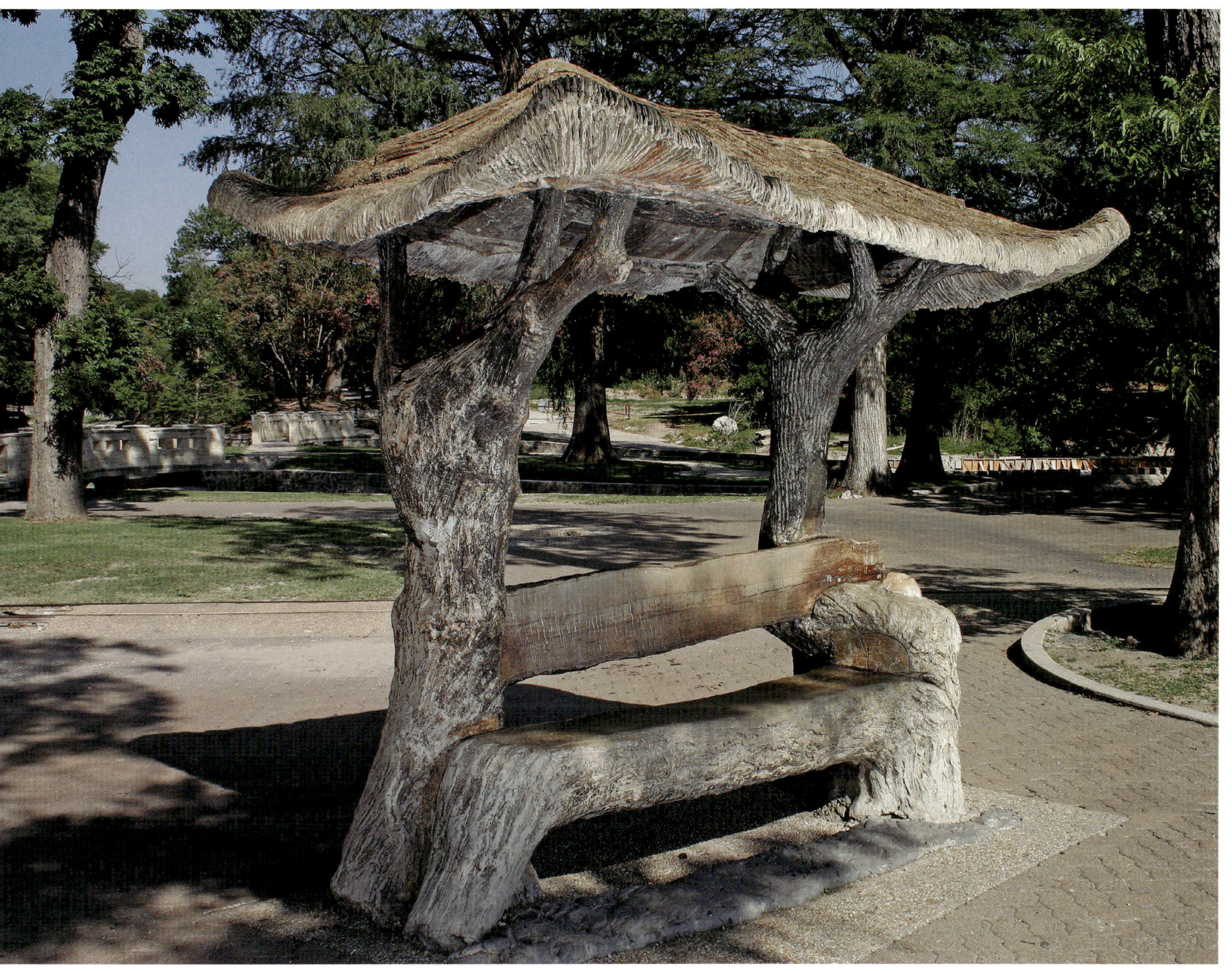

Opposite Above: *Palapa table and benches, Brackenridge Park, ca. 1925. Institute of Texan Cultures, University of Texas at San Antonio. Courtesy of Juanita Herff Chipman.*
Opposite Below: *Palapa table and benches, Brackenridge Park, San Antonio, 2006. Photo: Bob Parvin.*
Above: *Palapa bench, Brackenridge Park, San Antonio. Photo: Bob Parvin.*

version of the gate, along with numerous other pieces, in Clayton, New Mexico in 1943 (see chapter 4).

A palapa with its thatched roof resembling a large mushroom shelters a table sited near the San Antonio River. A huge tree trunk supports the hipped roof, made of three concentric layers of thatch bundles. The round table surface that surrounds the trunk is made of mortised boards, and has incised graffiti. One seat is a textured bark log that appears to have grown at a right angle and has two branch legs, and the other is a smooth curved slab with a back support. Rodríguez repeated this design, with slight variations, at six additional sites.

A palapa-roofed bench, an oft-repeated Rodríguez design, stands in the park at the terminus of St. Mary's Street across from the entrance to the San Antonio Zoo. The roof corners curve upward, similar to the oriental roof design of the Japanese Tea Garden entrance. On the lower edge on the inside of the roof is a small applied concrete plaque that reads "D. Rodríguez."

Alamo Plaza

Photographs of Alamo Plaza made about 1959 reveal a large hollow tree structure and a small bench similar to those in Brackenridge Park and at Miraflores, both attributed to Rodríguez. The tree house was removed from Alamo Plaza and is now in Brackenridge Park.

Buckeye Park

A structure of two curving tree trunks provides an unusual entrance to Buckeye Park on Wildwood Drive, northwest of downtown adjacent to Interstate 10. At the apex, one of the large curved trunks is notched, and the corresponding trunk passes through the notch. Although the work has no signature, the structure bears trademarks of Rodríguez's work—heavily textured bark with knots and insect holes. The log on the right front of the gate bears a portion of an inscription that reads "Hugo Traupmann, Director of Parks," and the numerals "83327-10." The gate was listed on the National Register of Historic Places in 2004.

Pittman-Sullivan Park

A dead tree sculpture attributed to Rodríguez once stood in Pittman-Sullivan Park on the eastern edge of downtown. Though demolished many years ago, it deserves mention because of its design relationship to faux sculptures built by Rodríguez elsewhere, particularly the dead trees in the flamingo exhibit at the Houston Zoo.

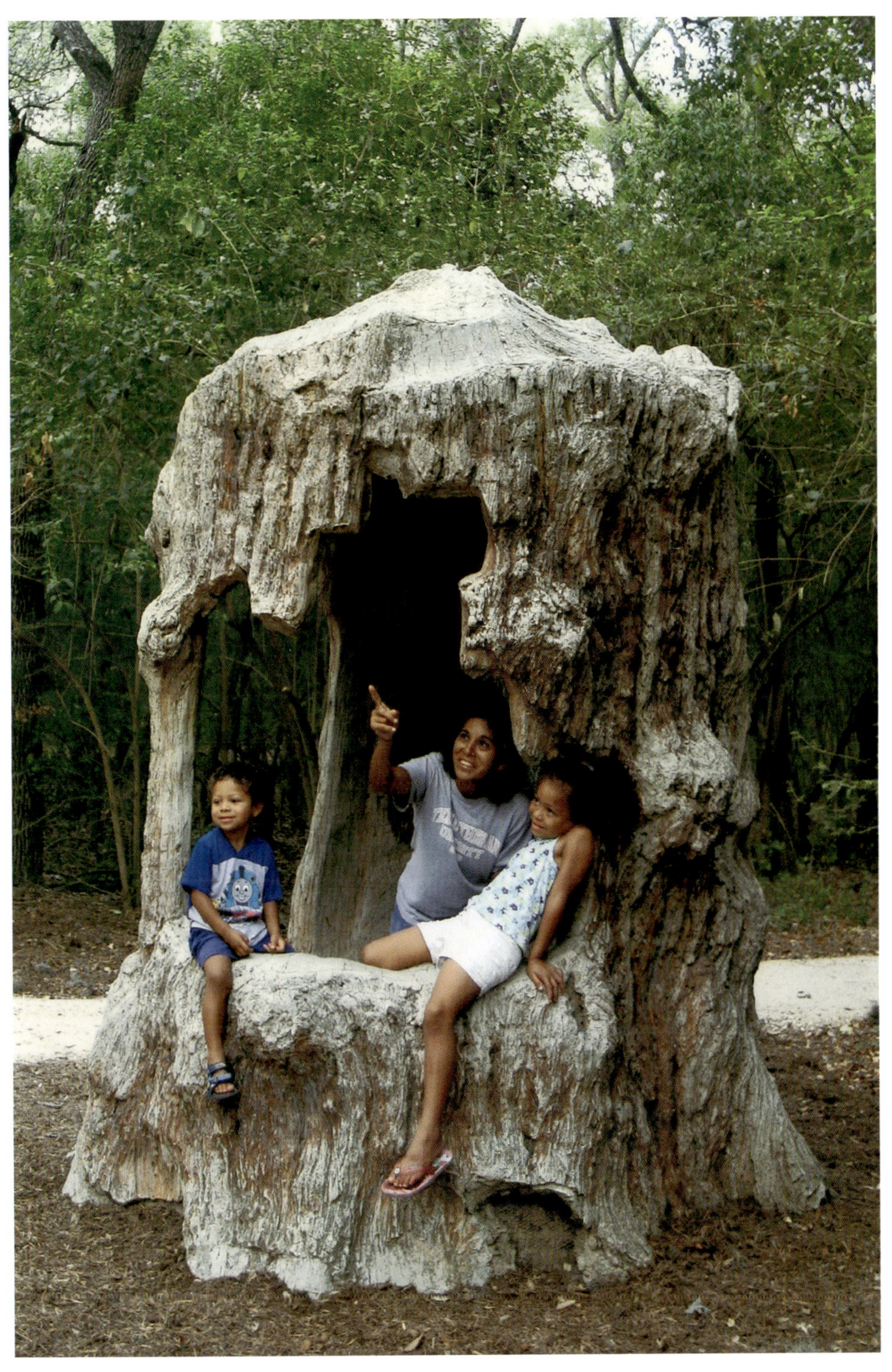

Hollow tree house, Brackenridge Park, San Antonio.
Photo: Bob Parvin.

Right: *Detail, Buckeye Park gate, San Antonio.*
Photo: Patsy Light.
Below: *Wood slab bench, Spanish Governor's Palace,*
San Antonio. Photo: Bob Parvin.

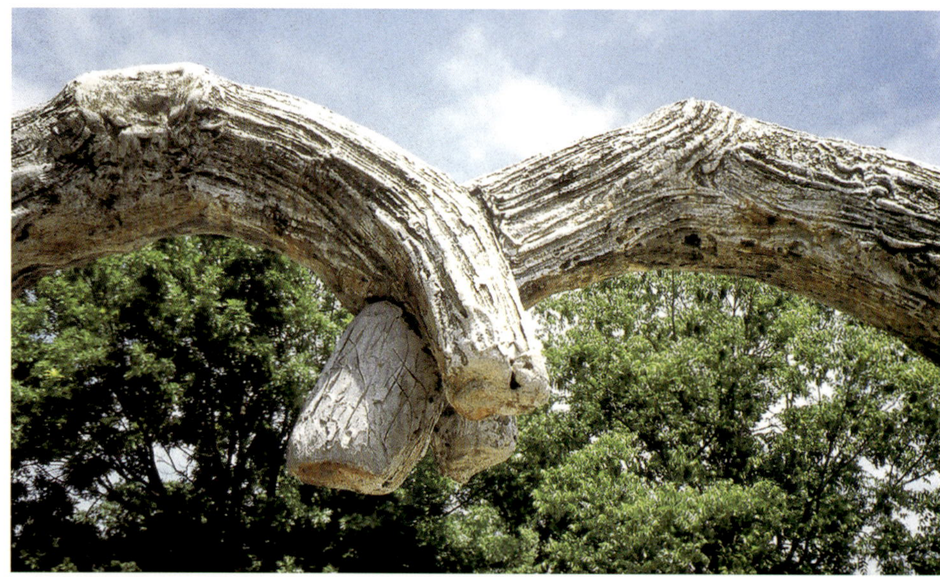

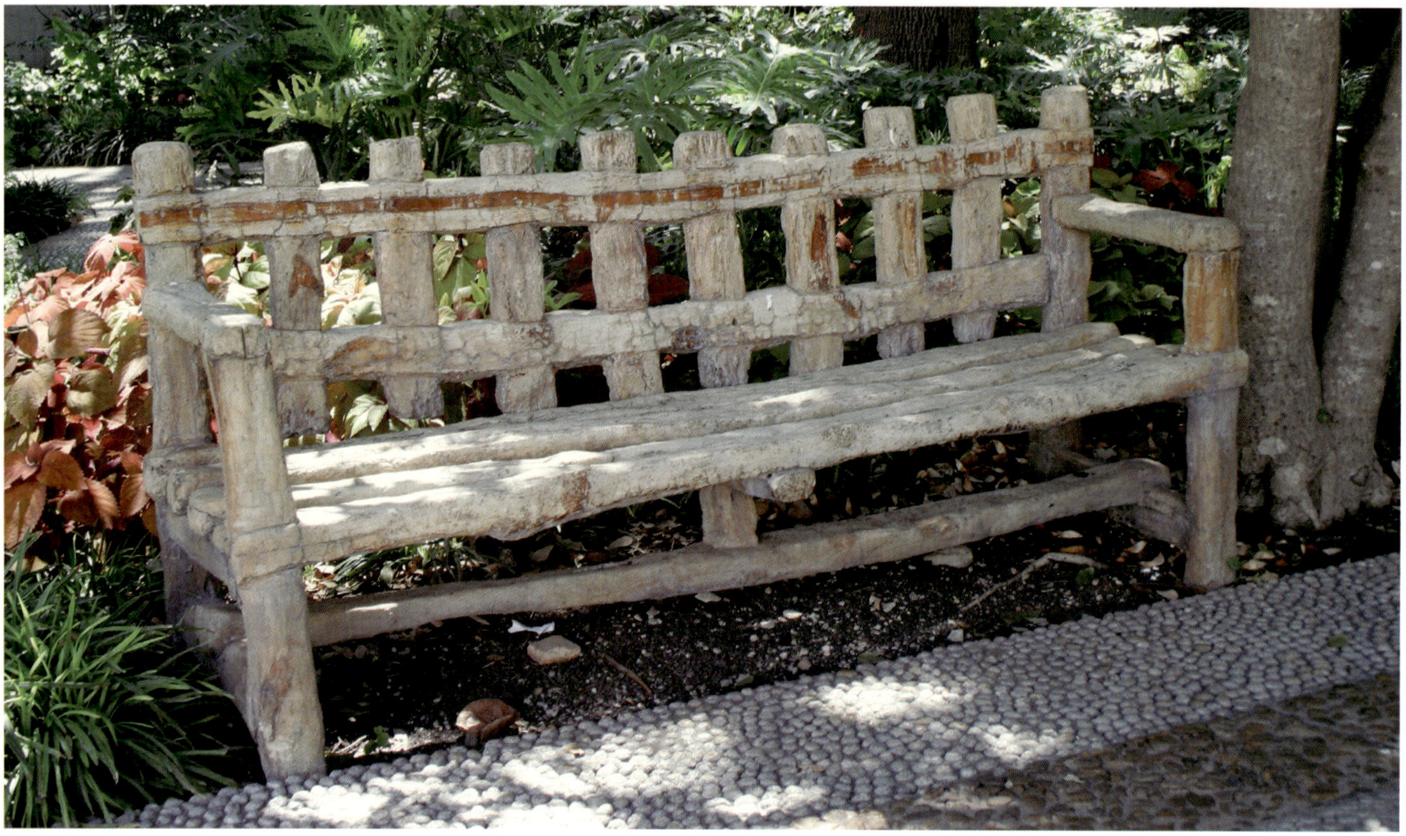

The Spanish Governor's Palace

At the urging of Adina de Zavala's Landmarks Association and early members of the San Antonio Conservation Society, citizens approved a bond issue in 1928 that allowed the City of San Antonio to purchase the Spanish Governor's Palace, the city's sole surviving secular building from the Spanish period. Architect Harvey Smith was in charge of restoration of the dilapidated building, while Dallas landscape architect Homer Fry designed the interior patio.[31]

Dionicio Rodríguez completed eight concrete pieces: four wood slab benches that encircle the fountain and four wooden light poles standing in the garden. The bench design, consisting of adjacent flat-planed slabs, is not seen in other Rodríguez work, but his technique of creating the texture of insect holes, knotholes, and rough and peeling bark is present. Additionally, countersunk screws appear on the back supports of the benches. The Governor's Palace inventory states: "Benches, wood-like in patio. Metal Frame with concrete. A man named Rodríguez about 1930."[32]

Additional Works in the San Antonio Area

When Alamo Portland Cement relocated its operations from the Brackenridge Park area to a site five miles north of the city, the company built ninety-one cottages and rented them to its employees and their families. Many of these families were Catholic Mexicans who had fled Mexico during the revolution. This settlement, Cementville, was several miles from the nearest Catholic church in Alamo Heights. In 1925, Archbishop Arthur J. Drossaerts assigned Reverend Peter Baque, a native Spanish speaker from the Basque area of Spain, to establish a church for these families. Realizing that there was no church named for the patron saint of the city, he named the shrine for St. Anthony of Padua.[33]

Stations of the Cross and Grotto at the
Shrine of St. Anthony of Padua

Father Baque supervised construction of the shrine—first, a wooden structure; later, in 1928, a stucco one; the grotto in 1933; and the Stations of the Cross in 1936. The Stations of the Cross and the shrine were placed on the National Register of Historic Places in 2004. Manuela Theall remembers that Rodríguez constructed the Stations and the grotto, either before or after she traveled with him in the 1930s.

The fourteen upright stations, built of Edwards Plateau honeycomb limestone rock, are capped by two pinnacles, and at eye level each has a relief-carved marble plaque with a scene from the "Way of the Cross," illustrating Christ's walk to Golgotha. Inscribed below each plaque is the name of the donor of the station. Rodríguez's patron, Charles

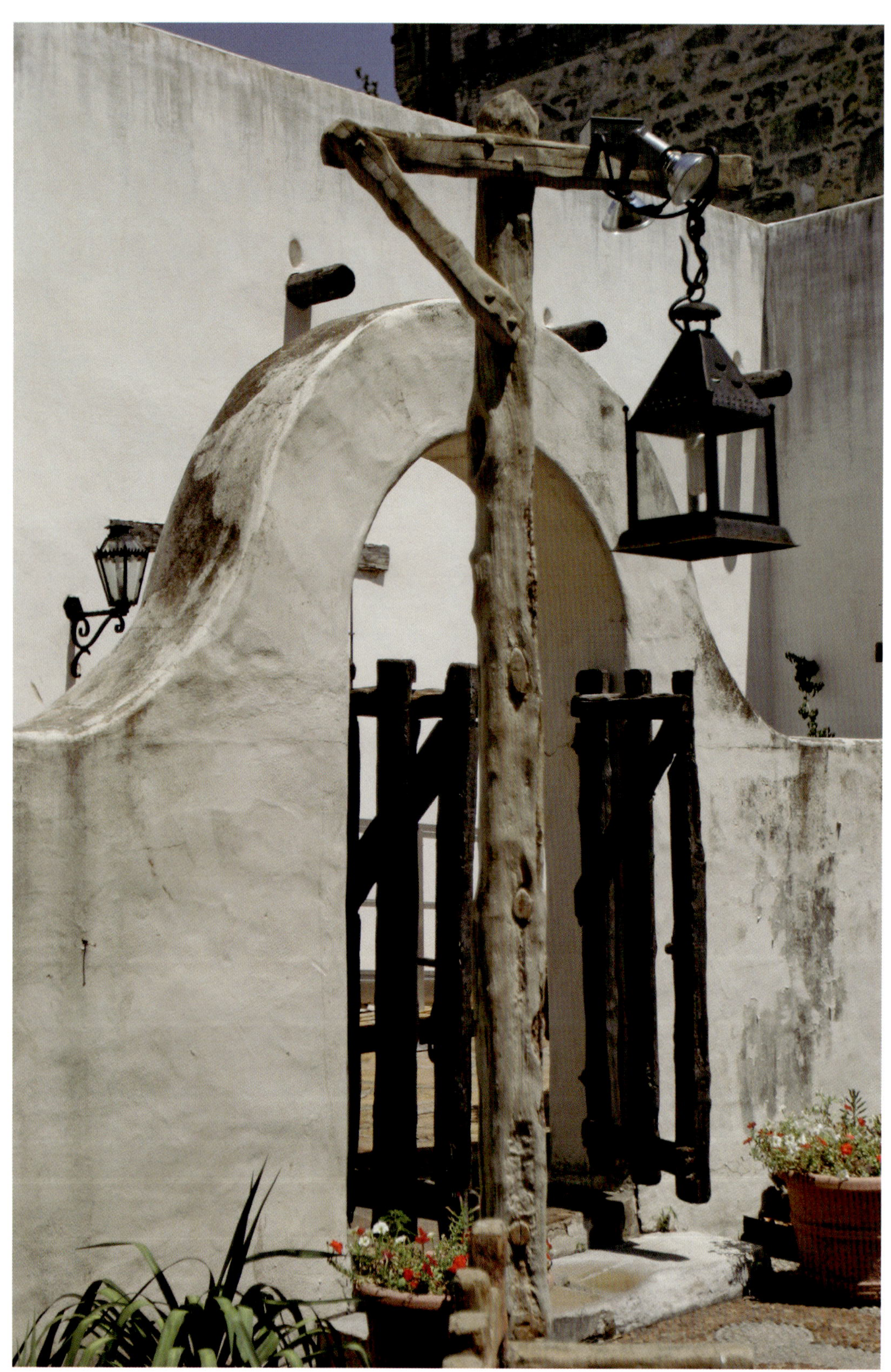

Wood light pole at Spanish Governor's Palace,
San Antonio. Photo: Bob Parvin.

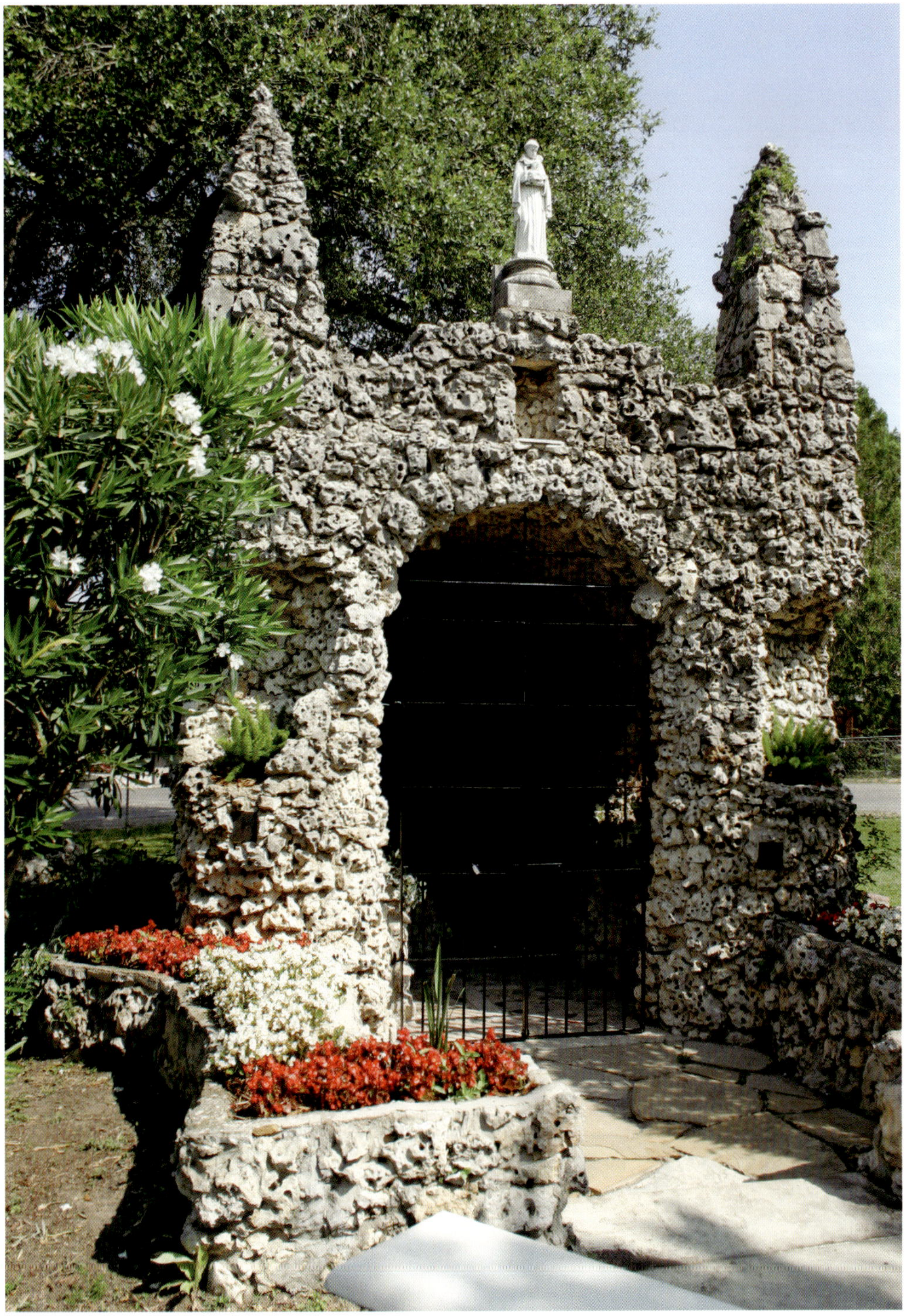

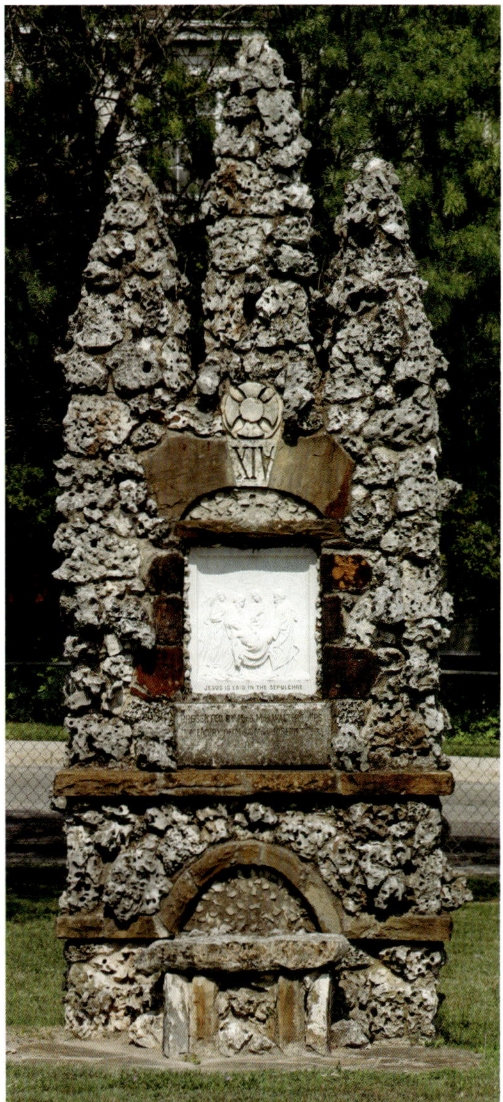

Left: *Grotto, Shrine of St. Anthony of Padua, San Antonio. Photo: Bob Parvin.*

Above: *Station of the Cross, Shrine of St. Anthony of Padua, San Antonio. Photo: Bob Parvin.*

Baumberger, donated one of the stations. These stations, grotto, and shrine are the property of the Missionary Servants of Saint Anthony, an order founded by Reverend Baque to serve the residents of Cementville.[35] The grotto, with a central gated arched opening, is constructed of the same rock as the stations and has an interior lined with seashells reminiscent of an earlier work at Eddingston Court in Port Arthur, Texas.

The construction style and incorporation of Edwards limestone make this similar to the grotto at Moye Retreat Center in Castroville, Texas, built and signed by Rodríguez in 1945 (see chapter 3).

Jacala Restaurant

Carlos Cortés, based on accounts by his father, Maximo Cortés, credits Rodríguez with the trabajo rústico false-front façade and attached palapa-roofed portico of the building at 2702 North St. Mary's. Lucille Quiñones Hooker, whose family's popular Mexican restaurant, Jacala, once occupied the building, says that the façade of board facing and log-trimmed windows and doors was applied when they remodeled an existing building in 1952. Their father thought the building "too plain" and engaged a group of artisans to apply the faux bois details.[36] Listed on the National Register of Historic Places in 2004, this is the only building façade by Rodríguez in Texas that has been documented at the time of writing.

Around 1926, soon after his arrival in San Antonio, Dionicio began to get work in other areas of the state—first in towns in near proximity to San Antonio and later in East Texas, including Port Arthur, Beaumont, Houston, and Sweeny.

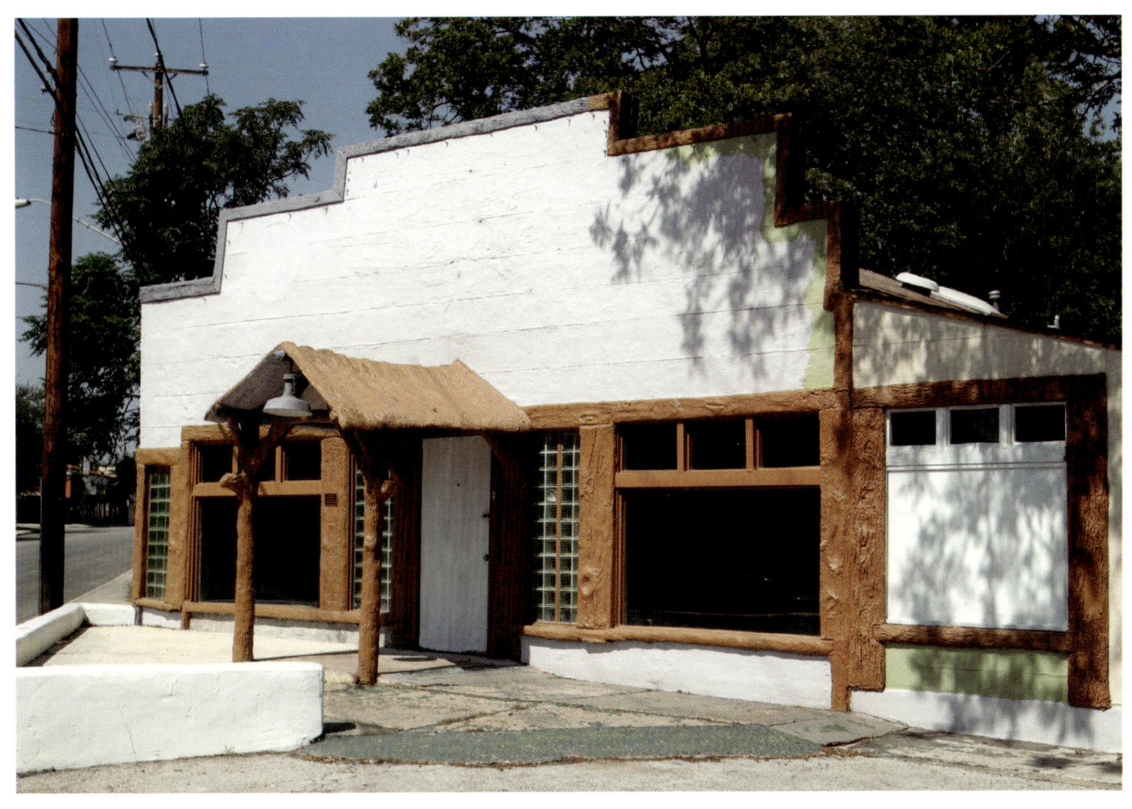

Façade of the former Jacala Restaurant, 2702 N. St. Mary's, San Antonio. Photo: Bob Parvin.

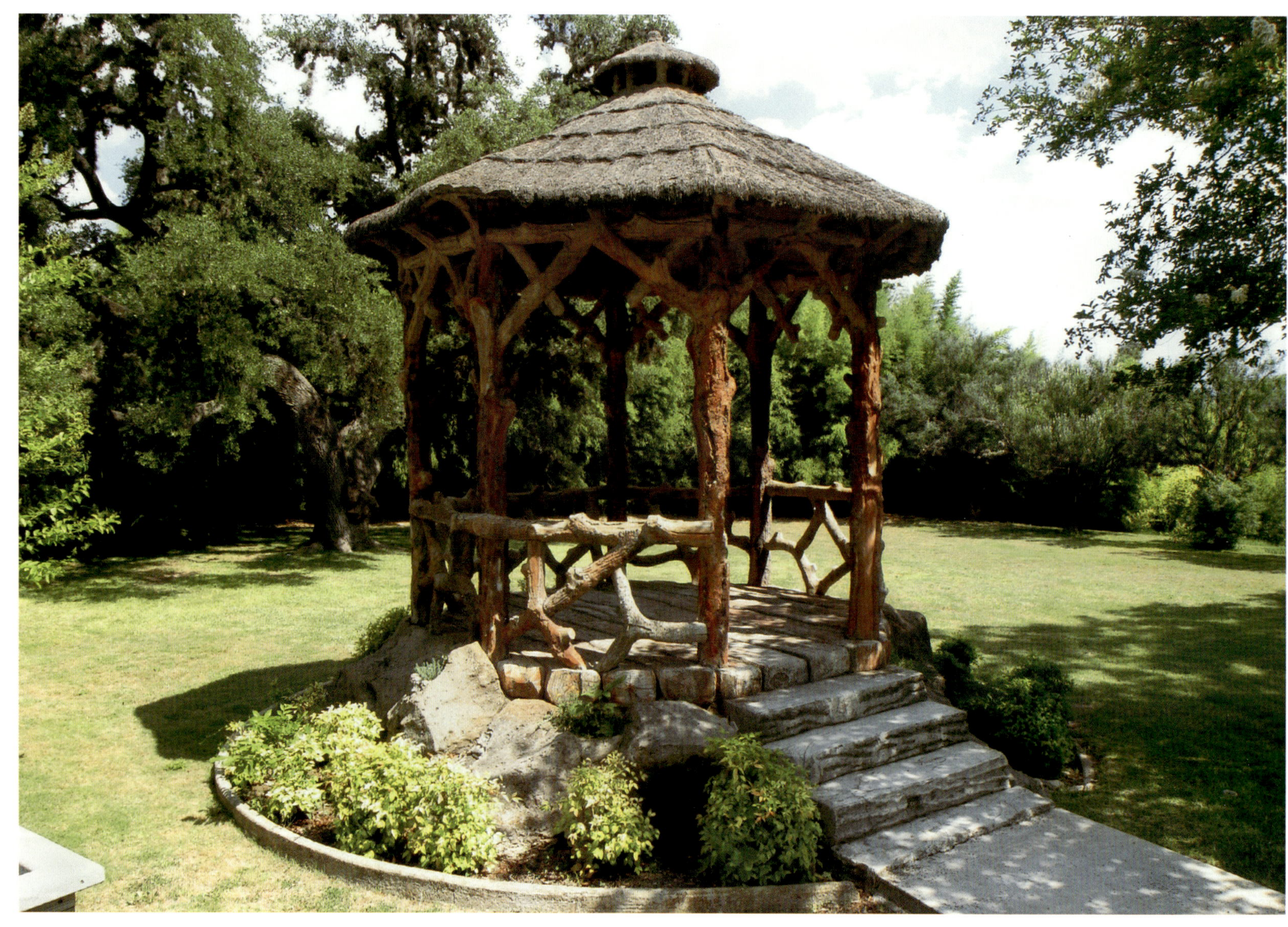

Albert Steves's gazebo, Comfort, Texas. Photo: Bob Parvin.

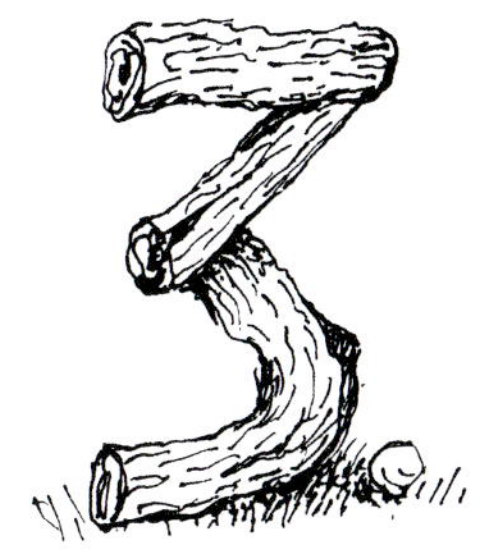

Expanding Work in Texas

In the three decades between his arrival in San Antonio in the 1920s and his death there in the 1950s, Dionicio Rodríguez completed a steady series of commissions in other parts of Texas. The projects span the spectrum from small scale to large and from residential and commercial properties to public spaces and religious sites.

Comfort: The Steves Ranch

Albert Steves was the son of German immigrants who settled in Comfort before moving to San Antonio, where they established a lumber business and became one of the city's leading families. In addition to working in the family business, Steves served as the "president of two railroads in Mexico, president of a Mexican mining company, vice-president of the City National Bank, and as a director of the Alamo National Bank." He was also a member of many civic, fraternal, social, and political groups.[1]

Steves wanted a summer home near his birthplace, and he bought land on the Guadalupe River near Comfort, twenty-five miles west of San Antonio. There he built a large house that he named "Aleswana," a combination of the names of his four children, and planted peach trees that he irrigated with water from the river.[2] It is presumed that Dionicio Rodríguez built the concrete tree-branch gazebo and four benches for Steves's large grounds. The octagonal structure is eighteen feet tall and is sited on a hillside overlooking the river. The main palapa roof, capped by a smaller lantern, also with a palapa roof, is supported by tree trunks that mimic the textures of pecan, cypress, pine, hackberry, and oak bark. The base is faced with concrete rocks similar to rocks at Lagos de

Chapúltepec, which are credited to Rodríguez. A family member, Margaret Lateer, recalled that the gazebo was built before 1931; that at one time it was used as an aviary; and that Steves stored his wine behind a small rock door underneath the sculpture.[3] Although there is no signature, the technique is unmistakably Rodríguez's, with his application of worm holes, peeling bark texture, and lichen.

It is an interesting parallel that Albert Steves and Richard Marmion built strikingly similar gazebos during the same period. Since both were involved in mining interests in Mexico, they may have known each other and could have shared knowledge of Rodríguez's artistic talent.

The Steves property is now the Haven River Inn, and the present owners relate that it is a popular site for weddings.

Sweeny: The James Richard Marmion Property

In 1910 San Antonio native James Richard Marmion bought approximately 360 acres of property adjacent to the San Bernard River, three miles east of Sweeny, as a retreat for his family. Marmion was involved in real estate, buying railroad rights-of-way for the New York and Texas Land Company Limited. Although he had moved to Houston, he traveled to towns in East Texas and to Sinaloa, Mexico, where he owned a silver and gold mine.[4] It is possible that he had seen Rodríguez's work in San Antonio or had learned about it from Albert Steves.

Oral tradition reveals that in 1926 Rodríguez built two faux structures for Marmion, both with palapa-type roofs: a wooden gazebo and a wooden table with two benches. The round gazebo, almost identical to Albert Steves's gazebo in Comfort, also rests on boulders, and bark-covered logs with recognizable textures of various trees support the octagonal roof. The gazebo was built on the largest island in a series of three islands in a manmade lake and was reached by a small rustic board bridge. Approximately a quarter of a mile away stands the other structure, a table, intersected by a bark-covered tree trunk support-ing the round thatched roof and flanked by two log benches. Marmion's daughter-in-law recalls that James Marmion was intrigued by the artisan's secrecy in not allowing his helper to watch while he applied the colors.[5]

Houston Zoo

Founded in 1920, the Houston Zoo opened in Sam Houston Park. By 1925 it had become the Houston Zoological Gardens and was moved to a thirty-four-acre site in Hermann Park.[6] The aviary, embellished with sculptural pieces of cement by Rodríguez, was

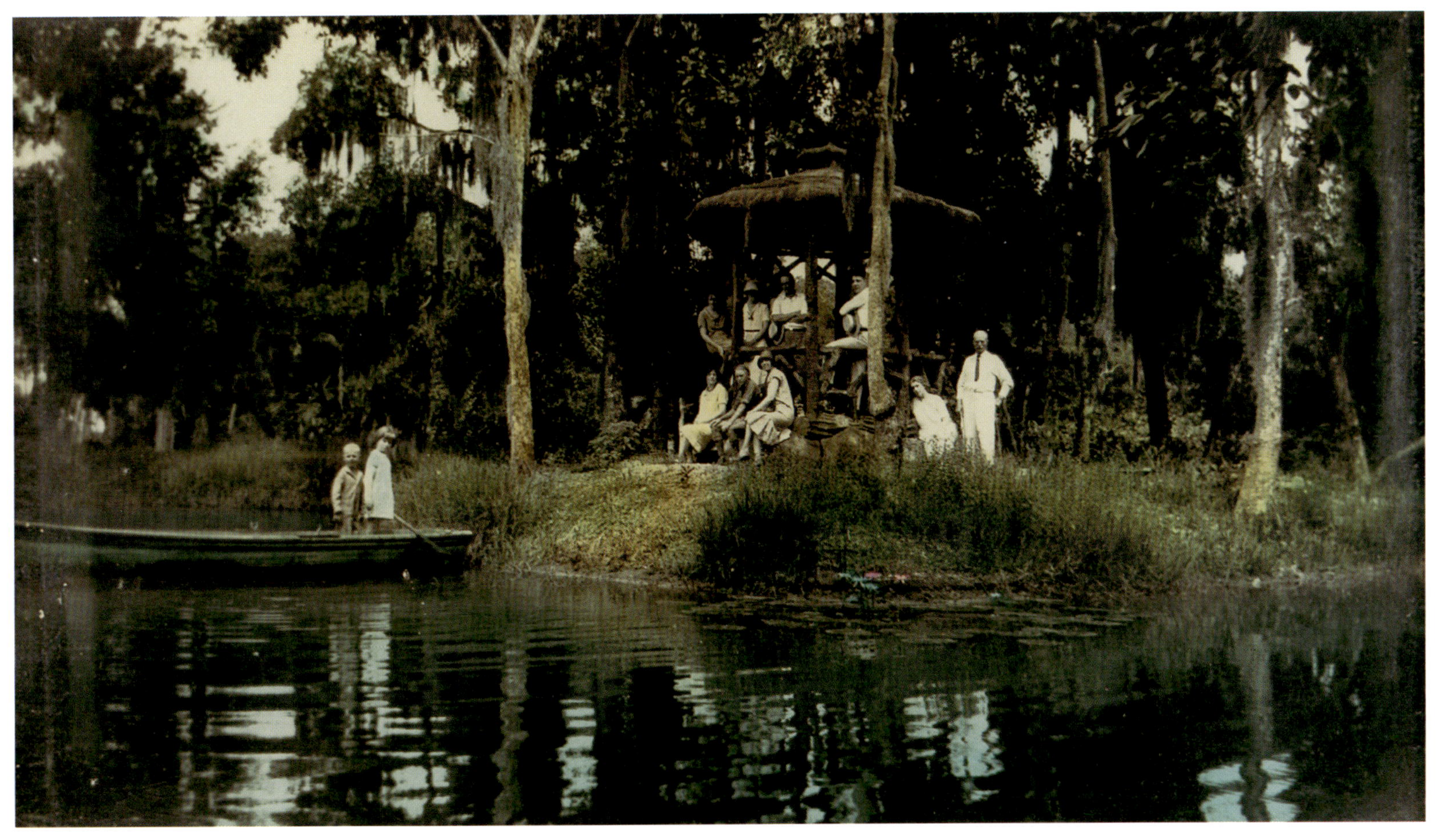

probably constructed near the entrance around 1926. Archival photographs identify the structure as a "flying cage."[7] A letter from Dr. Aureliano Urrutia to the mayor of Houston, dated November 24, 1925, states: "I take myself the liberty to introduce to your consideration Dionicio Rodríguez, of whom I had the opportunity to tell you."[8] This contact probably led to the city's commissioning of Rodríguez for work in the zoo.

The aviary, "said to be one of the largest in the United States," was a large convex-shaped screened metal frame enclosing Rodríguez's cement works.[9] It housed two tall bare tree sculptures, approximately twelve feet high and bark-textured, exhibiting many knot-holes, decayed areas, and protruding branches. A rustic fountain with sections of rocks in horizontal layers drips water into a rock-bordered pool. The rear of the fountain (not visible to the public) resembles a hollow tree house, an often repeated Rodríguez design, and has two apertures that open to an interior space housing the mechanical equipment for the fountain. A small decayed stump protrudes from the pool, which is surrounded by rock

"J. R. Marmion's Summer Camp on the San Bernardo [sic] River-Brazoria Co. Tex. July 4th, 1926." Courtesy of Mrs. Richard Marmion.

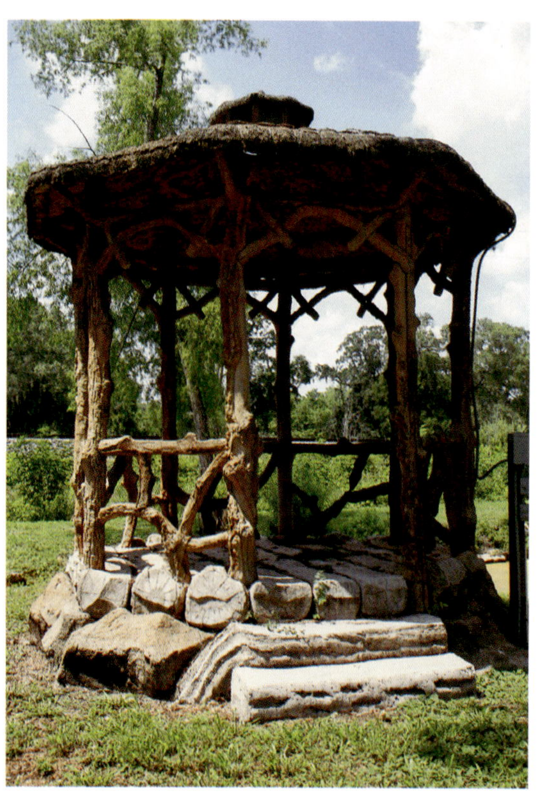

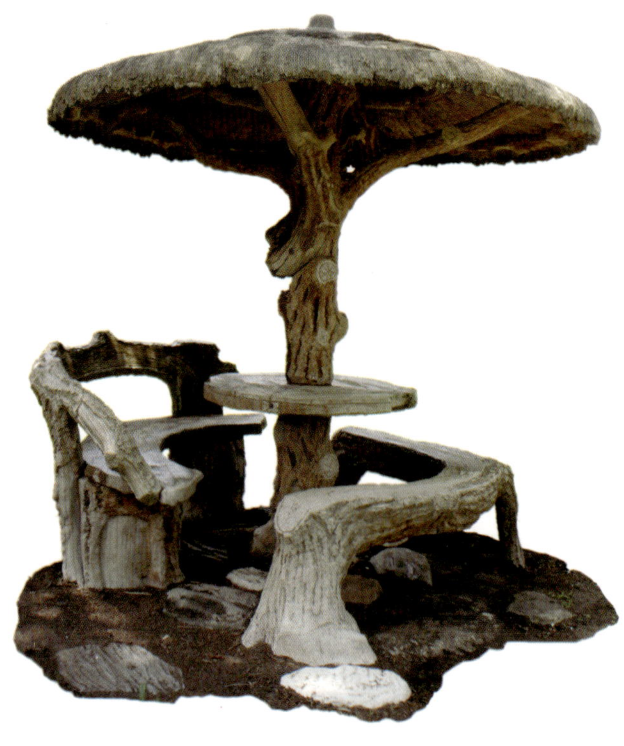

Above: *James Richard Marmion's gazebo, private property, Brazoria County, Texas. Photo: Bob Parvin.*
Above right: *James Richard Marmion's palapa table, private property, Brazoria County, Texas. Photo: Bob Parvin.*
Right: *Underside of James Richard Marmion's palapa, private property, Brazoria County, Texas. Photo: Bob Parvin.*

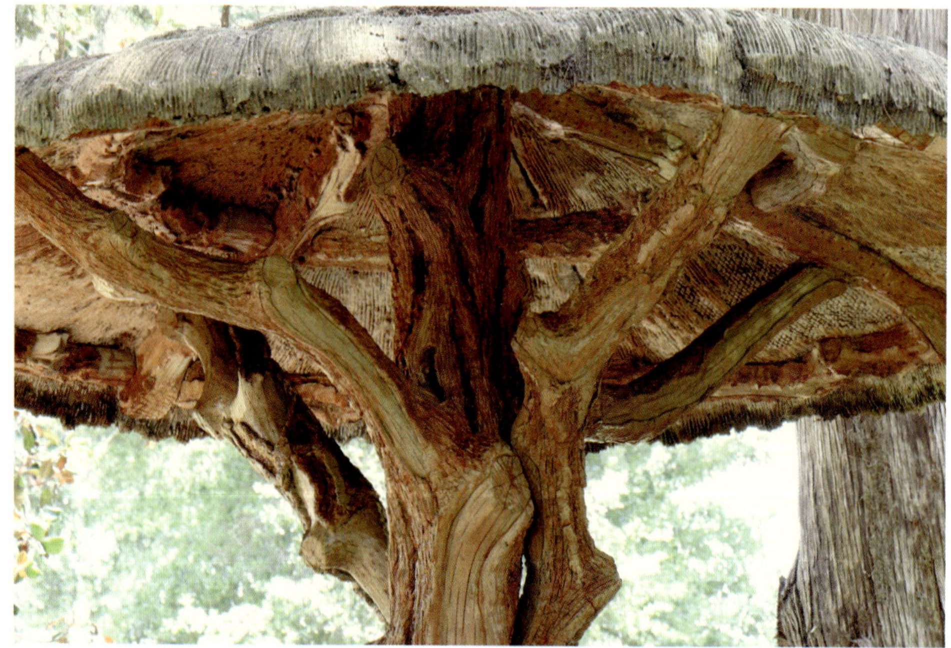

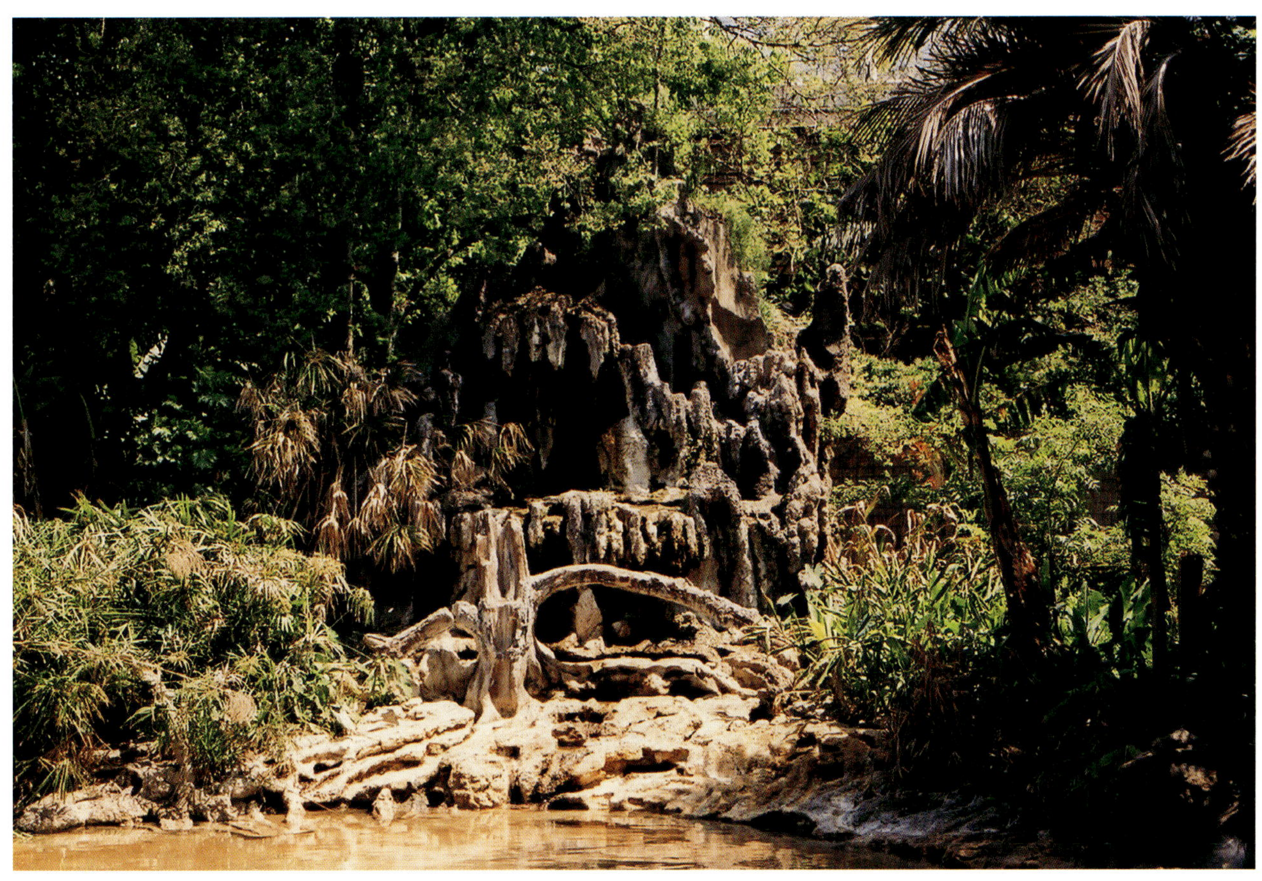

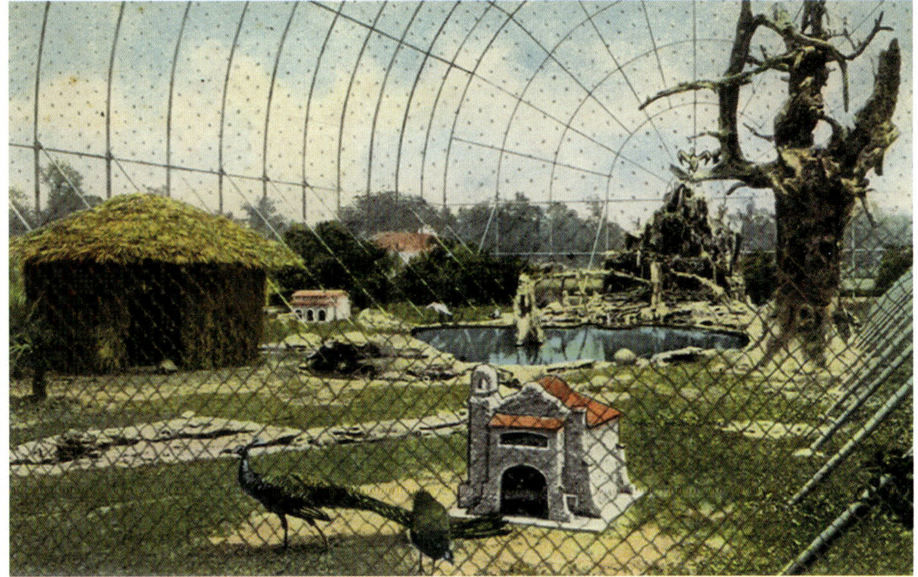

Above: *Rock fountain, Houston Zoo flamingo habitat.*
Photo: Myssie Light Acomb.
Left: *Postcard: "Bird House, Hermann Park Zoo,*
Houston, Texas." Collection of Rick Barongi.

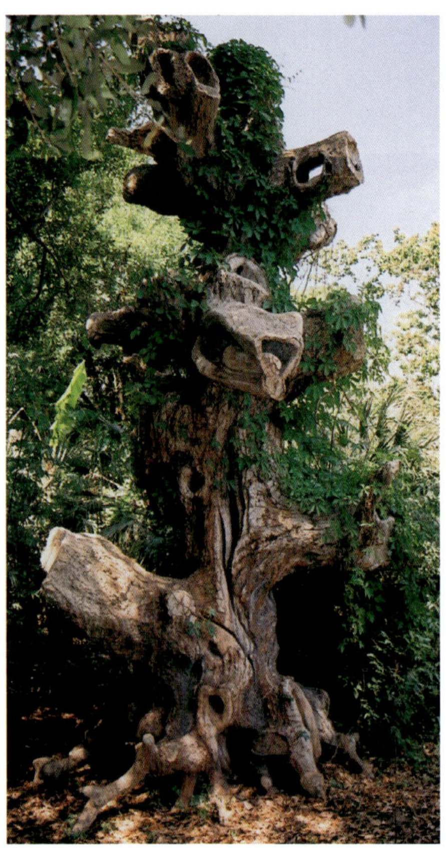

Bare tree, Houston Zoo flamingo habitat.
Photo: Myssie Light Acomb.

ledges and grassy areas. Perched on one of the ledges in the original design was a round hut made of palm fronds. A small, rock-lined stream with small cactus plants in crevices completed the composition.

The enclosure was destroyed by Hurricane Carla in 1961, but the fountain, one of the tree trunks, and the stump were incorporated into the existing flamingo exhibit. The remaining tree trunk and the stream are separated from the pond by a small bridge, probably built at a later date. Fred Maier, former facilities manager of the zoo, described the scene as "a unique fantasy shape, and I have always admired the way the artist left hollows in the trees that have been occupied by raccoons and other wild animals as well as beautiful pink blooming coral vine. On cold winter mornings the warm water that flows from the caldera (fountain) produces a surrealistic cloud of steam. Numerous small pools of water cascade down the face . . . perfect for the birds to play and shower in during hot summer days, delighted to find such a perfect spot to cool off."[10]

Port Arthur: Eddingston Court

In 1929 Dionicio Rodríguez, his wife Sara, Guadalupe Del Toro and her husband Mauro, Sara's brother George Cardosa, and Rafael (Ralph) Corona went to Port Arthur, Texas, to work on landscape embellishment features for the Eddingston Court apartments. According to Mrs. Del Toro, who was then an eighteen-year-old bride, Dionicio bought a new DeSoto car that year. They rented rooms for lodging, and although she relates that she occasionally helped with the concrete work, she and Sara spent much of the time at the rented rooms, where Sara taught her to embroider and sew. She said Rodríguez was a jealous husband and did not want Sara to leave the house.[11]

The group worked for tugboat captain Ambrose Eddingston, who had come to the port of Sabine Pass in 1907 with his wife, Eurina, along with other immigrants from the Cayman Islands.[12] Eddingston first served as the cook on the Sabine pilots' boat, later becoming captain.[13] He became a partner in the Sabine Ice, Coal and Water Company, which supplied these commodities to the shipping industry. This company later became the Sabine Transportation Company.[14] Other Caymanians were captains for Texaco and Gulf Oil fleets.[15]

In 1908, the Eddingstons moved to Port Arthur, and Captain Eddingston, realizing the need for additional rental housing as the town grew, built a rooming house for teachers, later purchasing a five-acre tract of land for a larger project, which he would name Eddingston Court. In 1929 he awarded a ninety-thousand-dollar contract to L. W. Lindsay of Houston to build four apartment buildings bordering the Sabine-Neches Ship Channel.[16] They would be similar to "picturesque manorial-style" projects that he was building in

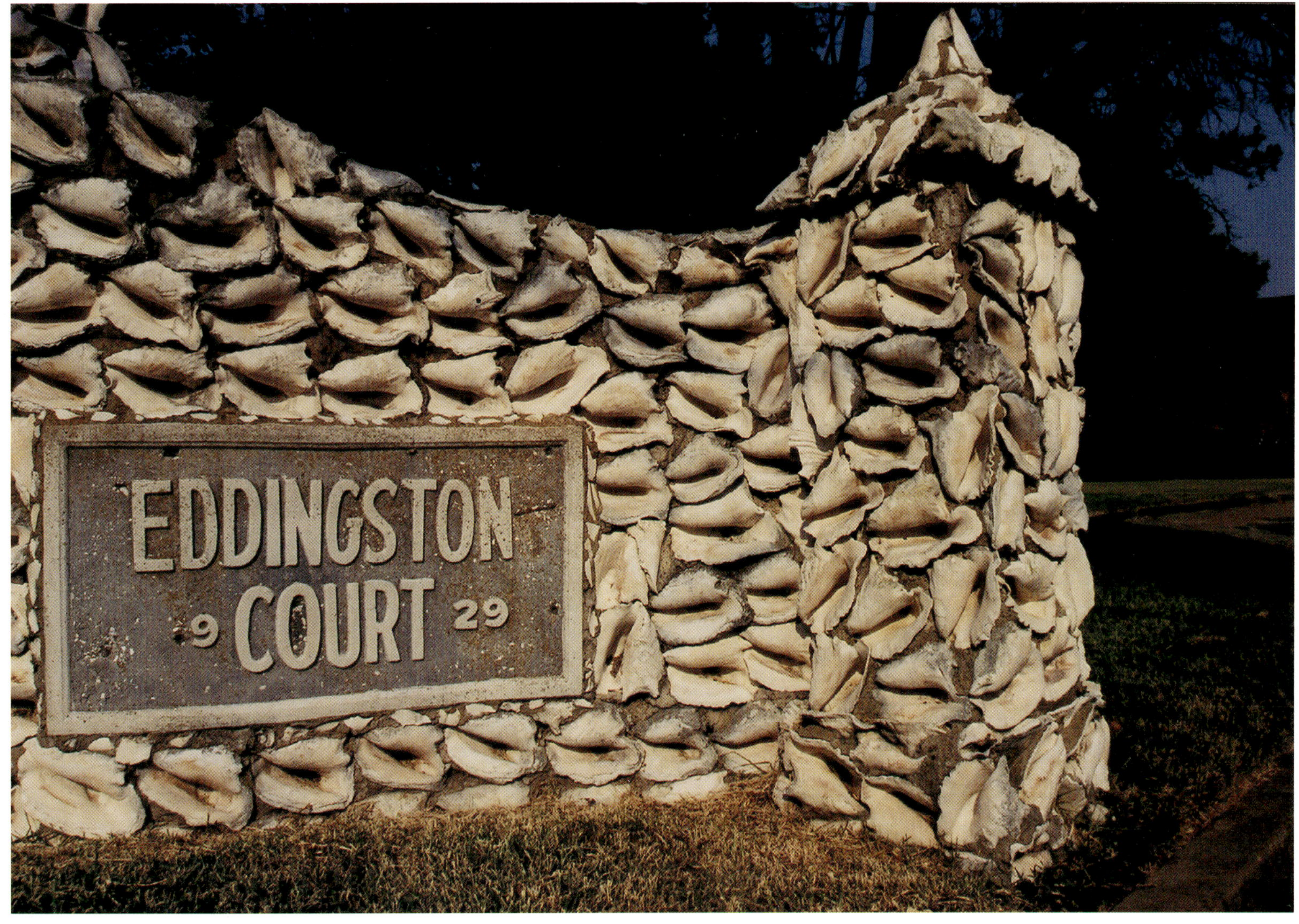

Houston.[17] The project included lavish landscaping with oak trees brought from Louisiana by Mrs. Eddingston, a boat slip (removed when the seawall was improved), a manmade lagoon, and a tennis court.

Eddingston commissioned his nephew, Captain Leonard Tibbetts of the ship *Smaland*, to bring five thousand conch shells collected by divers off of the coast of Eddingston's birthplace, Grand Cayman Island, to decorate the project.[18] Rodríguez was hired to build the landscape features of conch shells and cement, which Eddingston described as "the garden spot of Texas."[19] Rodríguez and his helpers built:

Conch shell gate, Eddingston Court, Port Arthur, Texas. Photo: Traci Middleton.

63

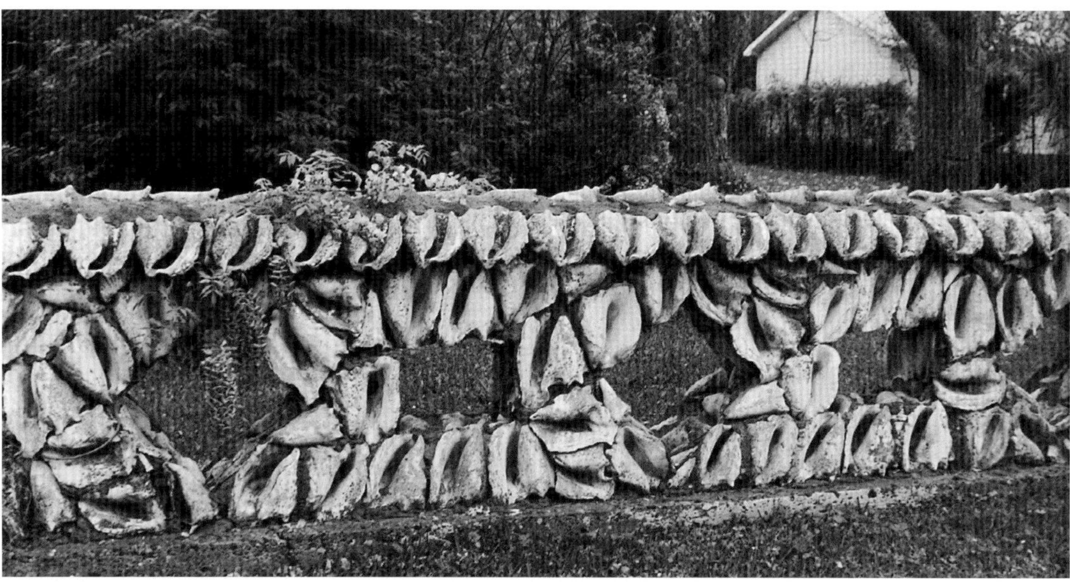

Fence detail, Eddingston Court fence, Port Arthur, Texas.
Photo: Traci Middleton.

• A conch shell–encrusted wall and entrance gate that border on Procter Street. The two main sections of the wall have alternating square- and diamond-shaped apertures along the ninety-eight-foot span. Two sets of conch shell pillars line either side of the entrance.

• A faux rock fishpond surrounded by rock ledges centered in the grassy median, which divides the boulevard between the apartments. A sculpted rock fountain with graduated layers dripping with faux stalactites provided water for the pond.

• A large lagoon in a section of the property called "The Garden of Tranquility"; the lagoon is now dry, but features surrounding it remain. One of the garden's main features is a large fountain of layered rock (similar to the earlier fountain at Miraflores, not extant), capped by a semicircular form, which dripped water into a pond over successive rock-lined ledges and finally into the wide kidney-shaped lagoon.

• The Cave of a Thousand Sounds, a grotto-like enclosure lined and faced with conch shells, a tranquil retreat on the eastern edge of the lagoon where apartment dwellers could enjoy the sounds of the seashells. The front entrance is decorated with a conch shell–encrusted stalactite and a stalagmite in the center. Similar in shape to Rodríguez's tree houses, it is open on three sides. The structure has a small bench attached to the solid back wall and was wired for electricity.

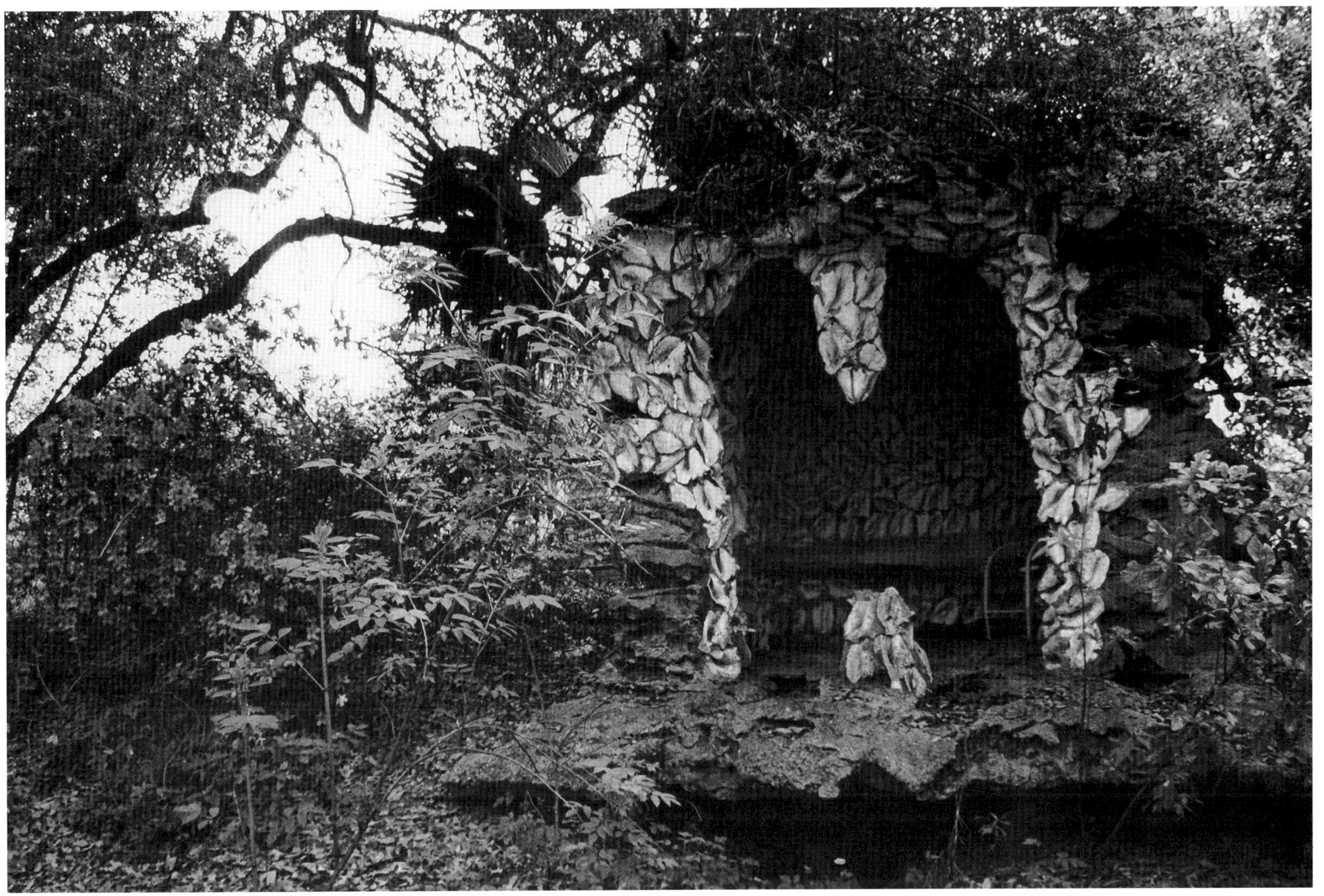

Cave of a Thousand Sounds, Eddingston Court, Port Arthur, Texas. Photo: Traci Middleton.

• A small stump seat with heavy bark texture near the "cave," with a portion broken away; it appears that this may have been a planned artifice by Rodríguez, as there is no exposed rebar or metal lath.

• A very large tree stump on the western side of the lagoon, with six large roots extending from the base, which raise the piece to a sitting height. The deeply grained bark seat is two feet in diameter.

• A wood plank with an attached stump similar in shape to a diving board, poised on the southeastern edge of the lagoon. Branch supports under the plank raise the structure above where the water level would have been.

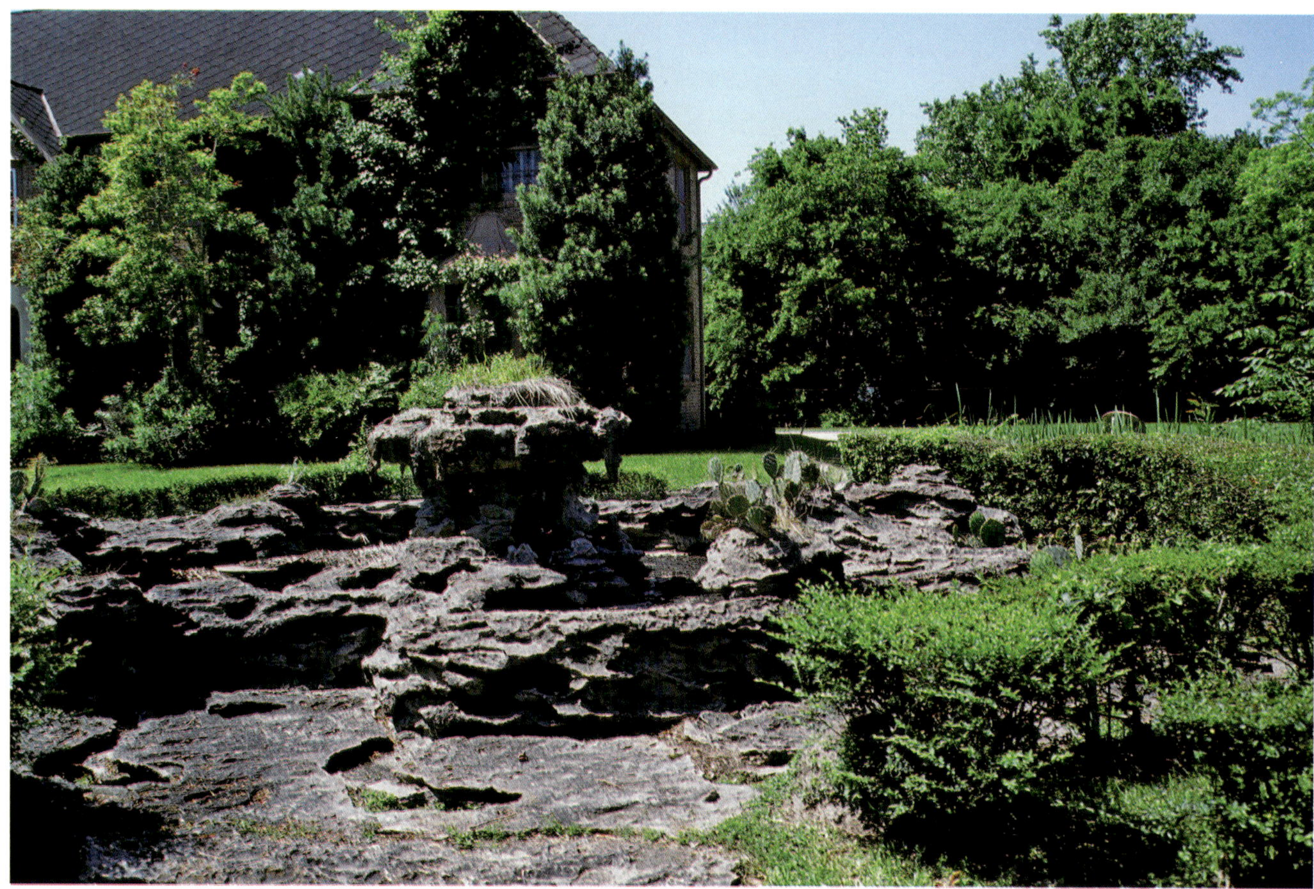

Rock fountain, entrance to Eddingston Court, Port Arthur, Texas. Photo: Jack Stansbury, AIA.

• Two textured wood seats and a flat-topped table supported by delicate, twisted small branches that converge into a stump base; this is next to the tennis court, near the seawall.

• A large stone-faced cement basket situated in a stone-lined planting bed east of the tennis court is typical of the basket shapes made by Rodríguez, surrounded by granite boulders once used as ballast on incoming ships. Plants in the bed include fifteen cement cactus forms, including two three-branched cacti, a prickly pear cactus, and a pincushion cactus.

After Captain Eddingston died, Mrs. "Mom" Eddingston managed the apartments for a few years before they were sold to John Aquilina, who built a home for his family on the property. His granddaughter, Angela Radusch, who lived there with her mother, Bertha, recalled that when her cousins visited, inevitably "one of them would fall into the goldfish pond." She remembers "running around the sculptures in endless games. We would hide and [the adults] couldn't find us." One of their favorite hiding places was the shell cave.[20] The property was listed on the National Register of Historic Places in 2004.

Beaumont: The Phelan Mansion

Guadalupe Del Toro and her husband and a group of helpers also accompanied Rodríguez to Beaumont in 1930–31, to construct garden embellishments for the John Henry Phelan mansion.[21]

Phelan and his wife were owners of the Phelan Coffee Company, a wholesale grocery firm, as well as investors with the Yount-Lee Oil Company, which developed the second Spindletop oilfield.[22] According to historian Bradley Brooks, the architect of the Phelans' large red brick colonial revival–style house, Owen Southworth, was the "creative mind of the landscape," and Homer Fry of Dallas was hired as the landscape architect.[23] Fry had designed the patio of the Spanish Governor's Palace in San Antonio, and it is possible that he recommended Rodríguez's work to Phelan.

The imaginative landscape plan for the property's fifteen acres featured a large free-form swimming pool with a spillway that flowed into a small pond and a three-hole putting green. The grounds were the scene of many social events, including a "doll party" where little girls had a doll parade, swimming parties for the Phelans' twenty-two grandchildren and their friends, a swimming party hosted by Mrs. Phelan for the Sisters of the Incarnate Word, and benefit style shows where the models strolled across the bridge that spanned the pool, accompanied by accordion music played by a local musician.[24]

The major decorative trabajo rústico features built on the grounds by Rodríguez and his crew included a gazebo similar to the Marmion and Steves structures; a bridge with realistic wooden railings and split log bridge bed; and a rock bath house featuring a wooden stairway with log steps and palapa-style roof. At a three-hole putting green, four palapa benches probably served as rest stops for the golfers. The seats of the benches are planed slabs, and the roof supports have patches of peeling bark, knotholes, and pyramid-headed bolts. Additional Rodríguez installations included a pine table, with a realistic bark trim and log legs, and a large hollow log planter.

The faux bois work at the Phelan house influenced other Beaumont citizens to embellish their landscapes, and it is possible that members of Rodríguez's crew built bridges, chairs, and ponds for at least one client.

When the Sisters of Charity of the Incarnate Word were given the property in

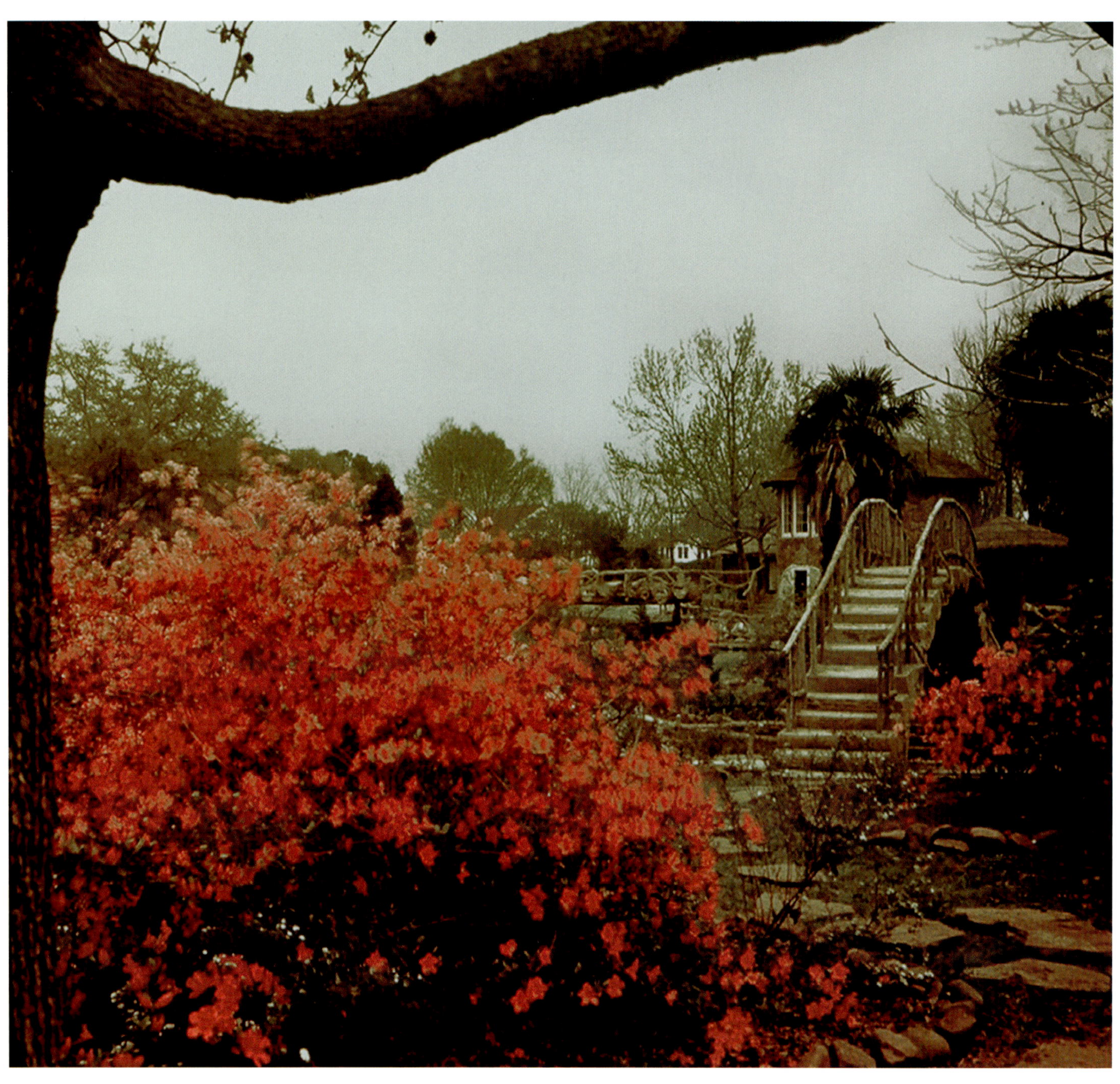

Log bridge, John Henry Phelan Mansion, Beaumont, Texas, ca. 1930 (not extant).
Courtesy of McFaddin-Ward House Museum Collection.

1957, they built St. Elizabeth's Hospital on the grounds, and most of the imaginative environment built by Rodríguez and his assistants was demolished, although the four palapa benches, the table, and the planter were retained.

Houston: Woodlawn Garden of Memories

When Woodlawn Cemetery was opened in 1931 on rural land on the outskirts of Houston on the then unpaved Katy Road, farmers occasionally had to drive their cattle away to preserve the dignity of burial services. Designed for upright headstones, the cemetery layout was planned with winding roads—a design made popular by Adolph Strauch with his landscaped lawn-park plans in the mid-1800s.[25] Original owners were J. W. Metzler, J. W. Metzler Jr., Ben Dancer, and Mrs. Phyklura Skalinder.[26]

In 1940 the name was changed to Woodlawn Garden of Memories when the cemetery joined the trend to become a memorial park, a movement begun by Hubert Eaton with an innovative approach at Forest Lawn Cemetery in Los Angeles. He initiated the use of flat grave markers and included the use of sculpture—original works and copies—as decoration.[27] It is understood to have been around this time that Rodríguez built decorative cement features for Woodlawn in special areas platted for flat markers. The embellishments he produced include:

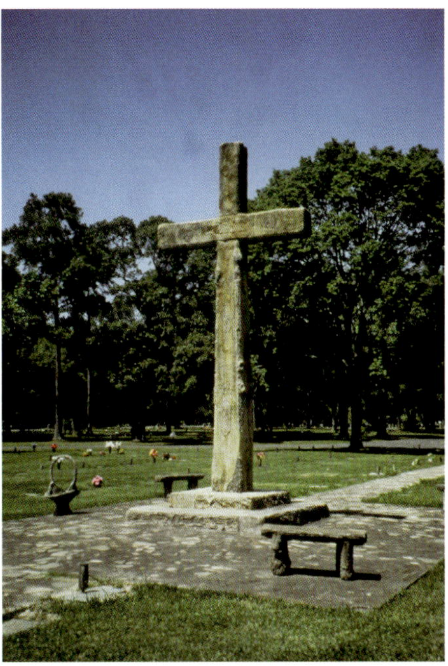

Wooden cross, Woodlawn Garden of Memories, Houston, Texas. Photo: Patsy Light.

- a twenty-five-foot high cross made of four split log planks and resting on a two-tiered base of horizontal timbers; pyramid-headed bolts are present in the cross, and both cross and base exhibit realistic textural surfaces and have retained much of their original color
- a tall woven basket with a twisted handle
- ten benches of split log planks with smooth seats and stump legs of deeply textured bark; four benches surround the cross, and six less detailed ones are elsewhere in the cemetery
- a mound-shaped fountain of honeycomb rock; water flowed downward from three horizontal layers into a semicircular pond
- a small honeycomb rock planter
- a thirty-five-foot-long fallen tree bench formed from a single textured trunk that splits, the two segments forming the back and seat; two stumps serve as legs, two pyramid-headed bolts are present, and the trunk is hollowed near the base to form a plant container
- the Annie Laurie Wishing Chair, with a bronze plaque mounted on the rear recounting the legend (see chapter 4, note 44); Rodríguez had made simi-

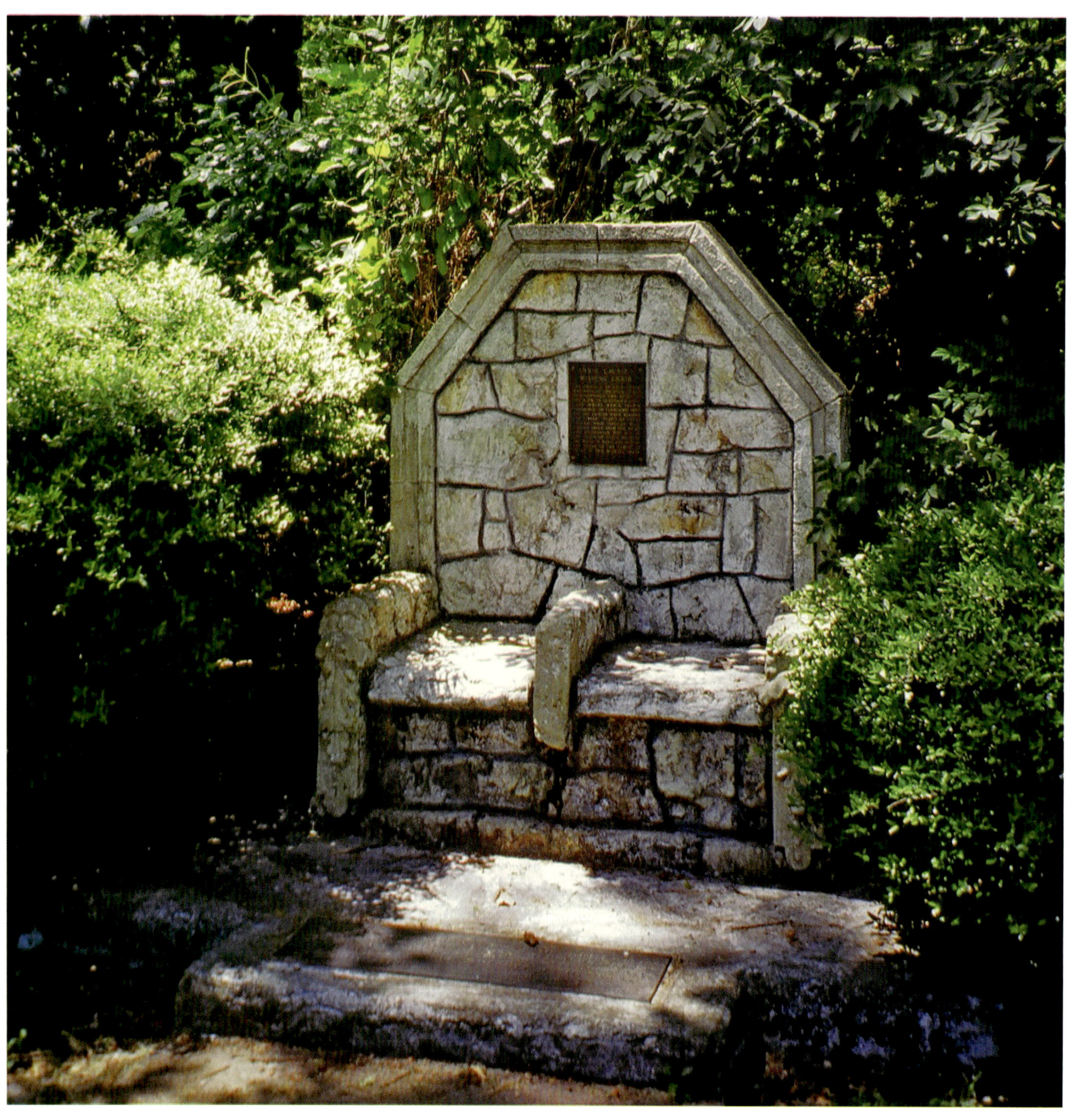

lar ones at Memorial Park in Memphis; Cedar Hill Cemetery, Maryland; and
Elmwood Cemetery, Alabama

Rodríguez's distinctive trademarks are present in Woodlawn, including rough- and
smooth-textured faux wood, with peeling bark, knotholes, insect borings, and pyramid-
headed bolts. An additional rustic work in the cemetery, a rose arbor, lacks his fine attention to detail and was probably constructed by one of his assistants. Although Rodríguez
worked in seven cemeteries throughout the United States, Woodlawn possesses his only
known cemetery work in Texas.

The Dallas Area

Details about Rodríguez's life in Dallas during the 1930s are sketchy, although
records indicate that he worked there in later years. It is possible that he or one of his
peers created a large sculptural piece at Laurel Land Cemetery in Dallas: a large faux wood
chair. The chair is attached to a tree trunk with horizontal branches, similar to the bare-
branched tree credited to Rodríguez in Pittman-Sullivan Park in San Antonio (not extant).
A postcard of Laurel Land Cemetery is in his collection of papers, furthering speculation
that Rodríguez worked there.

Manuela Theall remembered that her uncle showed her a small wishing well he had
built around 1932–34 on the east side of White Rock Lake, about 150 yards from the
edge of the lake, and some baskets in front yards of residences around Dallas. She added
that he was married when he was in Dallas.[28]

Castroville: Moye Military Academy Grotto

The Rodríguez grotto in the small town of Castroville, a few miles west of San
Antonio, is built of honeycomb Edwards Plateau limestone and bears a bronze plaque with
the inscription: "Donated by the Mothers of the Moye Military School Cadets, May 13,
1945." Dionicio Rodríguez's signature is incised in the concrete. Sister Martha Vrba, prin-
cipal of the school during the 1940s, remembers that she and some of her "Moye boys"
watched Rodríguez work on the grotto.[29]

A 1946 monthly newsletter published by the Sisters of Divine Providence reports on
the opening of school in September of 1945: "The boys were quite candid and outspoken
in their appraisal of improvements. The older Cadets pointed with pride to the beautiful
Grotto, a gift made last spring by their mothers. It is constructed of honeycomb rocks
gathered from the vicinity and is located near the music studio."[30]

The property, adjacent to U.S. Highway 90 West in Castroville, was originally the
site of St. Louis School, run by the Sisters of Divine Providence. In 1873, the first Mother-

Opposite: *Annie Laurie Chair, Woodlawn Garden of
Memories, Houston, Texas. Photo: Patsy Light.*

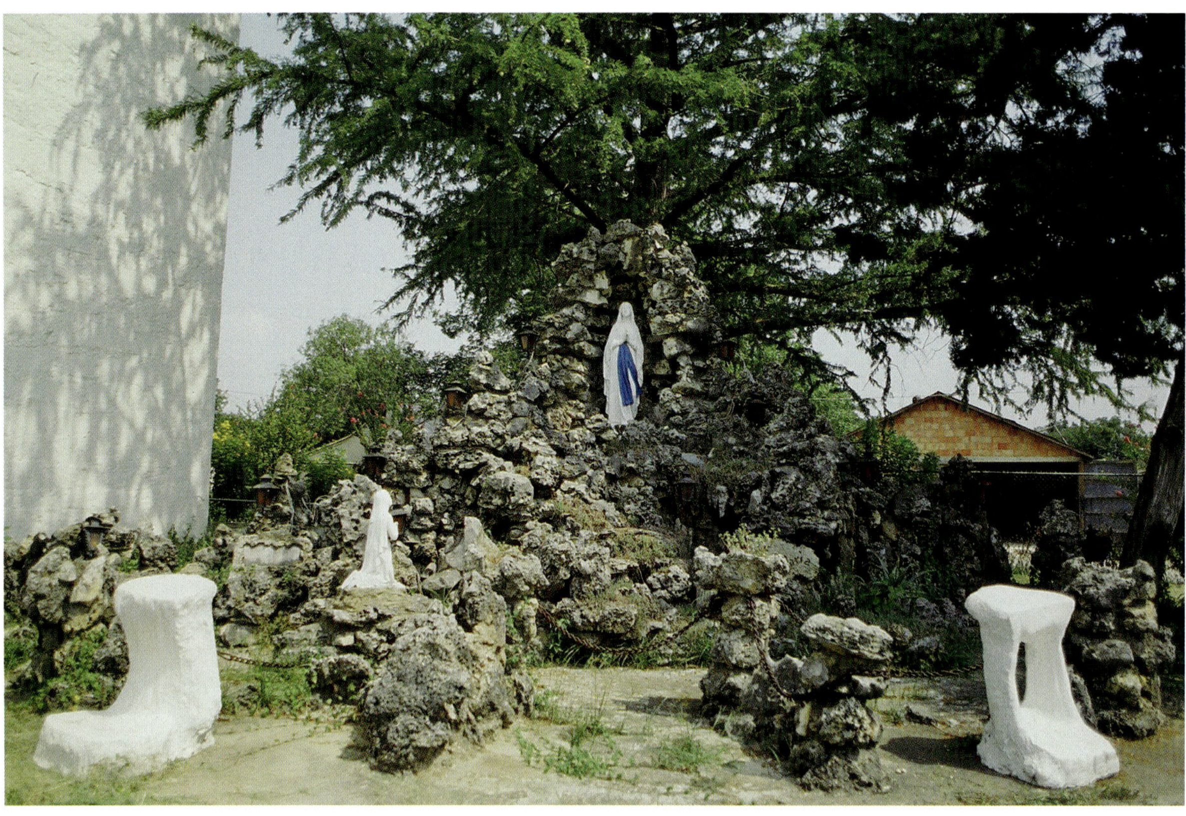

Grotto at Moye Retreat Center, Castroville, Texas.
Photo: Patsy Light.

house of their order in the United States and their first convent were built on the property. The property was owned for a time by the Oblate Fathers and was repurchased by the Sisters of Divine Providence in 1938. They operated the Moye Military Academy, "one of the finest in the state," for twenty-one years. When the academy closed, the property once again served as a convent for a few years, and since 1985 it has been a center for retreats and renewal.[31]

The twelve-foot-high grotto is constructed of the same material as the Stations of the Cross and grotto at the shrine of St. Anthony of Padua in San Antonio, and the masonry technique is similar to that in the St. Anthony work. The Moye grotto's twenty-eight-foot base tapers to a conical apex. Eleven wrought-iron lamps placed on the grotto provide illumination, and two concrete tree trunks with cut-out niches serve as kneelers facing the grotto; the trunks have been painted white. Several hundred feet outside the Moye property, on the north side of U.S. 90 West, is a planter outlined with wood planks and signed by Maximo Cortés, leading to speculation that Cortés might have accompanied Rodríguez to Castroville for the Moye project.

Much of the commissioned work described in this chapter is recognized in the National Register of Historic Places. Although San Antonio is a focal point, six of the fifteen Texas sites of Rodríguez's work that are included in the National Register are in other parts of the state: the Albert Steves gazebo at Comfort; Houston's Woodlawn Garden of Memories Cemetery and the flamingo habitat at the Houston Zoo; Eddingston Court in Port Arthur;[32] and the gazebo and palapa table for James Richard Marmion at Sweeny.

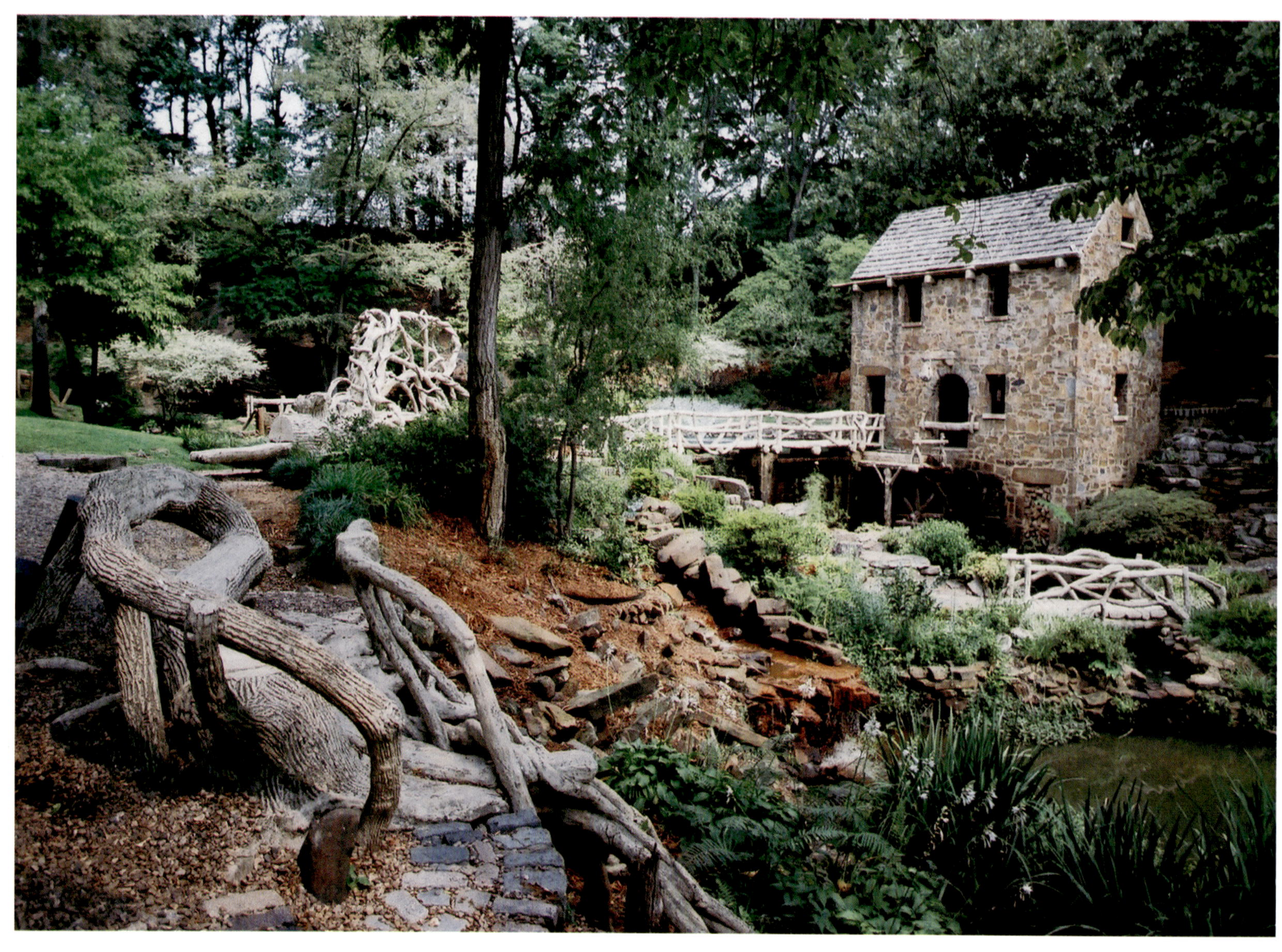

Old Mill, T. R. Pugh Memorial Park, North Little Rock,
Arkansas. Photo: Myssie Light Acomb.

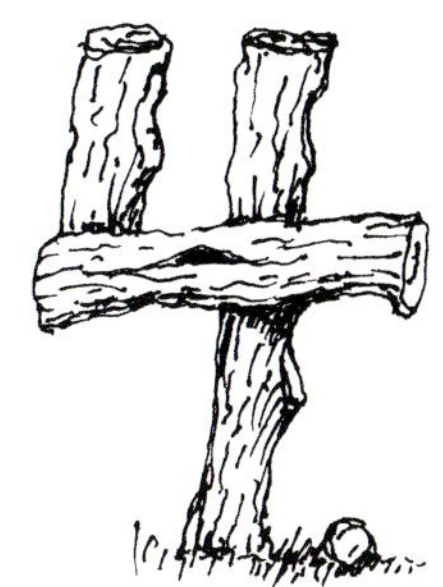

Projects throughout
the United States

Around 1932 Rodríguez began working on large projects outside Texas for several clients with whom he developed personal relationships that continued for many years. Two of these clients were Justin Matthews and Elliot Clovis Hinds. The collection of nine years of correspondence between Rodríguez and Hinds, who built Memorial Park Cemetery in Memphis, Tennessee, provides many details of the artisan's work and travels. Today these letters are in the collection of Hinds's granddaughter, Katherine Hinds Smythe. From the letters it is apparent that Rodríguez was first hired by Matthews, and later by Hinds, although he worked concurrently for both of them for a few years.

North Little Rock, Arkansas, 1932–36

Rodríguez worked for Justin Matthews in Arkansas from 1932 to 1936 at three parks: Crestview, Lakewood, and the T. R. Pugh Memorial Park. Previously involved in the cottonseed oil business, Matthews moved to North Little Rock, where he became a real estate investor and was responsible for much of the city's residential development, including Lakewood and Park Hill subdivisions and a series of six lakes.[1] He was an imaginative developer, who planned parks as open spaces in his subdivisions. He employed a company architect, German immigrant Frank Carmean, to design buildings for his projects, and Matthews planned promotional gimmicks to attract public interest.

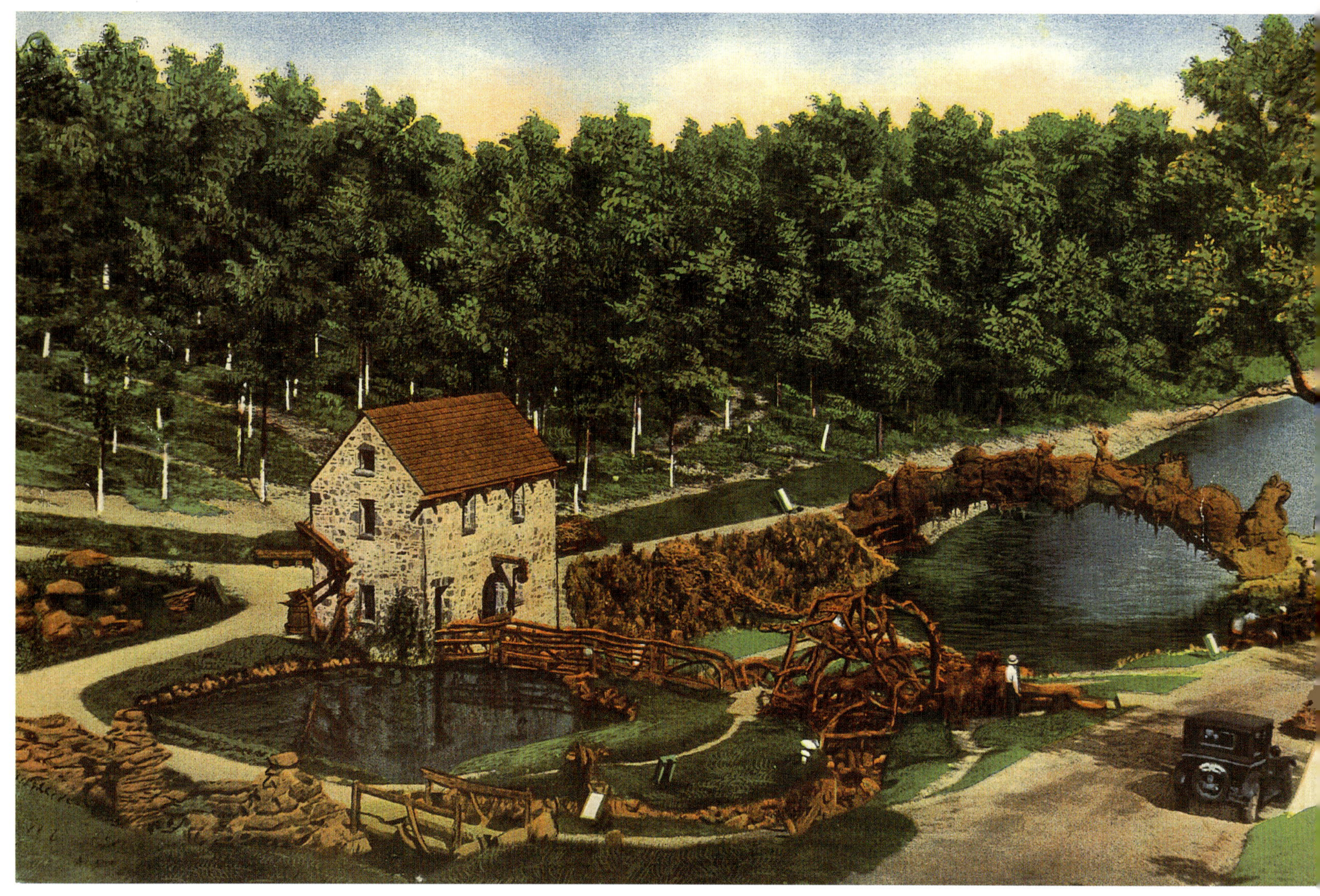

Looking south through Pugh Memorial Park, North Little Rock, Arkansas, souvenir photo by Justin Matthews Company, ca. 1935. Courtesy of Manuela Vargas Theall.

There are two theories as to how Matthews found Rodríguez. According to sources in Arkansas, Matthews sent Carmean "on a tour of southwestern states in search of new architectural styles," and he "found" Rodríguez.[2] Another source, Julie Vosmik, believes that Matthews saw Rodríguez's work at the Chapúltepec palace in Mexico City and contacted him in San Antonio. She relates that at the time Matthews was not interested in paying the price Rodríguez wanted; however, later, during the Depression, the two were able to work out a deal. Rodríguez's condition in working for Matthews was that the developer would place the artisan's work in public parks.[3]

The best known of Matthews's undertakings is the Old Mill at the T. R. Pugh Memorial Park, named for an early Arkansas settler, Thomas Robert Pugh.[4] Approached from a higher elevation at street level, the scene below is a lyrical fantasy land with a background of tall trees. A stone mill building, waterfalls, pools, rock ledges, and sculptures of convoluted shapes are set amid blooming flower beds and trees. The project was designed to appear as an actual mill of the 1800s would have appeared in its neglected state in the 1930s.[5] Matthews said of his project: "We have endeavored to produce something that would preserve in a picturesque manner, the memory of Arkansas' pioneers."[6]

Carmean designed the two-story building on the edge of a small pond that was a drainage area for Lake Number Three. This pond drains into a lower lake, Lake Number Two. Rodríguez created the mill's interior and exterior details, including plank floors, log railings, log stairs, an interior wall and gate (with metal hinges) of vertical planks, the hopper for the grain, and window sills. Numerous cement sculptural pieces enhance the grounds.

Actual historical relics used in the project are the grist mill, large mill rocks, milestones from a road laid out by Jefferson Davis, and sections of an iron shaft from the sternwheel of a steamboat.

The stone mill has a ten-thousand-pound working concrete waterwheel built by Rodríguez. In addition, he sculpted a pump with a water trough, a sluice gate, a winch, and a rain barrel with gutters and a drain spout, all very realistic imitations of actual wooden objects. Other faux components of this park that are Rodríguez's original designs, including six bridges, are:

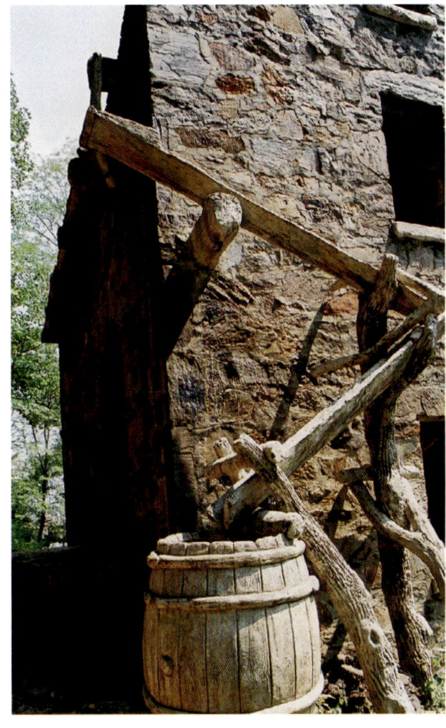

Wooden rain spout and barrel, Old Mill, North Little Rock, Arkansas. Photo: Myssie Light Acomb.

> • A bridge spans the water below the mill building in a arching configuration that Matthews described as "depicting two bent swamp persimmon trees joined together"; it is accented by a knurled wood and thick rock surface texture, hanging vine branches, and dripping stalactites.[7] The railings are bark-covered logs and the walkway is made of large stone ledges. Prickly pear and saguaro cactus appear in crevices. A hollow rock entrance on the western end has a built-in seat—a popular trysting place for young couples, judging by the incised graffiti.
>
> • A fallen black locust tree log, from which rises a canopy of entwined branches, serves as the access point for a log bridge with branch railings leading to the main entrance of the mill.
>
> • A wagon bridge spans the water and provides entrance to the mill. The railing is made of textured straight logs, and the flooring is planed wooden planks.

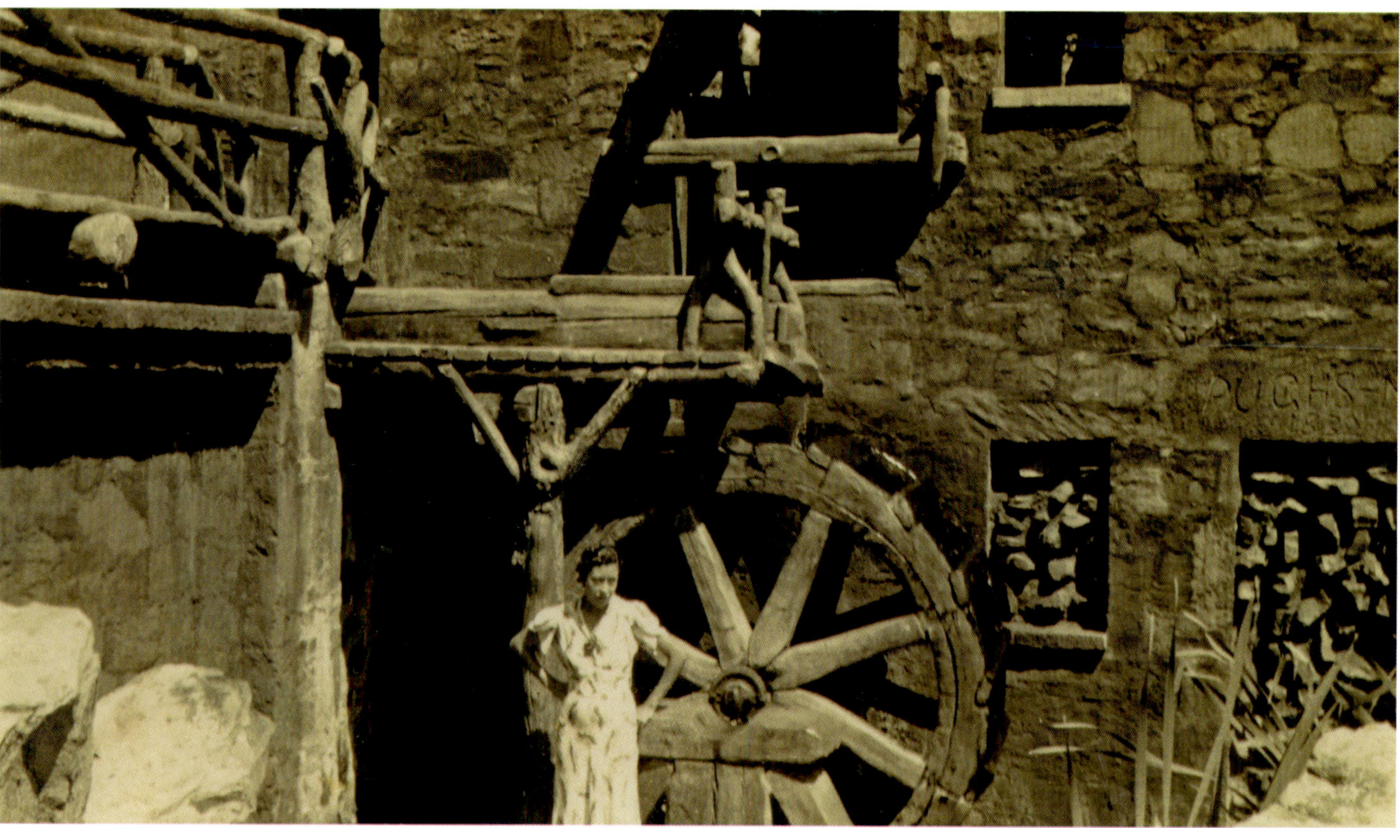

Manuela Vargas Theall at the waterwheel, Old Mill, North Little Rock, Arkansas. Courtesy of Manuela Vargas Theall.

• Larger-than-life toadstools appear in rock crevices and in groupings throughout the garden.

• Wood rail fencing lines the path from the mill to the persimmon tree bridge. Two rows of planed logs are supported at intervals by upright square wooden posts. Wooden shims fill in gaps where the rails are inserted into the posts.

• A fallen tree bench is perched overlooking the mill, the bridges, and the two waterfalls. The backrest is a single curving branch with smaller branch supports, culminating in a very naturalistic sharply broken end, and the seat is a heavier log. Sinuous roots taper down the hill from the base.

• Another bridge consists of two parallel planed logs with branch supports that appear to grow from the log. One side of the walkway has been "mended" with horizontally cut boards.

• Two smaller bridges provide additional crossings over the stream; both have curving branches as railings and split-log floors.

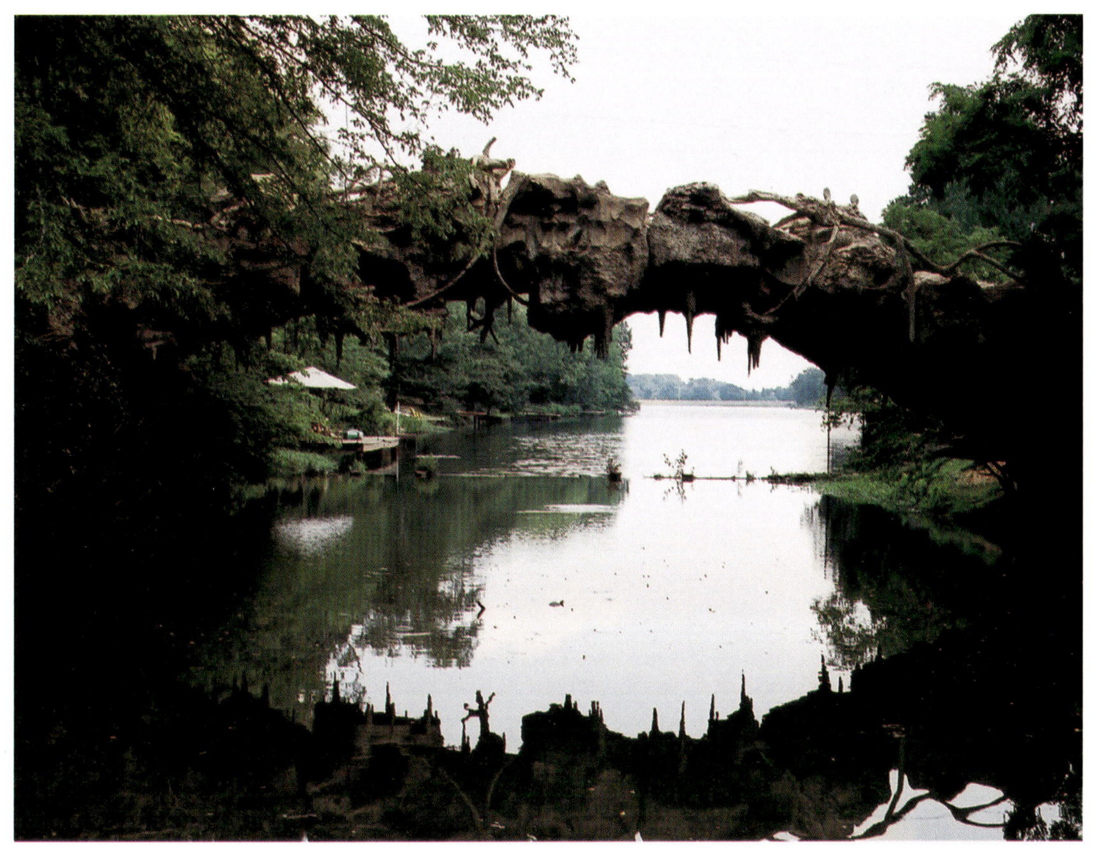

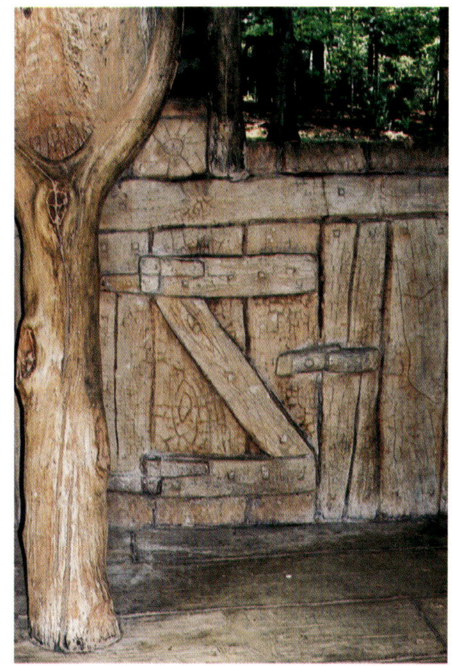

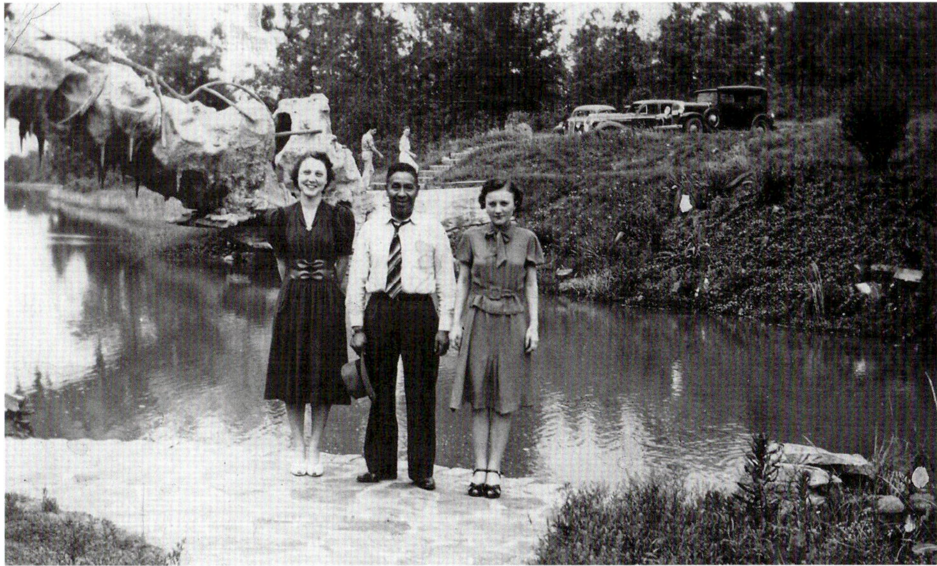

Top Left: *Bridge of two bent persimmon trees joined together, Old Mill, North Little Rock, Arkansas.*
Photo: Myssie Light Acomb.
Above: *Wooden gate, interior of the mill, Old Mill, North Little Rock, Arkansas.*
Photo: Myssie Light Acomb.
Below Left: *Rodríguez with Manuela Vargas Theall (right) and unidentified woman, near persimmon tree bridge, Old Mill, North Little Rock, Arkansas.*
Courtesy of Manuela Vargas Theall.

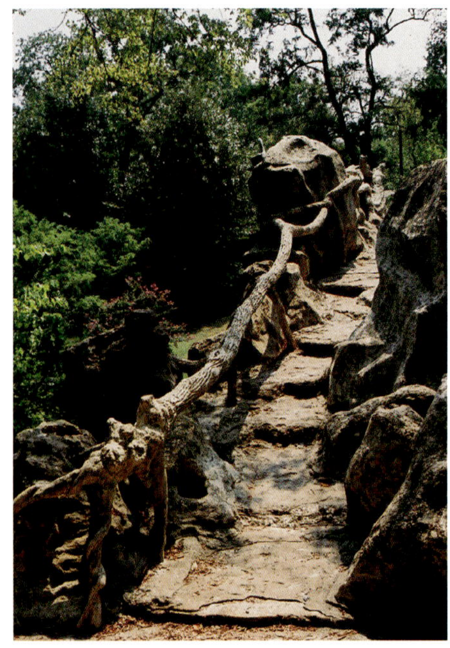

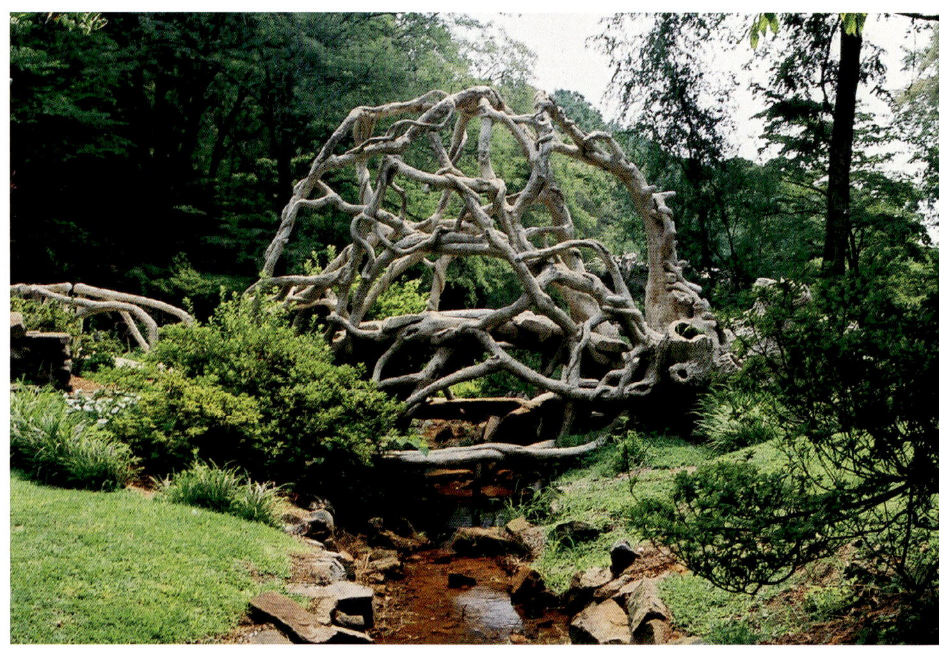

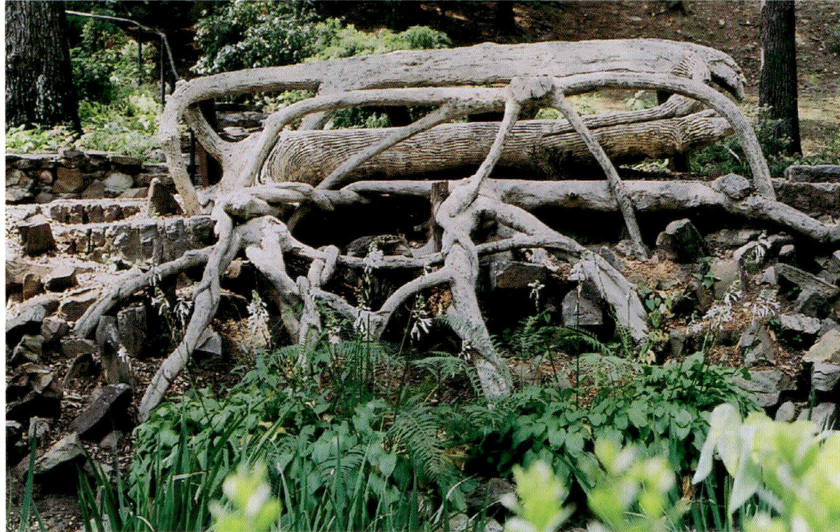

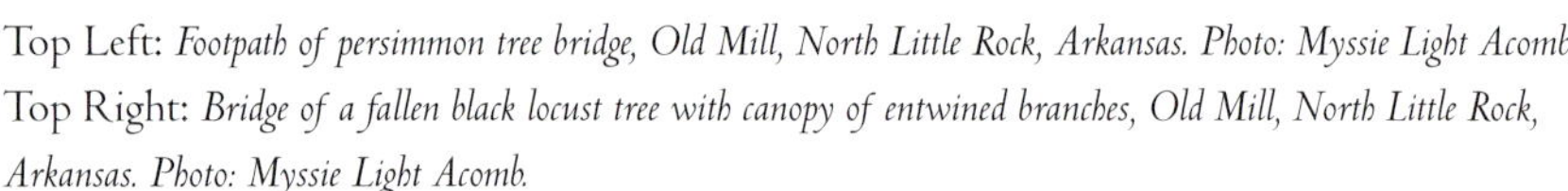

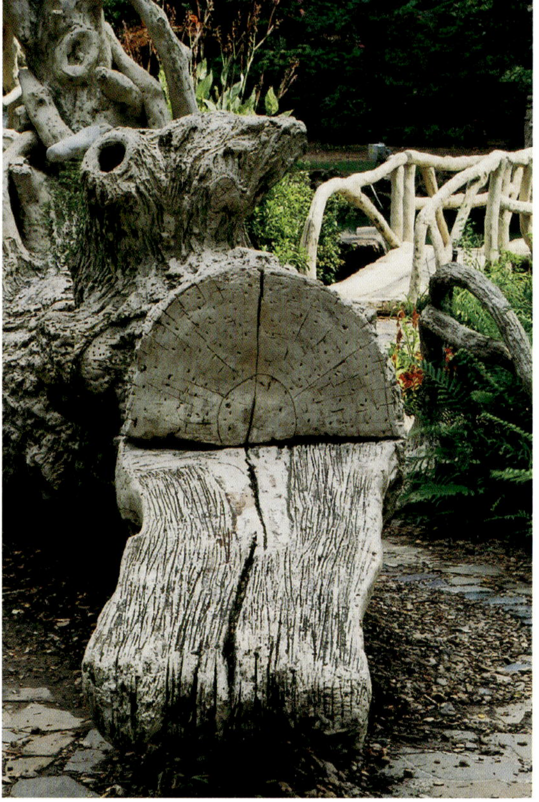

Top Left: *Footpath of persimmon tree bridge, Old Mill, North Little Rock, Arkansas. Photo: Myssie Light Acomb.*
Top Right: *Bridge of a fallen black locust tree with canopy of entwined branches, Old Mill, North Little Rock, Arkansas. Photo: Myssie Light Acomb.*
Above: *Fallen tree bench, Old Mill, North Little Rock, Arkansas. Photo: Myssie Light Acomb.*
Right: *Split log section, Old Mill, North Little Rock, Arkansas. Photo: Myssie Light Acomb.*

When the park was dedicated in August of 1933, Rodríguez, Matthews, and others gave speeches. The ceremony included speeches by a justice of the Arkansas Supreme Court, Justice Turner Butler, and former governor Charles H. Brough, who praised Justin Matthews for his development of subdivisions where more than $5 million was spent for water systems as well as for Matthews's tenure as a state highway commissioner when "more than 6,000 miles of hard surfaced roads were built in the State and approximately $100,000 was spent."[8]

Rodríguez "told of similar work he had done in Texas, but said he believed the work here was his greatest achievement. He expressed the hope that the mill would be durable as only the highest grade of cement, structural steel and copper were used in its construction."[9] Matthews "declared that the place selected for the Mill Park was the most unsightly in Lakewood and that the water supply caused him to decide on the Park. He said he expected the mill to last 'for many centuries' due to its heavy construction."[10] Eugene Villareal, who translated Rodríguez's speech, "became a well-known Little Rock investment banker in later years. Villareal had a more than nodding acquaintance with Rodríguez, as Villareal's father had come up from Mexico to assist Rodríguez in his work and lived in his son's home while this work was in progress."[11] After the park was constructed, the mill was used for the opening scenes of the 1939 movie *Gone with the Wind*.

Lakewood Park, built on the edge of Lake Number Three, is a short distance from the Old Mill and has seven Rodríguez cement sculptures:

- A palapa shelter near the front entrance to the park with a mushroom-shaped roof of bound straw bundles, secured at the apex with a knotted rope. The large tree trunk base has seats, which appear to be part of the root system, with planed log surfaces, and rough bark outer edges that curve around the trunk.
- A hollow tree house of roughly textured bark. Decayed knotholes serve as windows, and there is a large opening for a door. A built-in seat encircles the interior. Several bare branches extend outward; a birdhouse is perched on the end of one.
- A bridge of a single crosscut log with a single curving branch rail on one side.
- A gracefully curved planed-log bridge supported by a bark-covered log.
- A small, heavily textured hollow log, with four human faces emerging from the wood, with knotholes for eyebrows and noses. A vertical pipe exten-

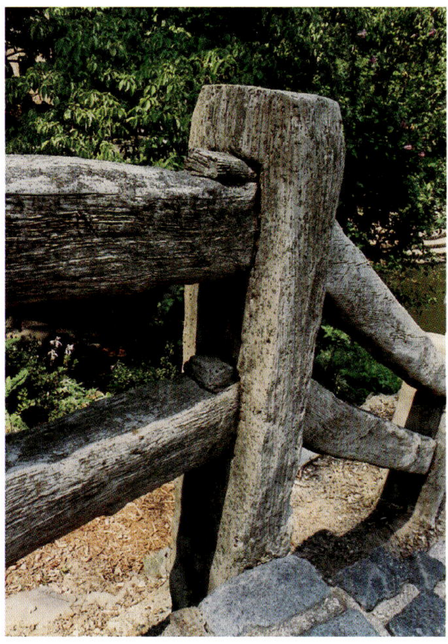

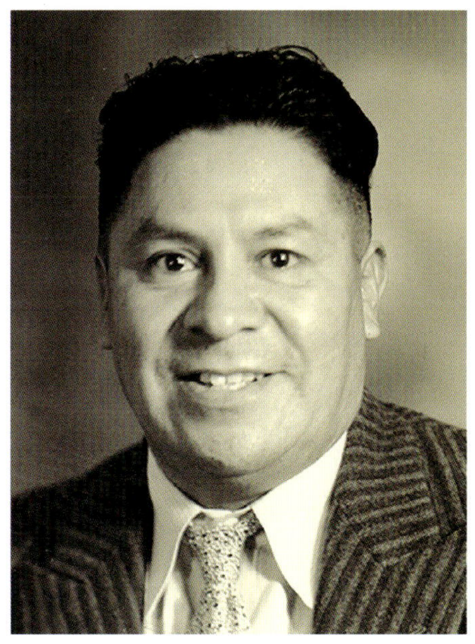

Top: *Wood fence detail with shims, Old Mill, North Little Rock, Arkansas. Photo: Myssie Light Acomb.*
Above: *Portrait of Dionicio Rodríguez, 1933. Courtesy of North Little Rock History Commission and* Arkansas Democrat-Gazette.

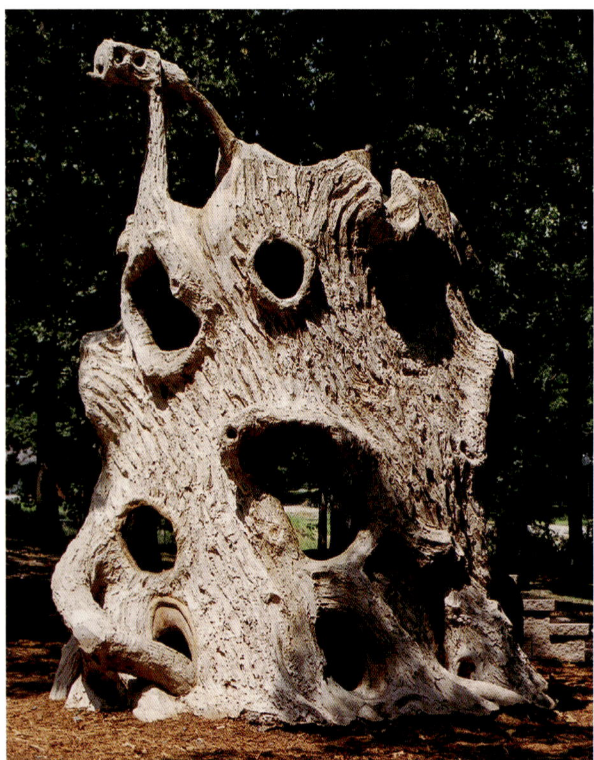

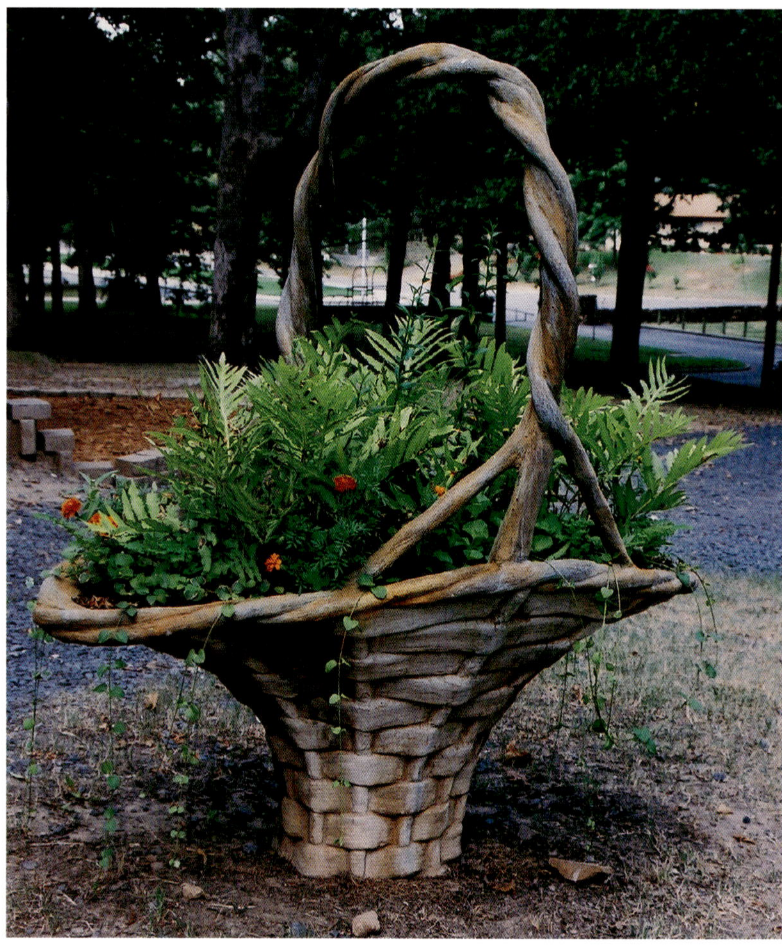

Above: *Hollow tree house, Lakewood Park, North Little Rock, Arkansas. Photo: Myssie Light Acomb.*
Right: *Basket with twisted handle, Lakewood Park, North Little Rock, Arkansas. Photo: Myssie Light Acomb.*

sion may have served as a water fountain and is now used as the water connection for an irrigation hose.

• A basket planter of sensitively woven thick straw with a handle and rim formed of three gracefully twisted thin branches. Carlos Cortés identifies this as Rodríguez's most beautiful basket sculpture.

• A bark-textured tree trunk trash container.

Crestview Park, another park planned by Matthews, is several miles west of the Old Mill and Lakewood Park. Reached by a long series of rock steps and sited at the base of a steep hill, the park contains two Rodríguez faux sculptures. One is a bridge with a bark covered log walkway. Lining either side of the bridge are two benches of logs that form backrests as they curve around upright log supports.

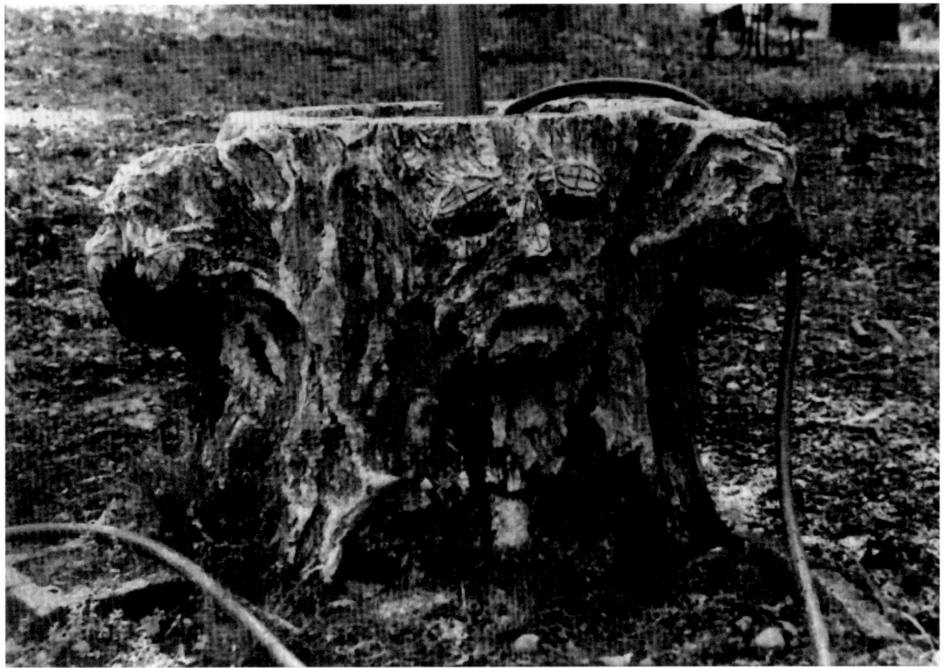

Hollow log with human faces, Lakewood Park, North Little Rock, Arkansas. Courtesy of Arkansas Historic Preservation Program.

The other installation is a rustic shelter with a front gabled roof of overlapping hollow logs, a unique Rodríguez design not duplicated at any other site. The top logs curve downward and the underside logs curve in the opposite direction, simulating a clay tile roof. Roof supports are four bark-covered log posts, which curve and meet at the apex of the roof. Attached to the supports on either side are narrow cut-out log benches with backrests of horizontal logs attached to the vertical log supports. Rodríguez's signature pyramid-headed bolts are present in the structure. The shelter rests on a textured wood base.

Cambridge Township, Lenawee County, Michigan, 1933

In the 1930s and 1940s, Michigan was a hotbed for faux bois work. In addition to Rodríguez's work at the zoo and a church in Detroit (discussed later in this chapter), several other sites exhibit rustic cement work. In 1933, Dionicio Rodríguez assisted Rafael (Ralph) Corona with work for St. Joseph's Church in the Township of Cambridge, Michigan. Originally a gabled structure that began as a missionary church in 1854, St. Joseph's Church has been altered through the years and presently has a Spanish mission revival–style exterior.[12]

A 1933 newspaper account read, "Dionetius [*sic*] Rodríguez, cement sculptor with special talent for reproducing artistic wood structures in cement, has been at the Irish Hills church grotto during the past week with his pupil Ralph Corona who has been here all

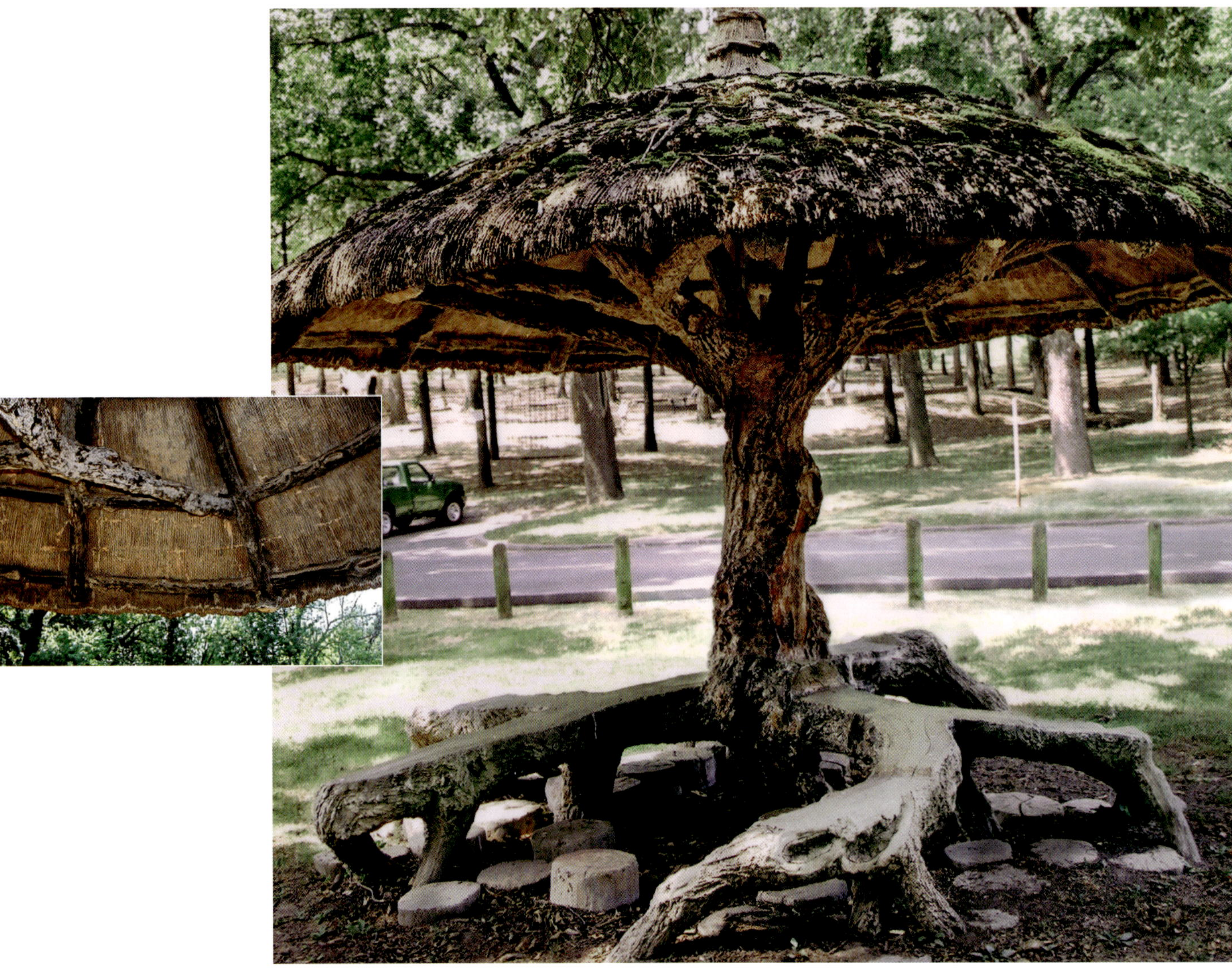

Above Right: *Palapa with rope detail at apex and root seats, Lakewood Park, North Little Rock, Arkansas. Photo: Myssie Light Acomb.*
Above Inset: *Underside of palapa roof, Lakewood Park, North Little Rock, Arkansas. Photo: Myssie Light Acomb.*

season at work on 'The Stations of the Cross.' It is expected that ten of the stations will be completed this season, the development proceeding under direction of Rev. F. Pfieffer."[13] A later account credits Dionicio with assisting with "some of the stations completed first."[14] For their work, the priest paid the artisans in gasoline money and farm produce.[15]

The historical marker for the shrine gives credit to Rodríguez and Corona for the "stone and timber" steps, archways, and railings for the stations. Situated near the shores of Iron Lake, existing outdoor stations are sited in an environment recreating old Jerusalem, with "Pilate's palace and courtyard, narrow cobblestone streets, balconied

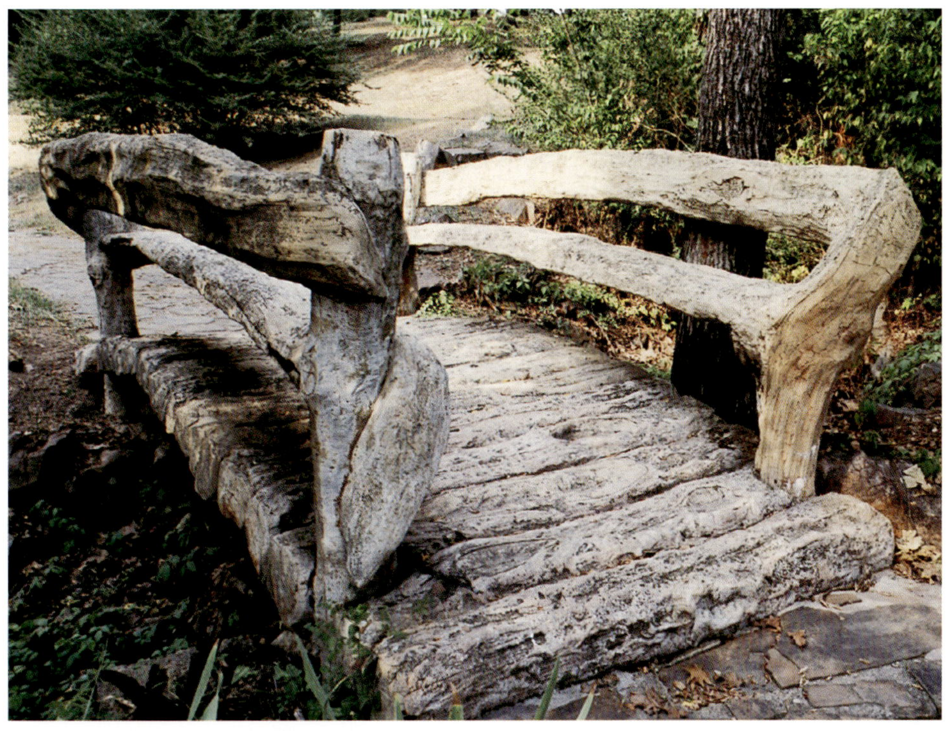

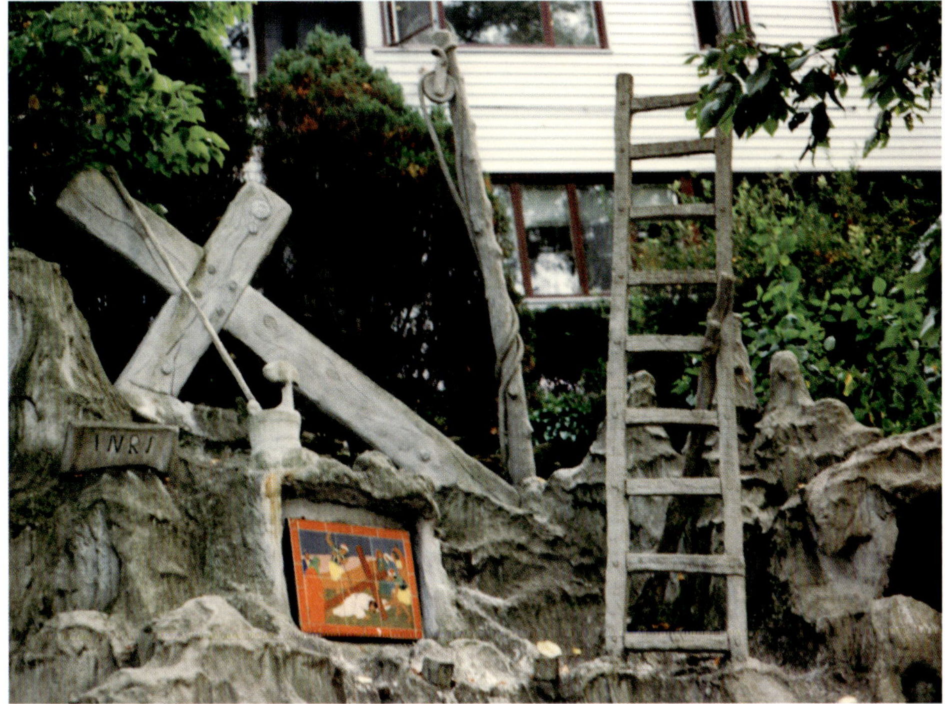

Top: *Log bridge with seats, Crestview Park, North Little Rock, Arkansas. Photo: Myssie Light Acomb.*
Left: *Station of the Cross, St. Joseph's Church, Cambridge Township, Michigan. Photo: Carlos Cortés.*

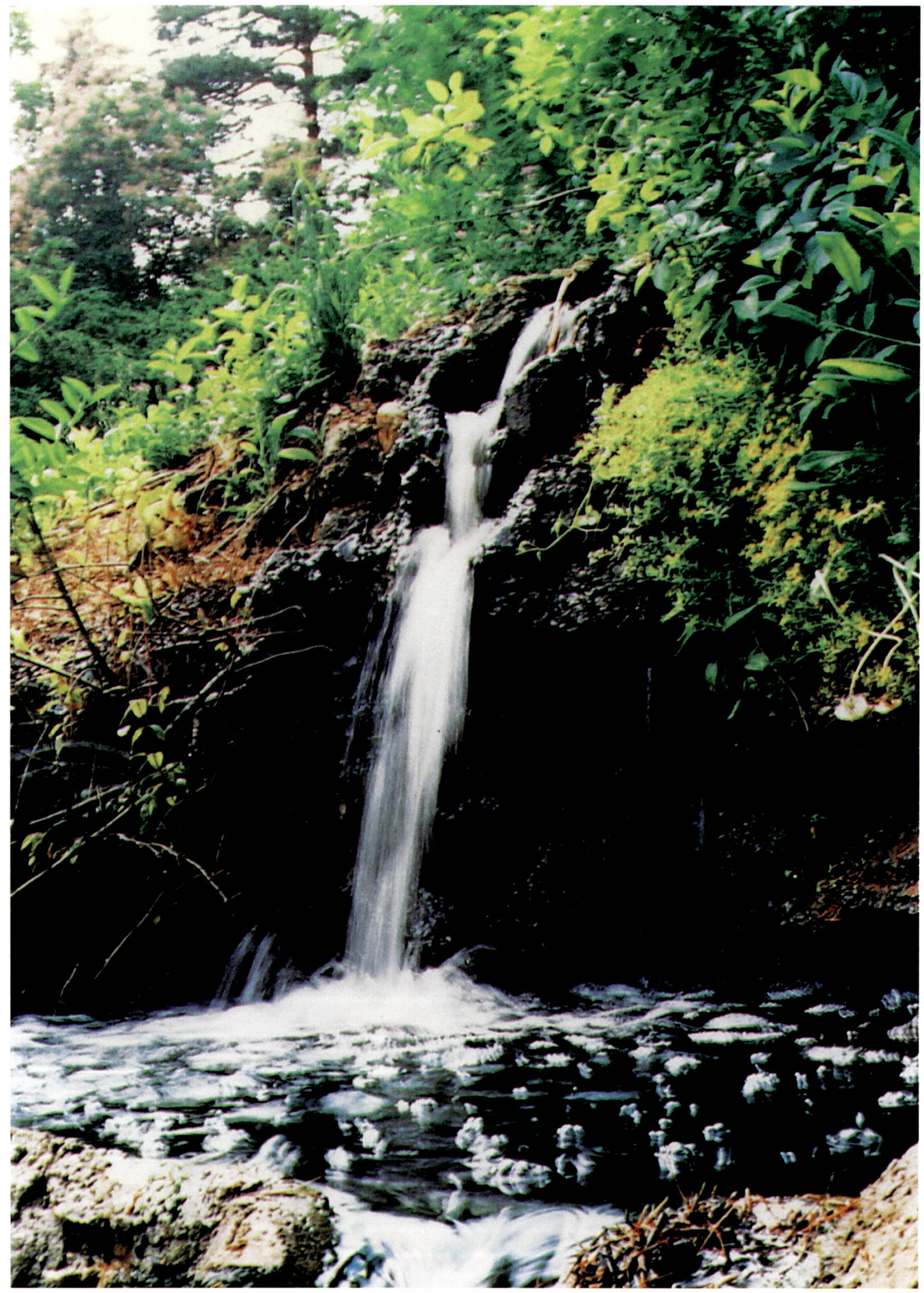

houses, . . . an image of the Judgment Gate, as well as a tomb, and masonry crosses, nails and ropes recalling biblically-inspired scenes and themes."[16] Each station is portrayed with inset glazed ceramic tile plaques that are mounted on various constructions, including a reclining wooden cross, a wooden ladder on artificial rocks, and a rustic hut similar to one in Crestview Park in Arkansas.[17]

There is strong evidence that Rodríguez worked with Corona and George Cardosa at Hillsdale College's Slayton Arboretum in Hillsdale, which was developed with the leadership of biology professor Bertram A. Barber.[18] Corona and Cardosa built two cement log bridges at the arboretum, which has a waterfall of concrete rocks where water cascades down a hill from a fieldstone gazebo. At the base of the waterfall, the initials "DR" are incised in one of the rocks.[19]

Corona and Cardosa also built seventeen rustic bridges and two bare-tree smokestacks for W. H. L. McCourtie's estate, "Aiden Lair," in Somerset Center, Michigan, ca. 1932–33. The Michigan-born McCourtie, who made his fortune from Trinity Portland Cement Company of Dallas, developed forty-two acres in his home town as a park, which was open to the public. The quality of the work at this site indicates that the artisans had perfected techniques learned from Rodríguez, who probably visited them while they were working on the project, as it is known that a third individual was with them.[20]

Rafael Corona said in an interview "that he and/or Cardosa worked at several other sites in the region . . . including at least one tree sculpture at the Detroit Zoo (indicating that they/he assisted Rodríguez on that project) and at Our Lady of Lourdes Convent in Sylvania Ohio."[21] Contractor John Angellotti and his crew (who may have been Rodríguez, Corona, and Cardosa) "worked for a group of Ford Motor Company employees and consultants for their country retreats in the 1930s and 1940s, specializing in concrete tinted and grooved to look like natural materials."[22] It is known that Henry Ford visited McCourtie in Somerset; he may have been familiar with the work there and told his associates about it.

San Antonio: Hollow Tree Shelter, 1935

In about 1935, Rodríguez built a trabajo rústico hollow tree shelter (not extant) for himself on property that he owned in San Antonio at 3602 Guadalupe Street. It was here that he stored his personal items while traveling around the country and that he later made his home. Simply furnished, it had a cot, two trunks and a stove.[23] Frank Tober, son of Julius Tober, who worked with Rodríguez, recalls the shelter being like both a tree and a cave.[24]

Albert Tober, Rodríguez's godson, has remembrances of the artisan and his tree

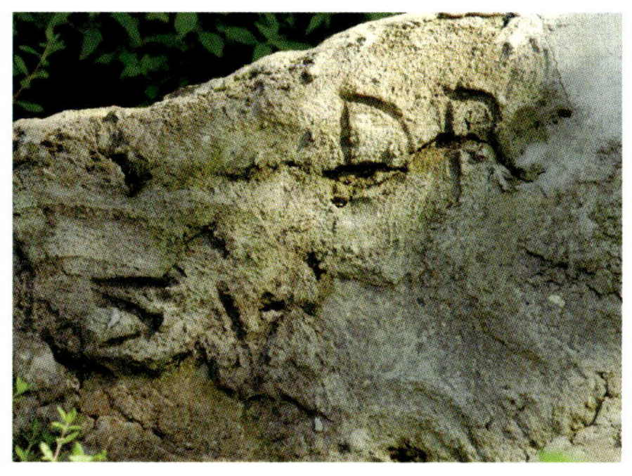

Above: *Dionicio Rodríguez's initials on fountain at Slayton Arboretum. Courtesy Hillsdale College External Affairs and Archives, Hillsdale, Michigan. Photo: Doug Coon.*
Opposite: *Fountain at Slayton Arboretum, Courtesy Hillsdale College External Affairs and Archives, Hillsdale, Michigan. Photo: Doug Coon.*

house. There was a plum tree in the front yard, and there was always money on the floor that Rodríguez would leave for the children to find. He recalls that the house looked like a hollow tree with a rounded dome roof that appeared like a broken tree on the top. It had a front door that locked, running water, electricity, a bathroom, and knotholes with glass for windows. Alicia Cortés, wife of Maximo Cortés, remembers that the girls did not go in the house—only the boys. She also recalls that there was a big flood one year: her family left their home on West Travis and went to the tree house to warn Rodríguez.[25]

Rodríguez was living in his house when he died. His property was sold, and the house was demolished.

Memphis: Memorial Park Cemetery, 1935

Elliot Clovis Hinds was the owner of the successful Cotton States Life Insurance Company, and according to his granddaughter, Katherine Smythe, he made many train trips around the country. On one of these trips he visited Carlsbad Caverns in New Mexico, the Garden of the Gods in Colorado Springs, and Herbert Eaton's Forest Lawn in Los Angeles, which was embellished with sculptural pieces and was the first cemetery in the country to replace upright tombstones with flat grave markers.[26]

Eaton, an unemployed engineer, had taken over the failed Forest Lawn Cemetery in 1904.[27] He initiated this new trend and included the English traditions of winding roads, paths, an abundance of landscape plantings—and sculpture, as found in the cemetery Père Lachaise in Paris.[28] The progression from dreary graveyards in United States churchyards had begun to evolve with Adolph Strauch's designs for landscaped lawn-park cemeteries toward the end of the 1800s. Eaton's project was the first of more than six hundred "memorial park" cemeteries that were built in the country by 1935.[29]

Influenced by Eaton's success at Forest Lawn, Hinds sold his insurance company and began making plans for a similar cemetery as early as 1924. He engaged John Noyes, a landscape architect with the George Kessler firm of St. Louis, who planned the site work and the planting. A local stonemason, Fred C. Andrews, was hired for the rock work, which included natural-appearing ledges and buildings.[30] Hinds corresponded with Rodríguez in 1933 while Rodríguez was working for Matthews in Arkansas, although he did not hire the artisan to work at Memorial Park Cemetery until 1935.

The correspondence between the two men is revealing of their resulting relationship. In a letter to Hinds in January, 1938, Rodríguez wrote that he wanted to work exclusively for Hinds in Memphis: "I can't do any kind of work in this town, only for you with exemption [*sic*] of the city."[31] There is speculation that Rodríguez may have worked at the Memphis Zoo, as Hinds had mentioned in earlier correspondence that Rodríguez might

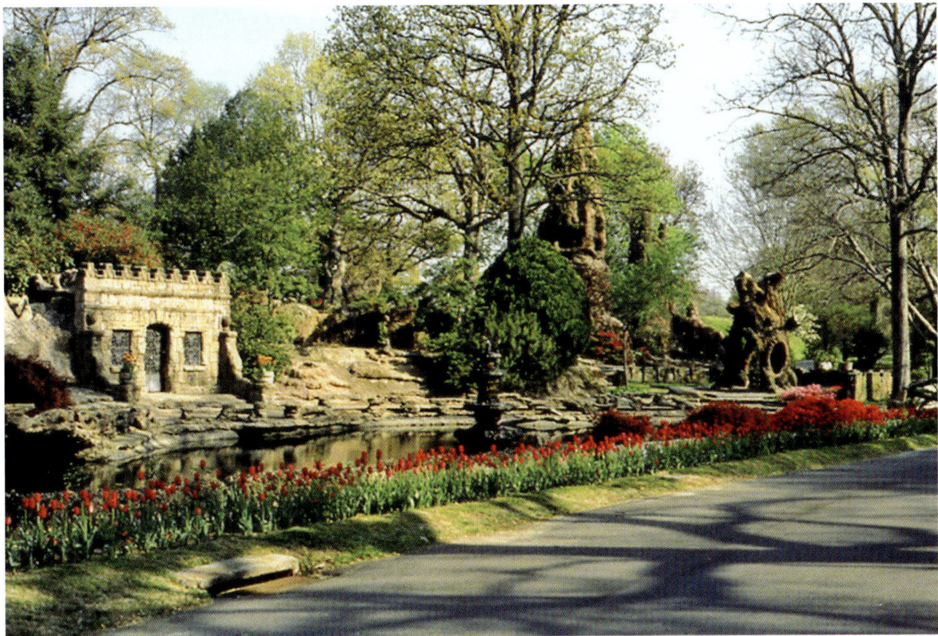

like "to work for Mr. Renfrow at the City Zoo."[32] A former zoo employee remembers a man who arrived on a bus with a suitcase, having come to work on the lion and bear moats (not extant).[33]

At the same time, his 1938 letter illustrates how protective Rodríguez was of his technique and work: "Please don't let anybody else try to perform or practice any of my artistical [*sic*] work."[34]

Many of the letters concern their financial arrangements—Hinds served as a kind of paternalistic financial manager for Rodríguez, depositing Rodríguez's earnings in the bank and then sending money when he needed it. Rodríguez would work on a credit basis when Hinds's collections were slow. On one occasion, when Rodríguez asked to receive three hundred dollars, Hinds sent him the money but wrote: "Would appreciate your forgetting me for awhile until I catch up on collections. In fact I want to keep in debt to you so you won't forget me."[35] In 1938 the Fair Labor and Standards Act was passed (which, according to Hinds, limited work to eight hours a day, five and a half days per week), at a time when Hinds was concerned about completion of the Crystal Shrine Grotto before the onset of inclement weather. He negotiated with Rodríguez for the artisan to work on a contractual basis, explaining that Rodríguez could then "work nine or ten hours if you like."[36] Rodríguez continued to work intermittently for Hinds until 1941, at times returning to touch up colors that had faded.

Memorial Park Cemetery, Memphis, Tennessee: Pool of Hebron, Cave of Machpelah, Guard of Machpelah, God's Garden, and Abraham's Oak. Courtesy of Tennessee Historical Commission.

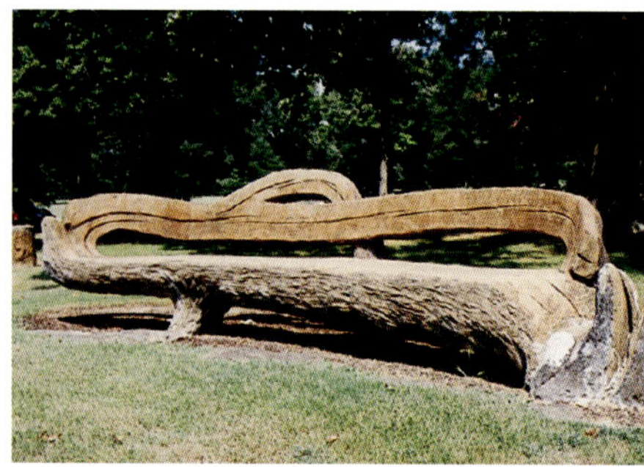

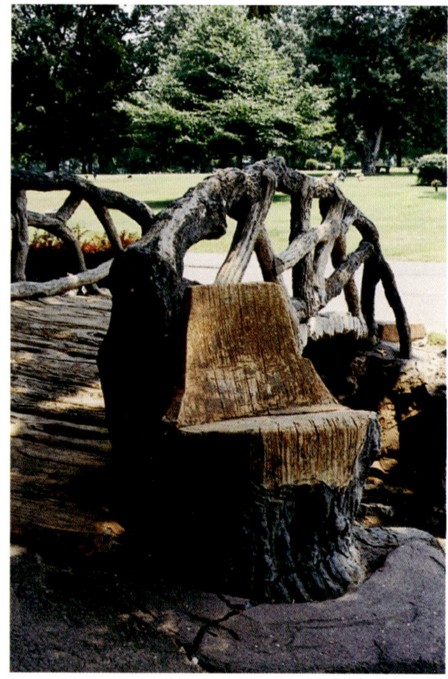

Top: *Fallen tree bench, Memorial Park Cemetery, Memphis, Tennessee. Photo: Myssie Light Acomb.*
Above right: *Cave of Machpelah, Memorial Park Cemetery, Memphis, Tennessee. Photo: Myssie Light Acomb.*
Above: *Log bridge and stump seat, Memorial Park Cemetery, Memphis, Tennessee. Photo: Myssie Light Acomb.*

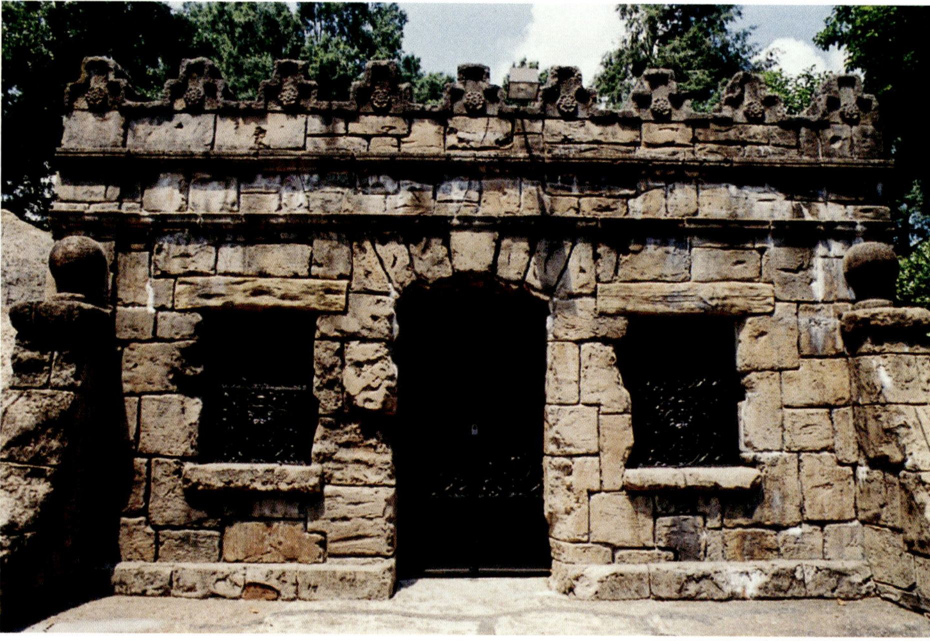

A brochure for the cemetery indicates that Hinds "envisioned a landmark cemetery marked by beauty and serenity." Rodríguez was hired by Hinds to "beautify the cemetery and reproduce certain bits of history, chiefly Biblical."[37] Clovis Hinds stated: "It is good business for me to make the park into a spot of beauty and art. We want to create something that will attract people. People usually don't go to cemeteries unless they have a special interest there. We shall try to change that."[38]

In 1935, Hinds addressed the annual convention of the American Cemetery Owners Association in Detroit in a speech titled "How to Make Memorial Parks Beautiful and Famous."[39] Memorial Park Cemetery remains a remarkable tourist attraction. The majority of the Rodríguez concrete sculptures, some marked with titles or plaques, are situated in a linear pattern along a road paralleling a rock-lined channel that traverses the cemetery from north to south:

- Abraham's Oak, a hollow tree sculpture; according to scriptural references, there was a large oak near the site of Abraham's tomb. Similar to other tree sculptures by Rodríguez, this one has two seats on the inside and knotholes providing openings. Fragments of cut branches protrude from the sides.
- A fallen tree bench. A single rough bark log seat curves and forms a smooth bark backrest with an extra branch, which curves to the ground.

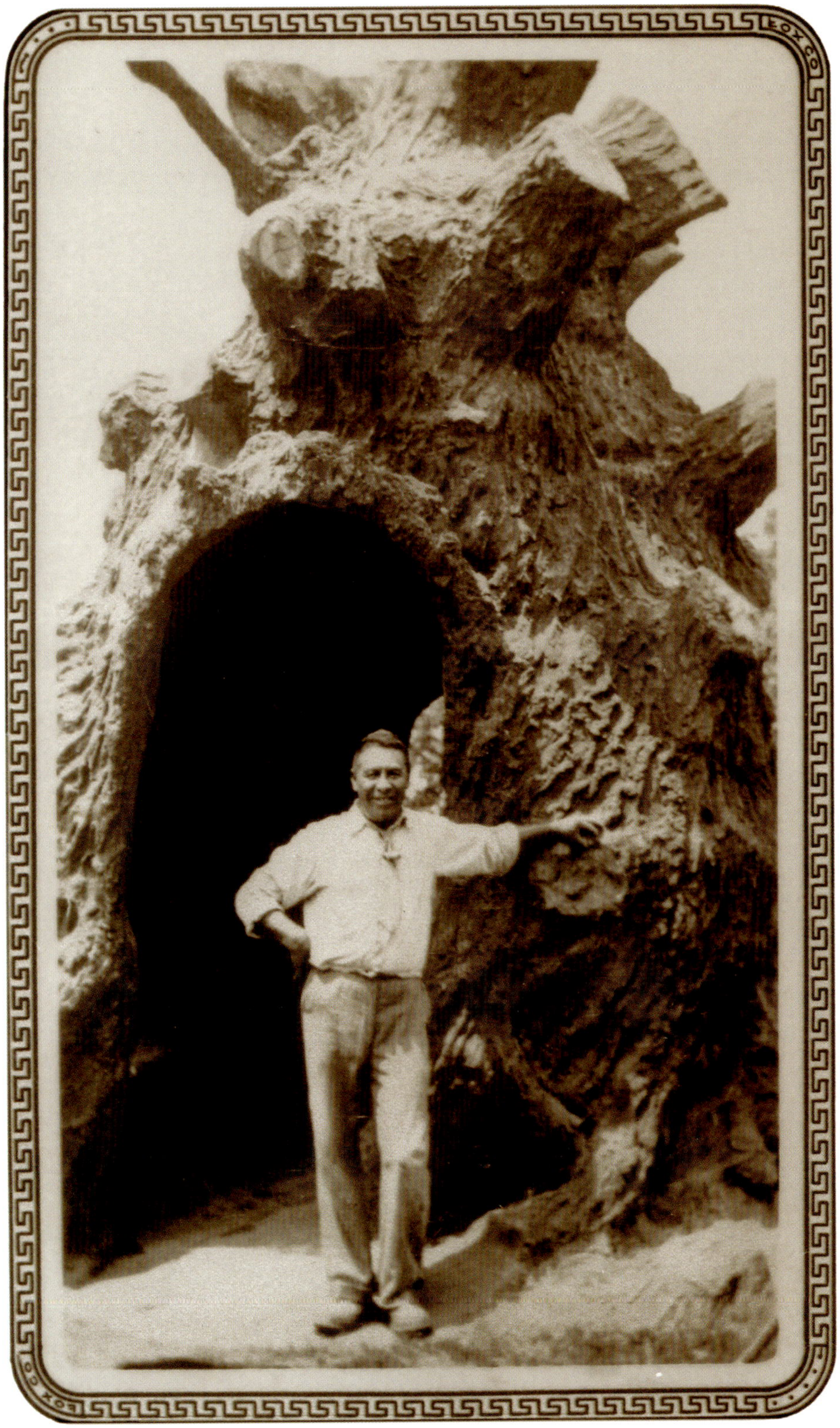

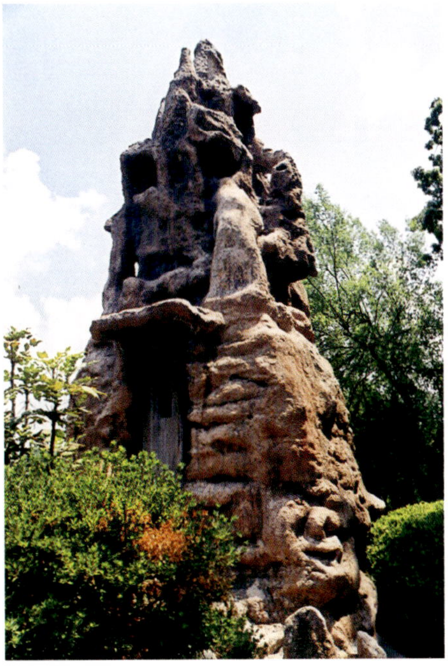

Left: *Rodríguez with Abraham's Oak, Memorial Park Cemetery, Memphis, Tennessee, late 1930s. Courtesy of Manuela Vargas Theall.*
Above: *God's Garden, Memorial Park Cemetery, Memphis, Tennessee. Photo: Myssie Light Acomb.*

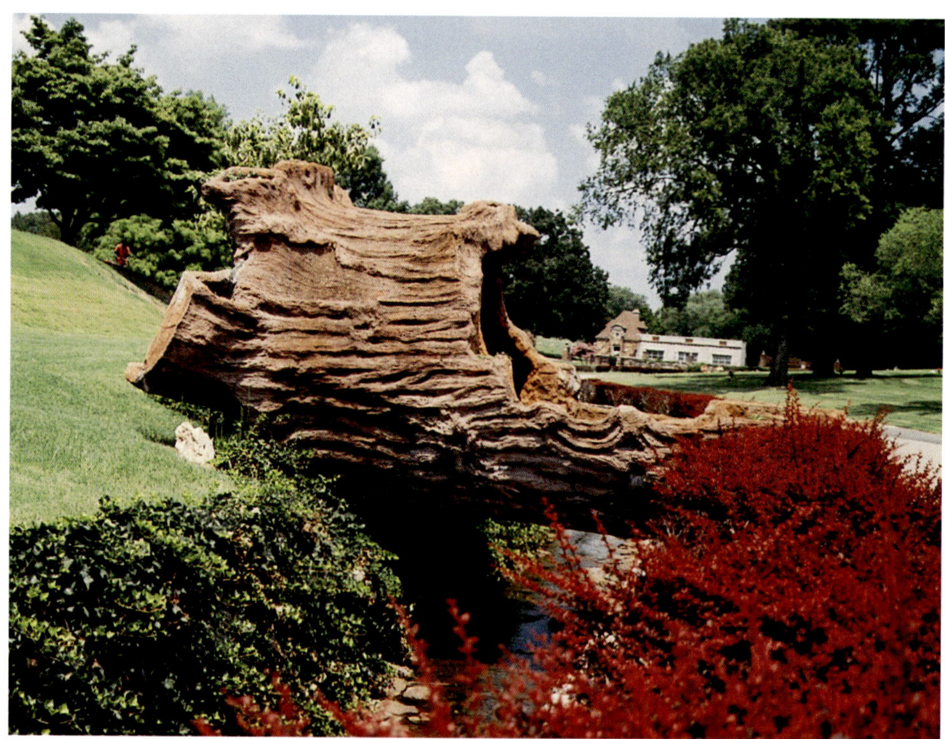

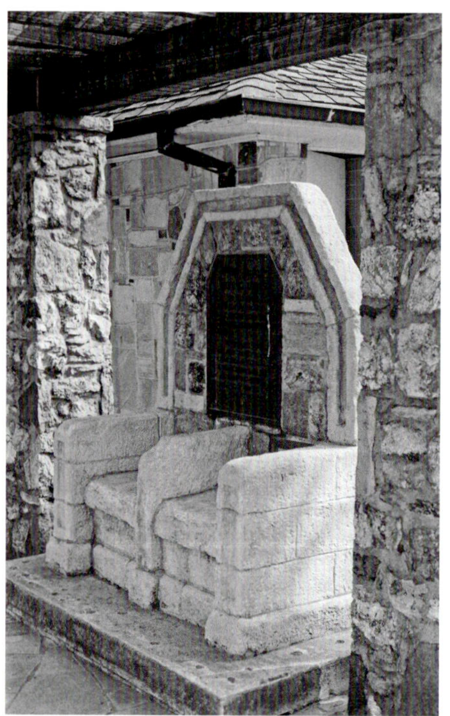

• The Fountain of Youth, a gabled palapa roof supported by four heavy timbers shelters a rock well, perhaps a replica of the one purported to have been found by Ponce de Léon. A glazed ceramic plaque of sailing ships and the inscription "Ponce de Leon's Fountain of Youth, 1513 St Augustine, Fla." embellish the fountain. A wooden sign incised with "Open Sesame" is suspended from the overhead beams. A raised carved stone planter bed extends on both sides of the shelter.

• The Cave of Machpelah, a rectangular-shaped building of simulated cut stone built into a hillside. Hinds instructed Rodríguez to build the structure representing the burial cave of Abraham at Hebron, as mentioned in the Bible, and it can be assumed that Hinds influenced the design of the building.[40] The crenellations capping the façade are reminiscent of designs on a building on the walls at Mitla, ancient Zapotec ruins in Mexico, and could have been Rodríguez's idea. The door and two windows are inset with decorative open grillwork, providing visitors a view inside the cave, which houses a cement replica of an oak tree coffin (the original, discovered in 1935, contained remains of a Danish warrior chief); a glazed ceramic tile wall plaque of an Egyptian scene; and two vaults (coffins) built into the north and south walls.[41]

• The Pool of Hebron, a large rock-lined pool sited in front of the cave. Biblical references are made to reservoirs or pools that served as water supplies. According to Beardsley, the original pool at Hebron was not one built by Solomon for this use.[42] Rather, it was "the place where David hung the bodies of the men who killed his rival Ishboseth, son of Saul."[43] A three-tiered fountain in the pool, embellished with faces (some speculate that they are likenesses of friends of Rodríguez), drips water from each tier.

• A rustic footbridge providing access to the pool and the Cave of Machpelah crosses the waterway that bisects the cemetery. Curving and intertwined branches form the handrails and split logs serve as the walkway. A small chair made of a cut-out stump with roots draping down toward the stream is at one end of the bridge.

• An Annie Laurie Wishing Chair. The large chair, with two seats separated by an arm rest, is made of cement cut stones and trimmed with a band of natural stones, which outline the shape of the seats. It is supposedly a copy of the original chair in the forecourt of a Scottish church. A bronze plaque is engraved with the legend of the Scottish lass, Annie Laurie.[44] Lisa Simpson notes that the chair is an exact copy of one found in the Wee Kirk of the Heather, a section of Forest Lawn, and that Hinds's papers contain a "blueprint of the chair which may have been given to Hinds by Eaton." The chair is built under a wood and limestone pergola, which may have been copied from one Hinds had seen in Tombstone, Arizona.[45] Julie Vosmik suggests that a source for the chair's design could have been one in Whitemarsh Memorial Park in Philadelphia, designed by French architect Paul P. Cret.[46]

• God's Garden. Three conical rock sculptures near the Cave of Machpelah resemble the rock formations at the Garden of the Gods in Colorado; the base of one serves as the entrance to the Crystal Shrine Grotto.

• Near God's Garden is a large tree stump with elongated roots extending toward the ground. The heavily textured bark surface and a knothole add to the realistic effect of the sculpture, which is similar to a smaller one at Eddingston Court.

• A rock bench with scrolled armrests, constructed to appear in ruins, stands near the rock towers. Alternate embossed tiles have designs of a four-petaled flower and a flying dragon. Rodríguez built a similar bench with these decorative features at Cedar Hill in Suitland, Maryland.

• One section (a dormer) of the cemetery's sales building's roof was covered with cement-bundled thatch.

• Simulated rock ledges appear around the Pool of Hebron and in other terraced areas of the cemetery.

• Guard of Machpelah. Hinds's notes state that the cave was guarded by "Mohammdan [*sic*] soldiers day and night," and if "one places the least value on his life he will not attempt to take a picture or enter the tomb."[47] The "guard" is represented by a large abstract rock form capped with a round shape for the "head."

• The Crystal Shrine Grotto was excavated fifty-nine feet back into the same hillside where the tomb of Machpelah was built.[48] The grotto planned by Hinds was "the high point of the entire production."[49] He purchased five tons of natural crystals from the Diamond Cave in Jasper, Arkansas, to line the interior of his cave, which had holes in the ceiling, allowing sunlight to sparkle on the rocks. Lining the interior of the grotto are ten niches for scenes from the life of Christ, with backgrounds created by Rodríguez; these are filled with ceramic and wooden figures, some of them stock figures purchased from a Boston firm and others created by Memphis sculptors.[50]

• A covered footbridge that resembles an enormous hollow fallen tree with heavily incised bark texture serves as an additional crossing over the cemetery's channel. Hollowed-out areas on the top and sides serve as planters.

• Groups of toadstools of exaggerated size.

John Richmond, who worked for the cemetery, recalled "great crowds of people coming out to watch Rodríguez work, especially on Saturdays and Sundays." Hinds would be there and "loved to talk to people, telling them about plans for the finished work and describing what Rodríguez was doing." Richmond also told of a sea lion with a ball on its nose that Rodríguez sculpted for the restaurant Davis White Spot. When the building was demolished, the sea lion disappeared.[51]

Washington, D.C.: Brentwood and Suitland, 1935–37

Rodríguez would continue to work intermittently for Hinds until 1939, interspersing this work with projects for other clients. Some presumably gave him commissions following referrals by Hinds. He was becoming something of a specialist in sculptural work for cemeteries.

Brentwood, Maryland: Lincoln Park Cemetery, 1935

Hired by an acquaintance of Clovis Hinds, Lobell O. Minear, owner of Lincoln Park Cemetery, Rodríguez worked just outside Washington, D.C., in Brentwood, Maryland, in

1935.[52] The cemetery's cloister garden features a truncated vault ceiling that is believed to have been made by Rodríguez. Cracks in the ceiling reveal his distinctive construction method—the use of steel reinforcing rods, metal lath, and cement.[53]

While Rodríguez was in the Washington area, Hinds wrote to advise him about his conduct there because he was "better acquainted with Washington and its customs" than Rodríguez, and confirmed that he would take care of Rodríguez's money for him, an arrangement that continued during their eleven-year association.[54]

Suitland, Maryland: Cedar Hill Cemetery, 1936–38

With a recommendation from Hinds, Rodríguez was hired to work in Cedar Hill Cemetery in Suitland, Maryland, which had been established by William H. Harrison and a group of farmer-merchants. Harrison was engaged in farming in Suitland, and he sold his produce in the Farmer's Market in nearby Washington, D.C.[55] Lobell Minear, owner of Lincoln Park Cemetery, was also the manager of Cedar Hill, and it is possible that he too recommended Rodríguez for this job.

Rodriguez wrote to Hinds in June 1936 that he was working in Cedar Hill, and according to a feature in the Sunday Gravure section of the *Washington Star*, he had completed at least six major pieces by the end of July.[56] Dorothy Richards, a fifty-year cemetery employee and manager for twenty years, related that when she was very young "we had family buried there so we visited [the cemetery] a lot."[57] In a 1990 interview, she recalled watching Rodríguez work. "I remember that he was very secretive. No one could see what he was doing because he worked in a tent and wouldn't let anyone near."[58] Rodríguez built numerous faux sculptural pieces at Cedar Hill, including:

- a fallen tree bench with a smooth planed seat, a richly textured base simulating the fallen trunk, and the backrest with a curved branch on one end; the initials "D.R." are incised in the seat
- two wooden bridges with branch railings and planked floors; one spanning a small pond evidences Oriental design influence and is flanked on either end by Chinese lanterns
- a wooden table of three smooth logs resting on a tree trunk base, sited under a rock-columned wooden pergola
- a hollow tree house approximately twelve feet tall, with two openings that serve as entrances; the exterior has heavy bark texture and several branch stumps that protrude outward
- an Annie Laurie Chair, built under a pergola similar to the one over the table

Right: *Rodríguez at Cedar Hill Cemetery, Suitland, Maryland, ca. 1937. Courtesy of Manuela Vargas Theall.*
Below: *Rodríguez (on right), J. M. Rocha Sr. (left of Rodríguez), and unidentified assistants with scaffolding for tree house, Cedar Hill Cemetery, Suitland, Maryland, ca. 1937. Courtesy of Manuela Vargas Theall.*

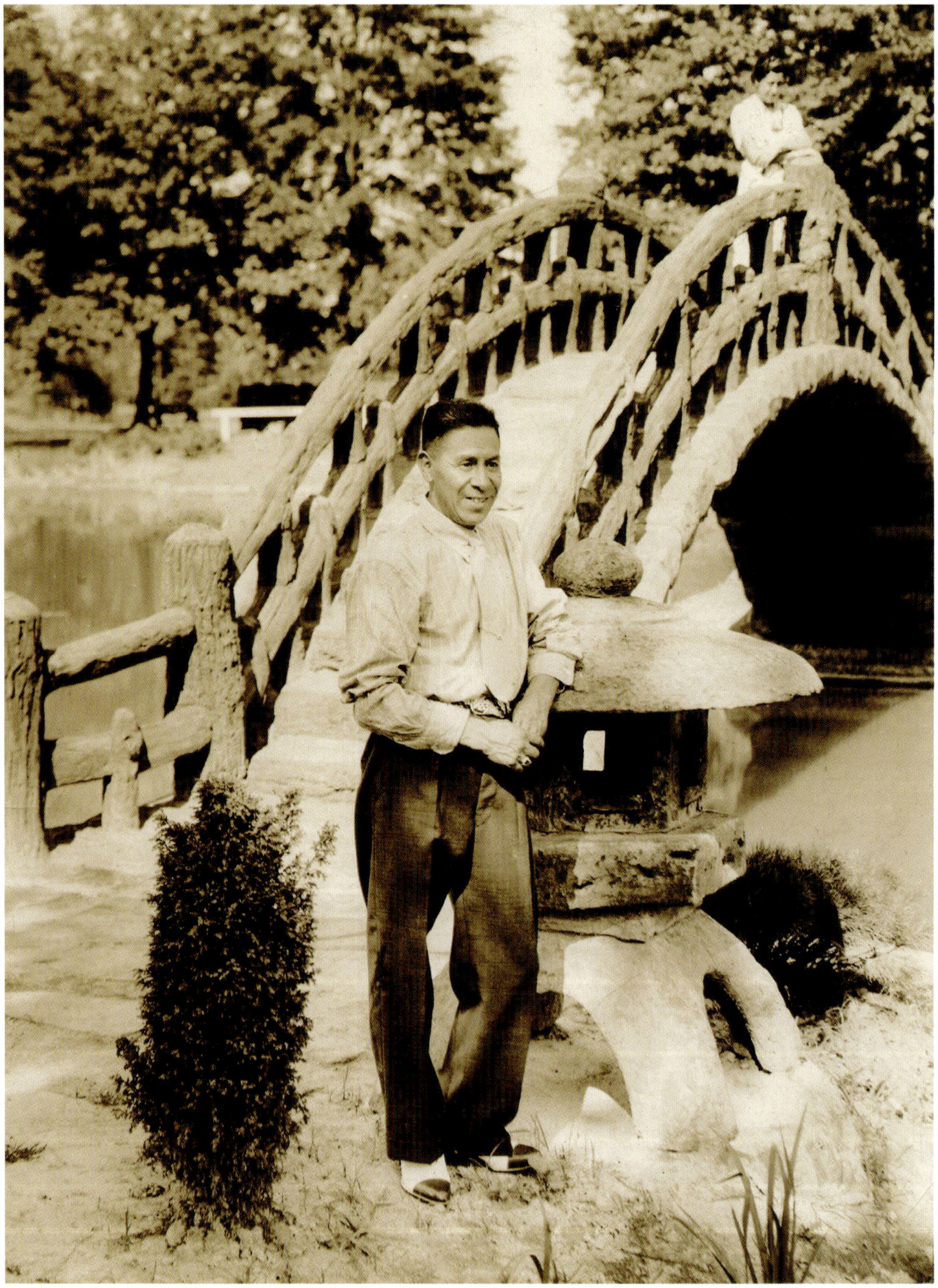

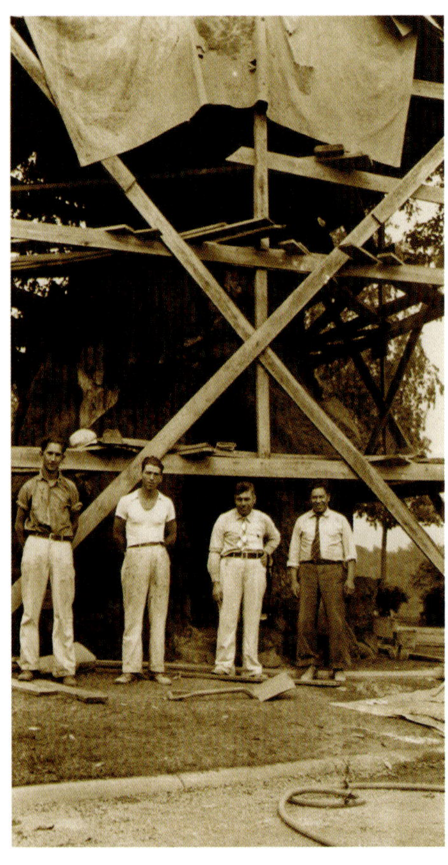

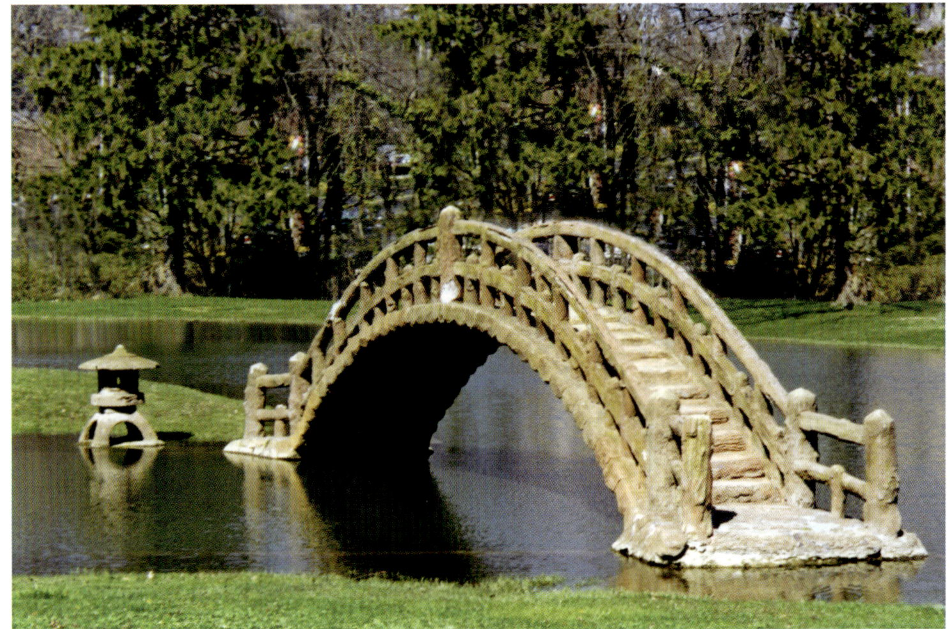

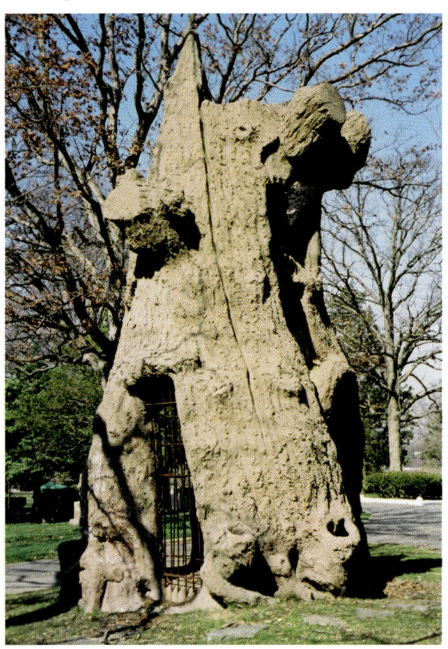

Left: *Log bridge, Cedar Hill Cemetery, Suitland, Maryland. Photo: Maria Watson Pfeiffer.*
Above: *Hollow tree house, Cedar Hill Cemetery, Suitland, Maryland. Photo: Maria Watson Pfeiffer.*

Early in 1937 Rodríguez visited his home town of Toluca on a driving trip with Maximo Cortés. He asked the mother and the aunt of his sixteen-year-old niece, Manuela Vargas (Theall), for permission for her to come to the United States and accompany him on his travels. Manuela later rode the train from Mexico City, with instructions from her family to the porter to take care of her. The train stopped in Laredo, and she then traveled on to San Antonio, where she was met by Maximo Cortés and his family. They took her clothes shopping and she spent the night before boarding the train to Little Rock, where Rodríguez was doing some work for Matthews. He was repairing sculptures that had been damaged by people scratching the surfaces trying to determine if the pieces were "real wood." Soon after Manuela arrived, they drove to Washington, D.C., in Rodríguez's 1936 DeSoto car.[59]

It appears that the manager of Cedar Hill wanted her uncle to sculpt a large seat with embossed designs similar to one he had seen in a magazine illustration. Manuela reported that she made the molds for the seat's decoration, including a dragon figure and floral motifs.[60]

During their stay, they lived in a boarding house on Northwest 24th Street, where they cooked some of their meals. She remembers visiting the U.S. Capitol building, where they climbed to the dome for more than an hour, where "everything was beautiful." Manuela said they spent their weekends at the movies, where they could see a double feature

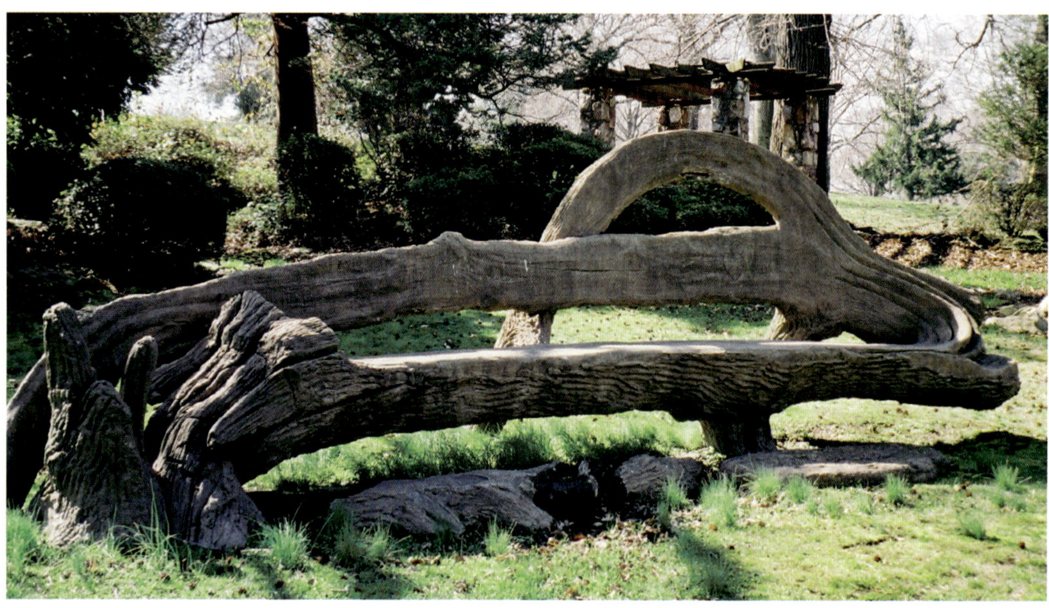

and a stage show for twenty-five cents. Harrison enrolled her in Holy Cross Academy, a Catholic school, which she attended for a short time.[61]

Manuela revealed that this phase of the Cedar Hill Cemetery work was completed between early May and the first week of August 1937. Rodríguez and his niece left Washington for Wheeling, West Virginia, where he created a bench for a "little lady," who said she would pay him what he asked. From there they went to Detroit, where he repaired earlier work on a church on Mack Avenue. From there they traveled to Chicago, St. Louis, Chattanooga, and Memphis, stopping in each city for a few days.[62] In Chattanooga, Rodríguez visited with a man who wanted him to build a rock garden, but the client was not willing to pay the price the artisan asked, and the deal was not finalized.

Little Rock, 1937

In 1937 Rodríguez was having injections for his diabetes in Little Rock, but he returned to work with Hinds. Hinds wrote to Rodríguez in December of 1937 that he wanted the artisan to wait until better weather to continue the work, as "we cannot afford to have any of this work go bad on account of bad weather." He added that he wanted the pending work to be "the best you have ever done, as it will be the work that will decide many new contracts for you in 1938, when we hold the National Convention of all the big cemeteries in the United States in Memphis."[63]

Although no records of this meeting have been found, it is probable that the delegates visited Memorial Park Cemetery and saw Rodríguez's sculptures.

Birmingham, Detroit, and Little Rock, 1938

According to Manuela Theall, she and Rodríguez were in Birmingham, Alabama, from January through March 1, 1938, where he worked in Elmwood Cemetery. The owner of Elmwood, John Jemison, was an investment banker and land developer.[64] Several of Rodríguez's trabajo rústico pieces for this project were almost identical to his previous work at Cedar Hill Cemetery.

He produced a curved wooden bridge with a Chinese lantern resting on a pedestal at one end. The footpath is of split logs and the handrails are rough timbers. A second sculpture was a fallen tree bench, with a horizontal trunk forming the seat. The backrest is formed by a split portion of the trunk, parallel with the seat. He also built a palapa-roofed shelter supported by a single tree trunk, with seats sculpted as roots radiating from the base of the trunk.

In 1938, Rodríguez returned to Detroit and completed a wooden bridge at the Detroit Zoo. It seems appropriate that he was hired by the zoo director, Frank McInnis, to build an organic-type sculpture of concrete for the naturalistic landscape that had been designed by Bostonian landscape architect Arthur Shurtleff, formerly of Frederick Law Olmsted's office. Shurtleff's design for the zoological gardens included sinuous paths built around native trees and around two lakes that were excavated from ditches formerly used for drainage.[65] Rodríguez worked for a week on the bridge, which spanned a trout stream. Although the sculptor continued to guard the secrets of his technique and worked inside a

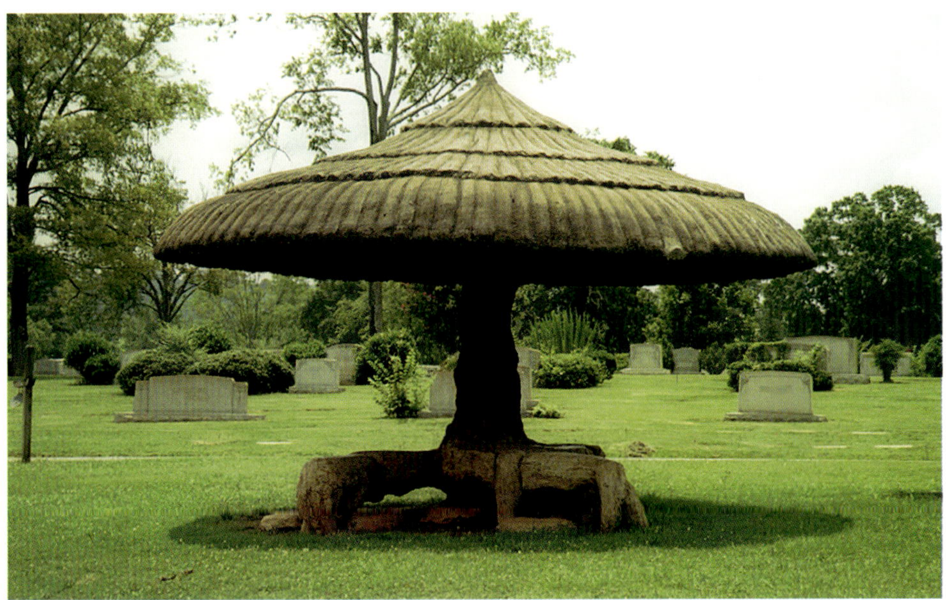

Palapa, Elmwood Cemetery, Birmingham, Alabama.
Photograph: Maria Watson Pfeiffer.

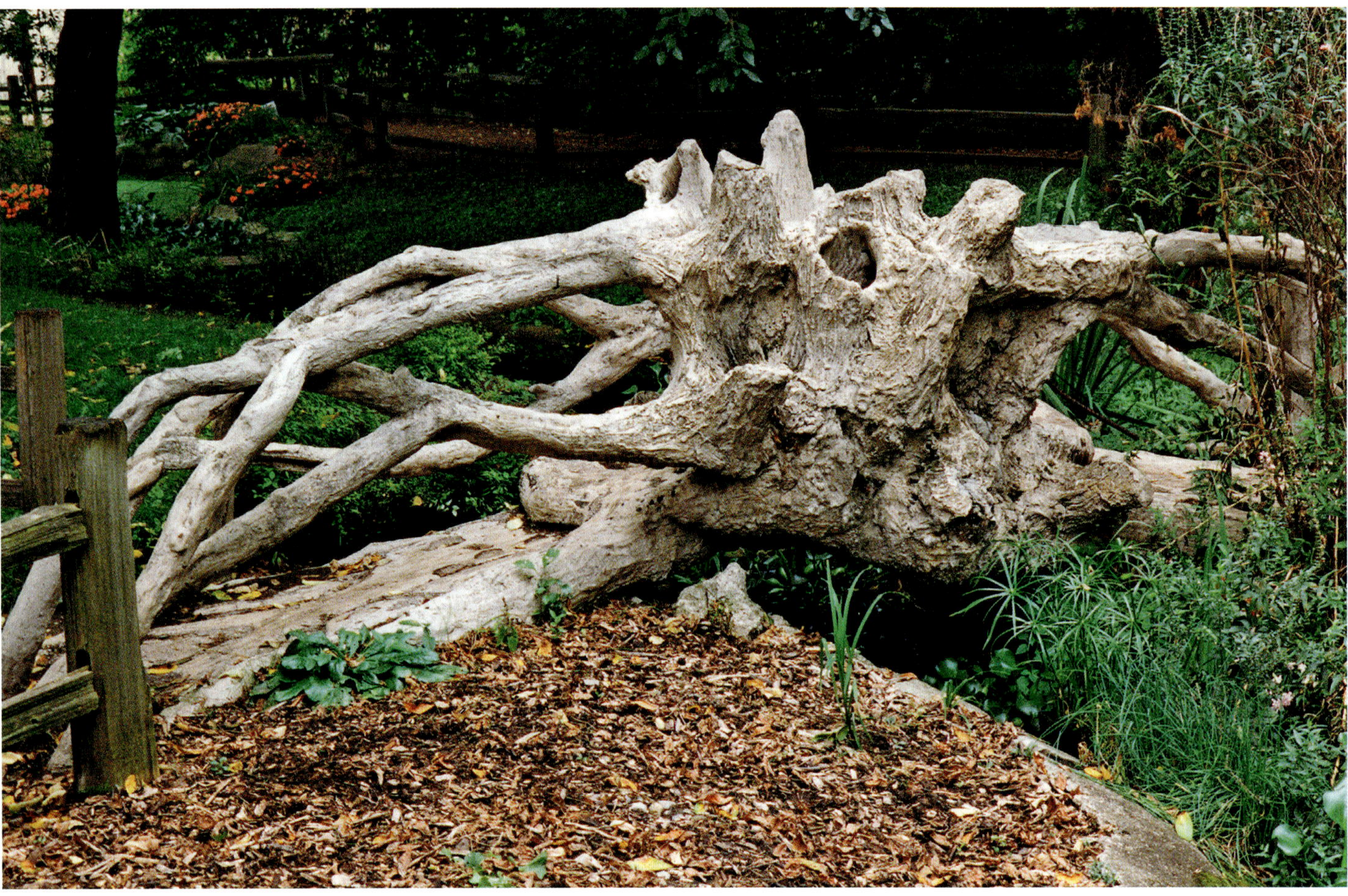

Log bridge, Detroit Zoo, Detroit, Michigan (not extant).
Photo: Carlos Cortés.

tent, he occasionally allowed his helper and Jack Truxton, an employee of the zoo, inside.[66] The bridge, signed by Rodríguez, was demolished in the 1990s.

Information in the Hinds letters indicates that in 1938, Rodríguez was again in Little Rock, planning to go to Mexico City. During this Mexico trip, he visited the Cacahuamilpa *grutas* (caves) in the state of Guerrero. His friend, letter writer, and translator, J. M. Rocha Sr., of Little Rock, reported to Hinds that Rodríguez had related to him "that those [caves] are wonderfool [*sic*] and he have in his mind to fix your cave with more experience with the grouts."[67] It appears that he returned to Memphis to work on the Crystal Cave.

Chicago and Memphis, 1939

Dionicio Rodríguez spent six or seven weeks in Chicago in 1939, where he worked for Leonard Cowan, who developed cemeteries including two burial parks for Masons: Cedar Park in Calumet Park and Acacia Park in Norridge, both Chicago suburbs.[68] Both cemeteries have cement thatch-roofed palapas with log seats. Half of Acacia Park, now Westlawn Cemetery and Mausoleum, Inc., belongs to Temple Shalom, Chicago, and the Rodríguez sculpture is in this area.[69]

In August 1939, Hinds wrote Rodríguez asking him to come back and touch up some of the colors that had faded. He would pay $1.50 an hour and $2.50 a day for the helper. It is apparent that Hinds knew the kinds of chemicals Rodríguez used for his tinting, as he wrote: "If you want me to order any coloring, send a list of colors, giving the number of pounds on the enclosed card."[70]

Rodríguez's reputation continued to grow, and in 1939 he was contacted by a group of individuals in New York City who wanted to commission a project. He modeled a maquette, but the work apparently never materialized.[71]

Arkansas: Couchwood and Little Switzerland, 1939

In a 1939 letter, Clovis Hinds wrote to tell Rodríguez that "Harvey C. Couch of Pine Bluff Ark President of Ark Power & Light Co. was here to see me about getting you to do a lot of work—beautifying his Summer Estate out at Couch Wood located near Hot Springs Ark. Mr. Couch is one of Arkansas big men of affairs and I have promised to send you to see him as soon as you can come. . . . From what he says think he wants big over shot wheel and some other rustic seats, features, etc."[72]

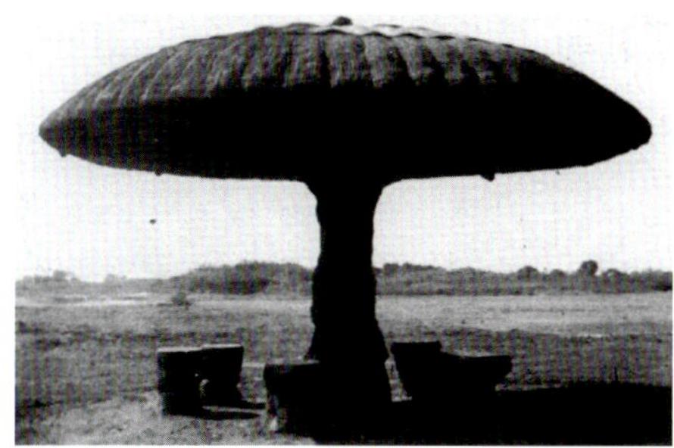

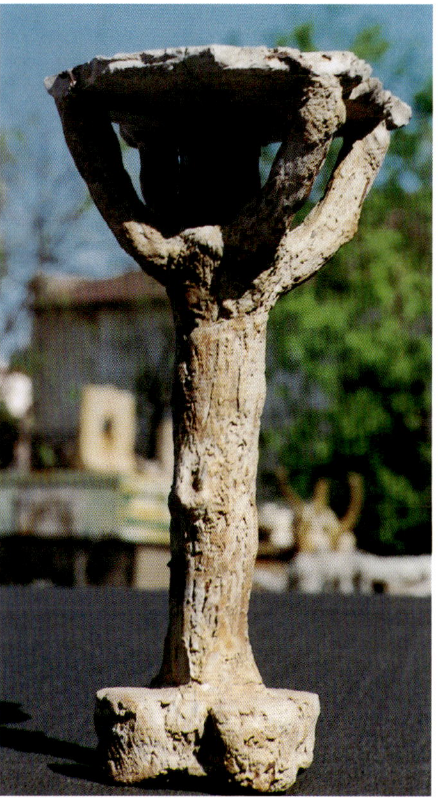

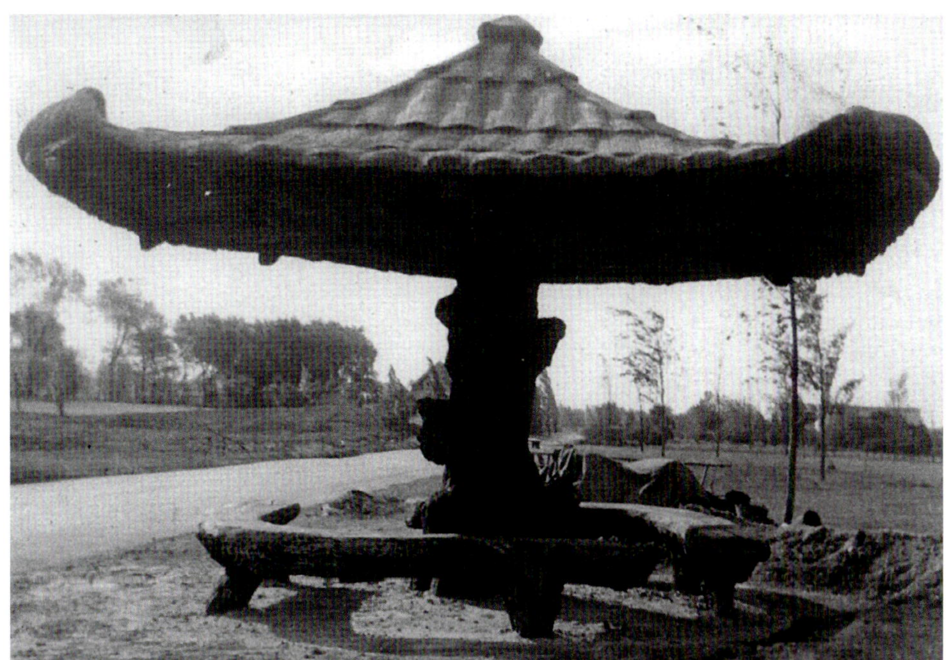

Left: *Palapa, Westlawn Cemetery and Mausoleum, Inc., Norridge, Illinois. Courtesy of Manuela Vargas Theall.*
Top: *Palapa, Cedar Park Cemetery, Calumet Park, Illinois. Courtesy of Manuela Vargas Theall.*
Above: *Maquette for New York City clients. Courtesy of Carlos Cortés family. Photo: Laurie Light Saunders.*

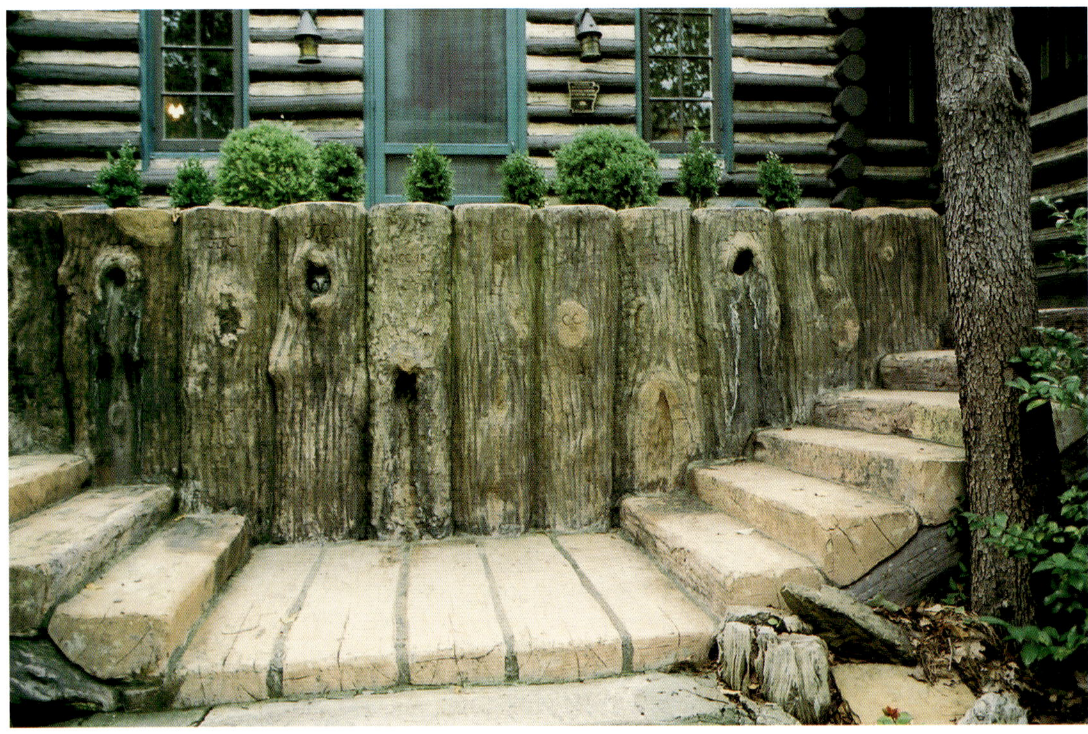

Couchwood steps, private property, Garland–Hot Springs counties, Arkansas. Photo: Myssie Light Acomb.

Through this recommendation from Hinds, Rodríguez was hired in 1939 by Couch to work at two sites: Couchwood on Lake Catherine in Hot Springs and Garland counties, and Little Switzerland, northwest of Couchwood in Garland County.

An early builder of telephone lines in Arkansas, which he sold to Bell Telephone, Couch was the organizer of the Arkadelphia Power Company, which developed hydroelectric dams and power plants on the Ouachita River, and was the owner of the Louisiana and Arkansas Railroad. Along with Jesse Jones, Couch was appointed by President Herbert Hoover as a director of the Reconstruction Finance Corporation, and he was also administrator of the Rural Electrification Agency.[73]

Couchwood, his retreat on Lake Catherine, had a large eight-room red cedar lodge and three additional guest houses that now accommodate thirty to forty people. There he entertained not only his eastern bankers but also President Roosevelt, former president Hoover, United States Postmaster General Jim Farley, Bishop Boaz of the Methodist Church, and vaudeville performer Bob Burns.[74]

The main house at Couchwood, designed by John Parks Almond, has faux bois concrete steps and planters at the front entrance and log steps at the rear. The front entrance is composed of twelve upright logs, with five knotholes: three are drain holes and one is home to a concrete owl with glass eyes. Family members' initials were incised into the logs,

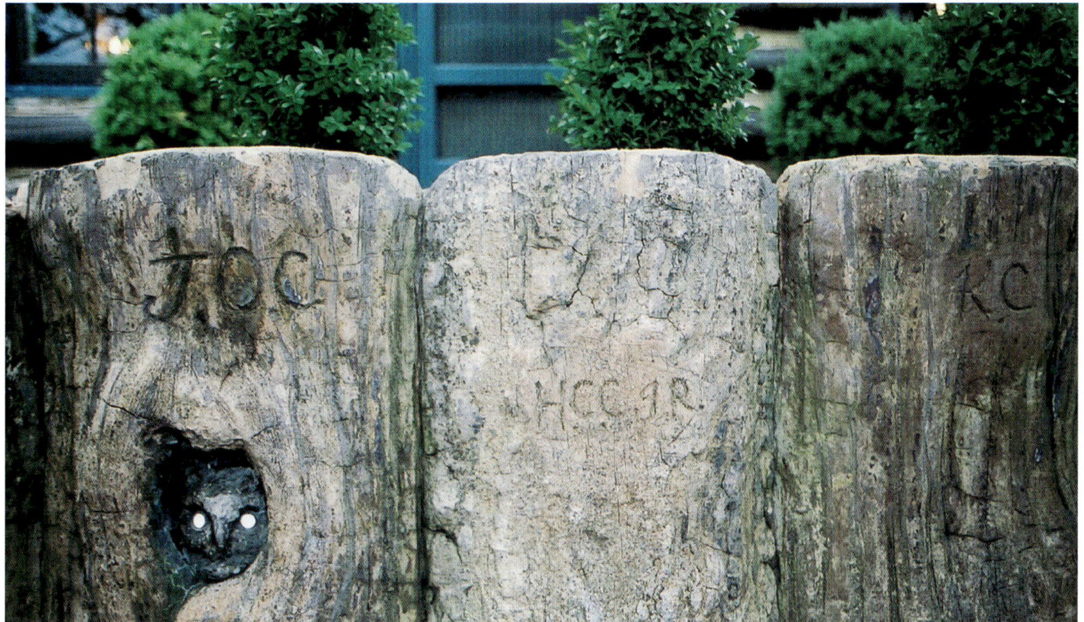

probably by Rodríguez or a helper at Couch's request.[75] These uprights are capped with a log planter. On either side of these logs, six steps made of cut logs provide entrance to a wood-planked porch, which has two additional log steps (flanked by wood planters on either side) leading to the front door. The rear steps are planed logs. These sculptural pieces, along with components on the Old Mill building, trim on the Jacala Restaurant, and the Miraflores gate, are the only architectural embellishments known to have been executed by Rodríguez.[76] A tree trunk drink cooler at the rear of the house's screened porch was the subject of a recurring question Couch asked his house guests. He challenged them to guess the type of tree from which the stump was cut; he would then tell them that it was a "cement tree."[77]

Behind an additional house, "Little Pine Bluff," the artisan constructed the largest fallen tree bench of his career, with a very realistic bark-covered trunk. The bench has two seating areas and three built-in planters. It rests on a bed of rocks and its forty-four-foot length corresponds to the full length of the rear of the cabin. An additional bench with two planters is eleven feet long. Couch's daughter, Catherine Remmel, remembered that her father and Rodríguez communicated about the artisan's work through hand signals, since neither spoke the other's language, and that Rodríguez used a curtain to shield the area where he mixed his tints.[78]

Couch was developing nearby Little Switzerland as a place to go fishing with his friends, but the project was not completed before his death.[79] Dionicio built the "over shot

Detail of owl and family initials in Couchwood steps, private property, Garland–Hot Springs counties, Arkansas. Photo: Myssie Light Acomb.

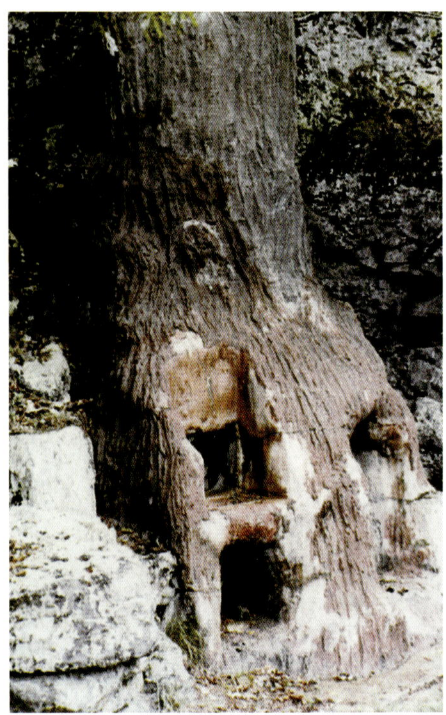

Barbeque pit and chimney, Little Switzerland, Garland County, Arkansas (not extant). Photo: Carlos Cortés.

wheel" (a water wheel) that was not finished near a lake that had been created with a dam of rock and stone; he also made a wood bench and a tall tree sculpture to be used as a barbeque pit (not extant). One of the largest pieces sculpted by Rodríguez, this tree had a thirty-seven-foot-wide base with three openings—an open pit and two recesses—all lined with firebrick. The trunk, which concealed the smoke stack, was fifteen feet tall.[80]

Clayton, New Mexico: The Froman House, 1943

Bayliss C. Froman, a land speculator and building contractor in Clayton, New Mexico, built an eclectic house for himself and his wife in 1933. Details of the house were influenced by his world travels: Greek columns, a Spanish façade, and "a Turkish style entrance" opening into an "Oriental-looking dining room."[81] According to Manson Edmondson, retired city manager of Clayton, Froman had a dream about the fence that he wanted to build around his house, and he talked about it long before it was built.[82]

While traveling through San Antonio around 1933–34, Froman arrived too late to visit the Alamo but stopped to look at Rodríguez's sculptures in Alamo Plaza. Several years later he sought out the "Mexican nationals who were familiar with cement sculpture, and brought them to Clayton," where they were reportedly paid $2,800 for the project.[83] There they built a Torii-style gate that is similar to the Chinese Tea Garden portal in San Antonio. The details of the gate, including the supporting log pillars and log lintel, are closely related to those of the portal built in 1942, although the Froman structure is slightly smaller in scale.

Froman commissioned a log fence. Surrounding three sides of the property, the intertwining branches supported by vertical logs echo the design of other Rodríguez fences, especially the one built several years earlier at the Alamo Cement Company. A third piece at the Froman house is a hollow tree sculpture with heavy bark texture. Although similar to other Rodríguez hollow tree sculptures, it is smaller in scale.

According to Edmondson, the artisans built a concrete footing for the fence and inserted metal rods, which they twisted to look like tree branches. Referring to the cement mixture, Edmondson said: "They concocted it in a box, kind of secret-like, and when you'd go up to talk to them, they would turn away."[84] Lucille Childers, who lived in a small cottage on the property, recalled that "Froman was always there with the sculptors, supervising the work."[85]

Clayton resident Dora Rodríguez Garcia remembers that as a young girl she lived two blocks down the street from the Froman house. On one of her frequent walks to town, she passed a man working on the wood fence at the house. She asked what his name was. When he replied, she said, "I'm Rodríguez, too." She recalls that he spoke to her in Spanish.

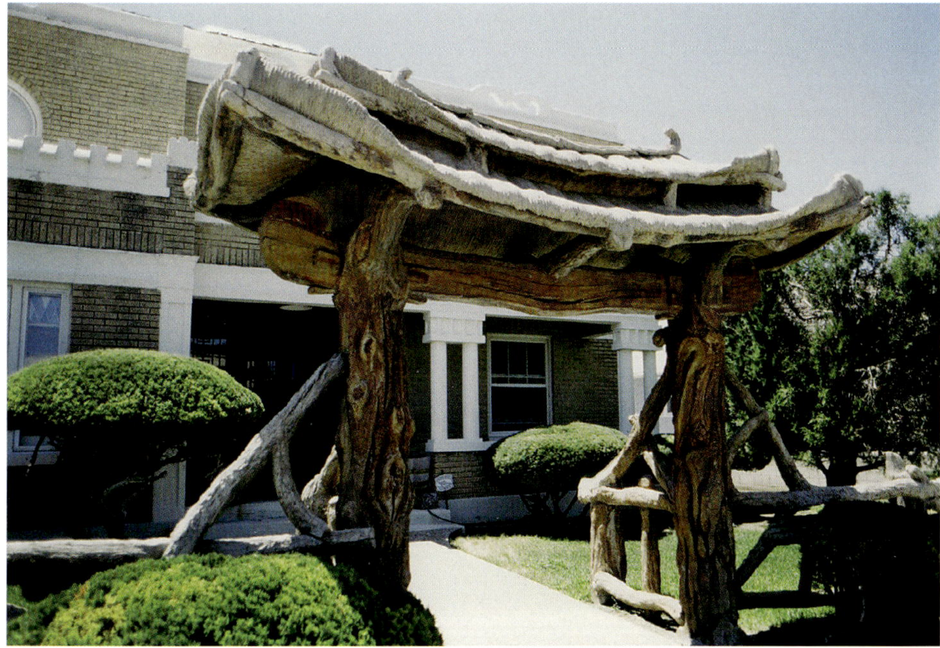

Wooden gate, Bayliss C. Froman House, Clayton, New Mexico. Photo: Patsy Light.

Clifford Sampier, now a resident of Colorado, recalls that when he moved to Clayton in May of 1943, the artisans "were putting on the exterior aspects of the logs." He was impressed with their technique and says he "couldn't believe it, to tell you the truth . . . especially making the intricate knots," and he noted that they added "a color to the cement" as the last part of the process.[86] Carlos Cortés stated that his father, Maximo, accompanied Rodríguez to Clayton to work on Froman's project. The two likewise collaborated on the gate in San Antonio.[87] Based on the Clayton project's similarity to the Chinese Tea Garden work, and the artisan's secrecy about his technique, there are good indications that these pieces were made by Rodríguez, but they are not signed.

The Later Years, 1942–55

In 1941 Dionicio Rodríguez's worsening diabetic condition prompted him to write that he was not well and was having treatments from a doctor.[88] A final letter from Hinds to Rodríguez was mailed to Dallas in 1942 as a response to the artist's request for an accounting of his 1941 wages owed by Hinds.[89]

Only a few records are available about Rodríguez's activities from 1942 until his death in 1955. Theall relates that he traveled infrequently after 1942 and returned to San Antonio to live in his tree house. Frank Tober remembers visiting him there, and Rodríguez would pay Frank and his siblings a penny for each gray hair they removed from his head.[90]

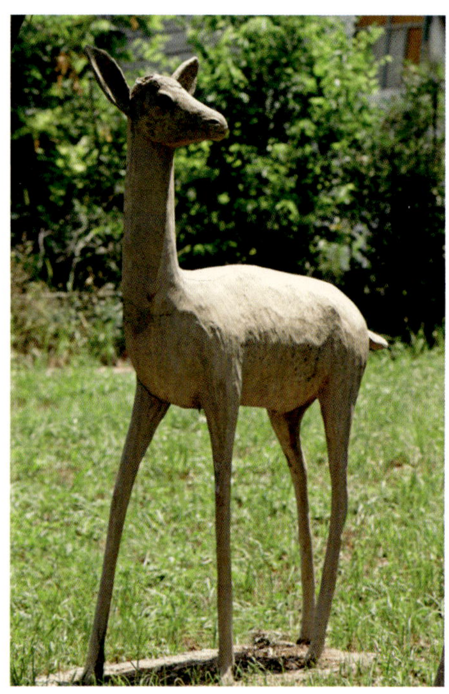

Above: *Rare deer figure. Private collection, Jennifer Robuck. Photo: Bob Parvin.*
Right: *Birdbath. Private collection, Judamaier-Neugebauer family. Photo: Bob Parvin.*

His niece recalls that during the war years he worked on smaller pieces because it was difficult for him to acquire steel and concrete for large projects. She remembers some of this later work, such as deer, baskets, and other decorative garden pieces (probably cast from molds) that were stored, along with work by Maximo Cortés, in a yard at a home on General McMullen Drive in San Antonio.[91]

As previously noted, two of Rodríguez's last projects were completed after he returned to the San Antonio area: the portal for the Chinese Tea Garden in 1941 and the grotto at the Moye Military Academy in Castroville, Texas, in 1945. In the late 1940s Rodríguez built a concrete bridge for the Lake View Motel in Little Rock, Arkansas. The bridge, now demolished, had realistic log rails along its length, with large plant containers at regular

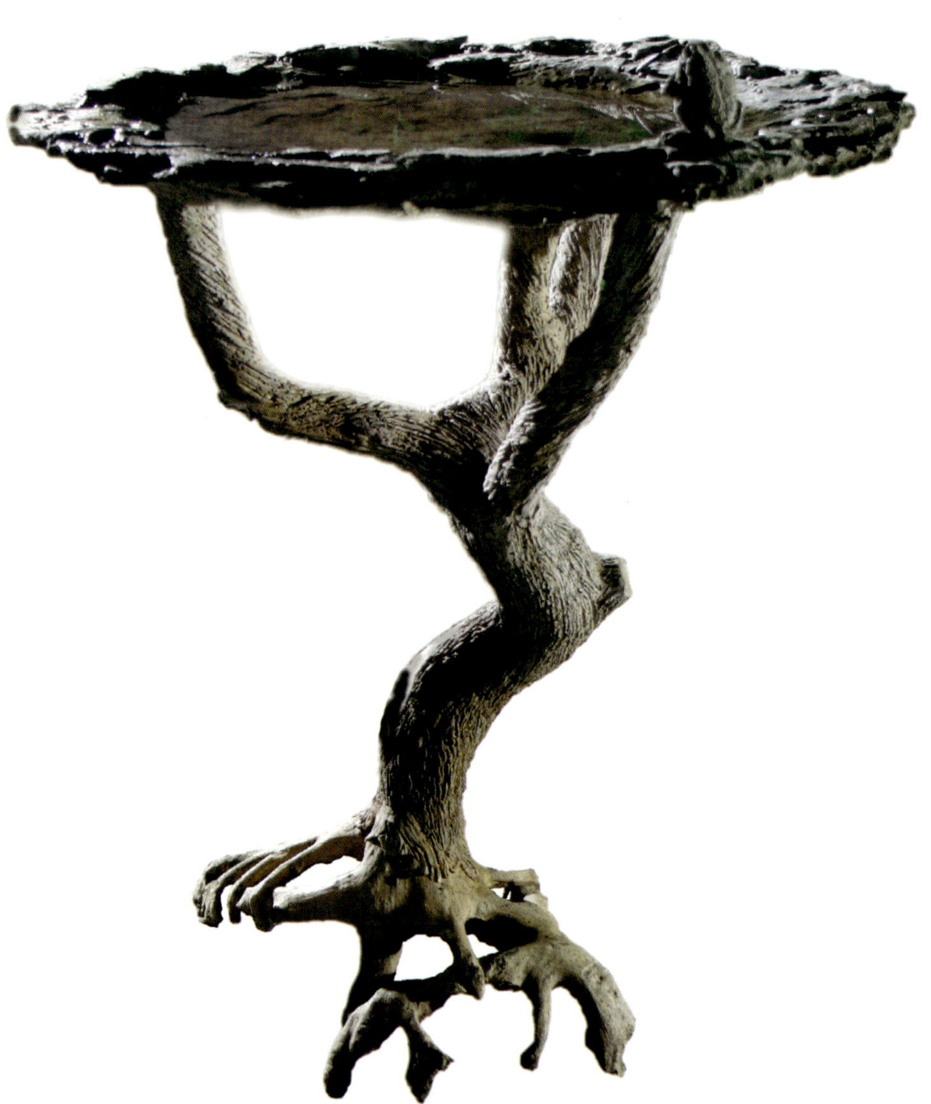

intervals.[92] He also worked on the façade of the Jacala Restaurant in San Antonio in 1952. In 1953 he purchased yet another automobile, a Buick.

Fellow artisan Sam Murray recounted that during Rodríguez's final years, his eyesight was failing. He would bring work to Murray for him to sell, and it lacked the quality of his earlier projects.[93] According to William Green, Rodríguez's health continued to decline; doctors wanted to remove one of his legs but instead amputated several of his toes.[94] When Dionicio Rodríguez was hospitalized during his last illness, he asked Maximo Cortés to go to his tree house and look in his Bible. Cortés found five hundred dollars that Rodríguez instructed be used for his grave marker.[95] He died at the Robert B. Green Hospital of coronary occlusion on December 16, 1955, and was buried in San Fernando Cemetery No. 2.

The art form perfected by Rodríguez endures in his existing works throughout the United States. For the most part, the pieces are in relatively good condition and remain as a legacy of this talented, unassuming artisan. An unknown number remain in private collections. Although there are numerous trabajo rústico craftsmen working today, Rodríguez's ability to recreate textures and patterns in nature has yet to be surpassed.

For more than seventy years his work has delighted, amused, and intrigued artists, architects, and students, but until a decade ago, his name and the enormous body of work that he created were relatively unknown to a wider audience. There has been a flurry of interest in Rodríguez's work; this could be attributable to the fact that there are contemporary creators of faux bois, Carlos Cortés in particular, working in the genre. Individual artisans are featured on Internet web sites, and an exhibit of the trabajo rústico work of Rodríguez and Carlos and Maximo Cortés was sponsored by the San Antonio Botanical Center in 2005. Rodríguez's artistry has been featured on web sites; in magazines, newspapers, and John Beardsley's 1995 book, *Gardens of Revelation: Environments by Visionary Artists;* and more recently in the television series *Rare Visions and Roadside Revelations* and a 2002 book by the same name.[96]

Japan designates artisans of exceptional talent as national treasures. If there were such designations in this country, Rodríguez would deserve the honor. Perhaps this book will serve as a celebration of his life and work for generations yet to come.

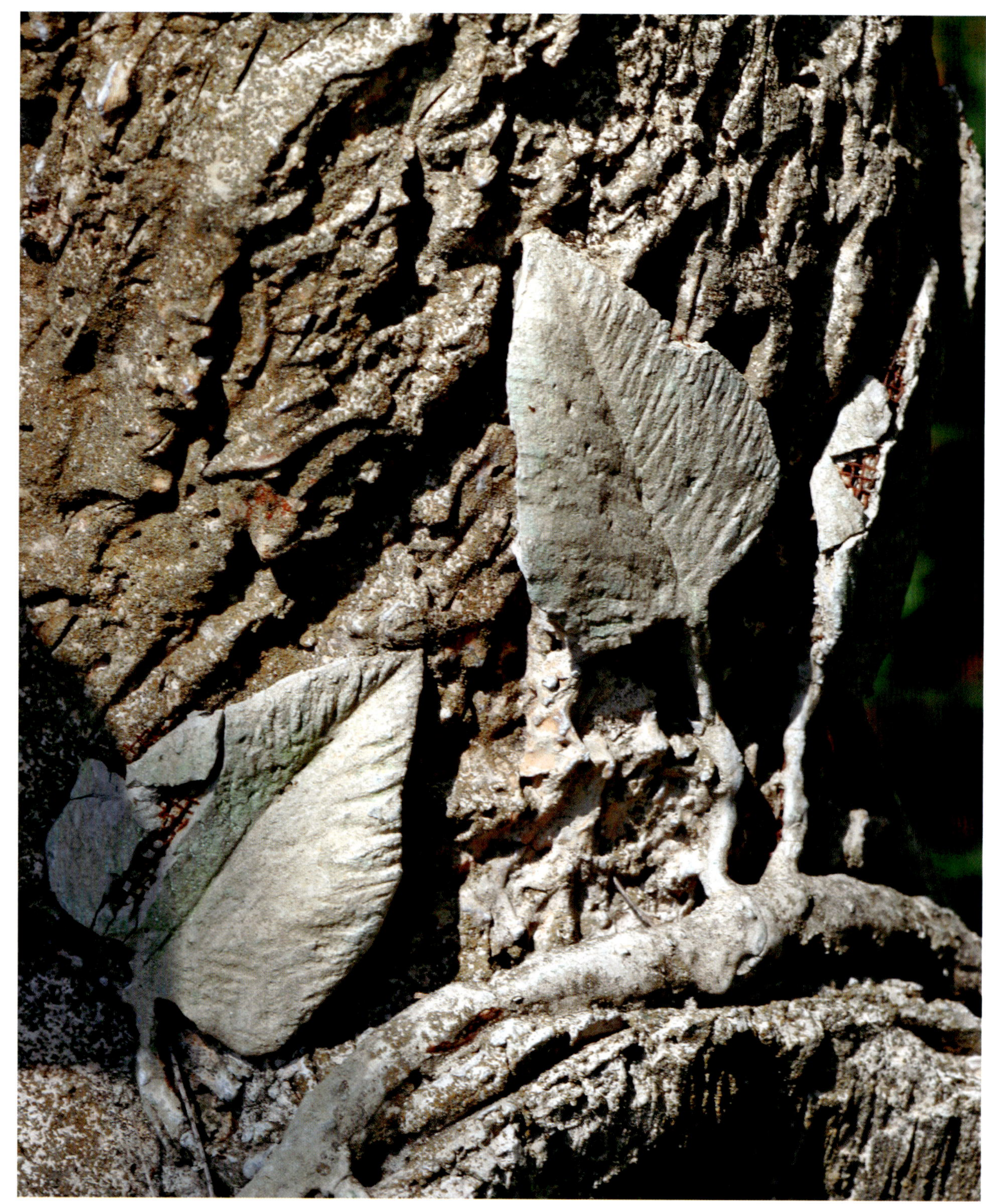

*Oak bark texture,
planter, private
collection, Jennifer
Robuck, Austin,
Texas. Photo:
Bob Parvin.*

Chronology of the Life and Work of Dionicio Rodríguez

1891	Born in Toluca, Mexico, April 11
1920s	Worked in Mexico City
1924	Left Mexico City to work in Monterrey, Mexico, and Laredo, Texas
1924	Began working in San Antonio, Texas
1925	Comfort, Texas (year uncertain)
1926	Sweeny, Texas
1926	Houston, Texas
1929	Port Arthur, Texas
1931	Beaumont, Texas
1932	Dallas, Texas (Manuela Theall's recollection is 1932 or 1934; records indicate 1934 and 1942)
1932	North Little Rock, Arkansas, and Cambridge, Michigan
1933	Michigan (projects in several sites)
1934	Dallas, Texas
1935–39	Memphis, Tennessee (intermittent work for Clovis Hinds, with absences to work on commissions for other clients)
1935	Washington, D.C. (Brentwood, Maryland), and San Antonio, Texas
1936	Suitland, Maryland
1937	Suitland, Maryland; Wheeling, West Virginia; Detroit, Michigan; Chicago, Illinois; St. Louis, Missouri; Little Rock, Arkansas; and Chattanooga and Memphis, Tennessee
1938	Birmingham, Alabama
1938	Guerrero, Mexico, and Detroit, Michigan (with additional travels to Mexico and San Antonio, ca. 1938–42, dates not known)
1939	Hot Springs and Garland counties, Arkansas; Chicago, Illinois
1940	Houston, Texas
1942	Dallas and San Antonio, Texas
1943	Clayton, New Mexico
1945	Castroville, Texas
1947	Little Rock, Arkansas (year uncertain)
1952	San Antonio
1955	Died in San Antonio, Texas, December 16

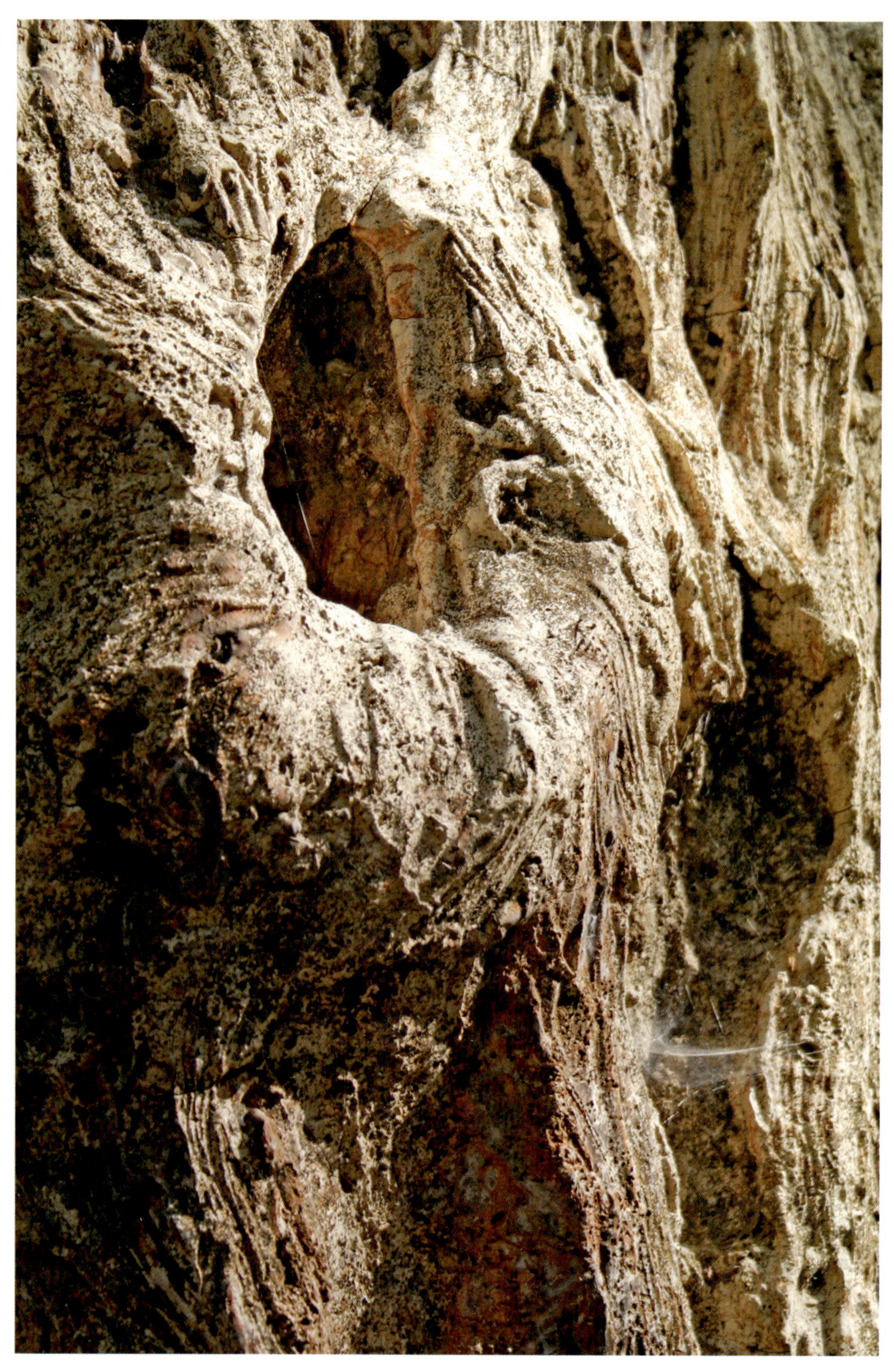

Tree house detail, Brackenridge Park, San Antonio.
Photo: Bob Parvin.

Acknowledgment of Donors

Generous grants from friends, foundations, organizations, and professional corporations made this book possible.

Graham Foundation for Advanced Studies in the Fine Arts

Professional Tour Guide Association of San Antonio

Quarry Coyotes, Ltd.

San Antonio Conservation Society Foundation

The Alfred S. Gage Foundation, *Roxana C. Hayne and Joan N. Kelleher, Directors*

The Betty Stieren Kelso Foundation

The Tobin Endowment

Thunder Exploration, Inc.

Myssie and Barry W. Acomb

Val Alexander

Mary Margaret and Chris Amberson

Anonymous

Wendy and Billy Atwell

Anne Pettus Bode

Aimee and Ernest Bromley

Phyllis and Jamie Browning

Sally and Bob Buchanan

Charles Butt

Laura and Bobby Cadwallader

Annie Mae F. Carrington

Chris Carson, FAIA

Aubrey and David Carter

Linda and Roger Christian

Robert S. Downey

Betsy and Brooke Dudley

Katy and Ted Flato, AIA

Claire Golden

John Gutzler, ASID, IIDA

Maria and Friedrich Hanau-Schaumburg

Chita Harris

Meta and Boo Hausser

Lynne Hendry

Rose Marie and John L. Hendry III

June and George His

Karen and Tim Hixon

Dan A. Hughes

Loyce and Raymond Ince

Bonnie Sue and Donald Jacobs

Cisi and Lloyd W. Jary, FAIA

Joan Kelleher

Sarah Westkaemper Lake

Suzy and Cappy Lawton

Rosemary and Jack Leon

James Lifshutz

Roy A. F. Lowey-Ball, AIA

Alice Lynch

John Mize, AIA

Nancy and Jeff Moorman

Guillermo Nicolas

Nancy Pawel

Carolyn S. Peterson, FAIA

Boone Powell, FAIA

Robert Price

Terry Gay Puckett

Verónica Prida and Omar Rodríguez

Laura and Jack Richmond

Carole and Louis Romano

Al Schwab

Linda Seeligson

Banks M. Smith

Lamar Smith

Jill and Steve Souter

Patsy Steves

Marjorie Strayer

Adair R. Sutherland

Patrick H. Swearingen Jr.

Tinka and Lewis Tarver

A. A. Urrutia, M.D.

Courtney and Mark E. Watson Jr.

Barbara and Ricks Wilson

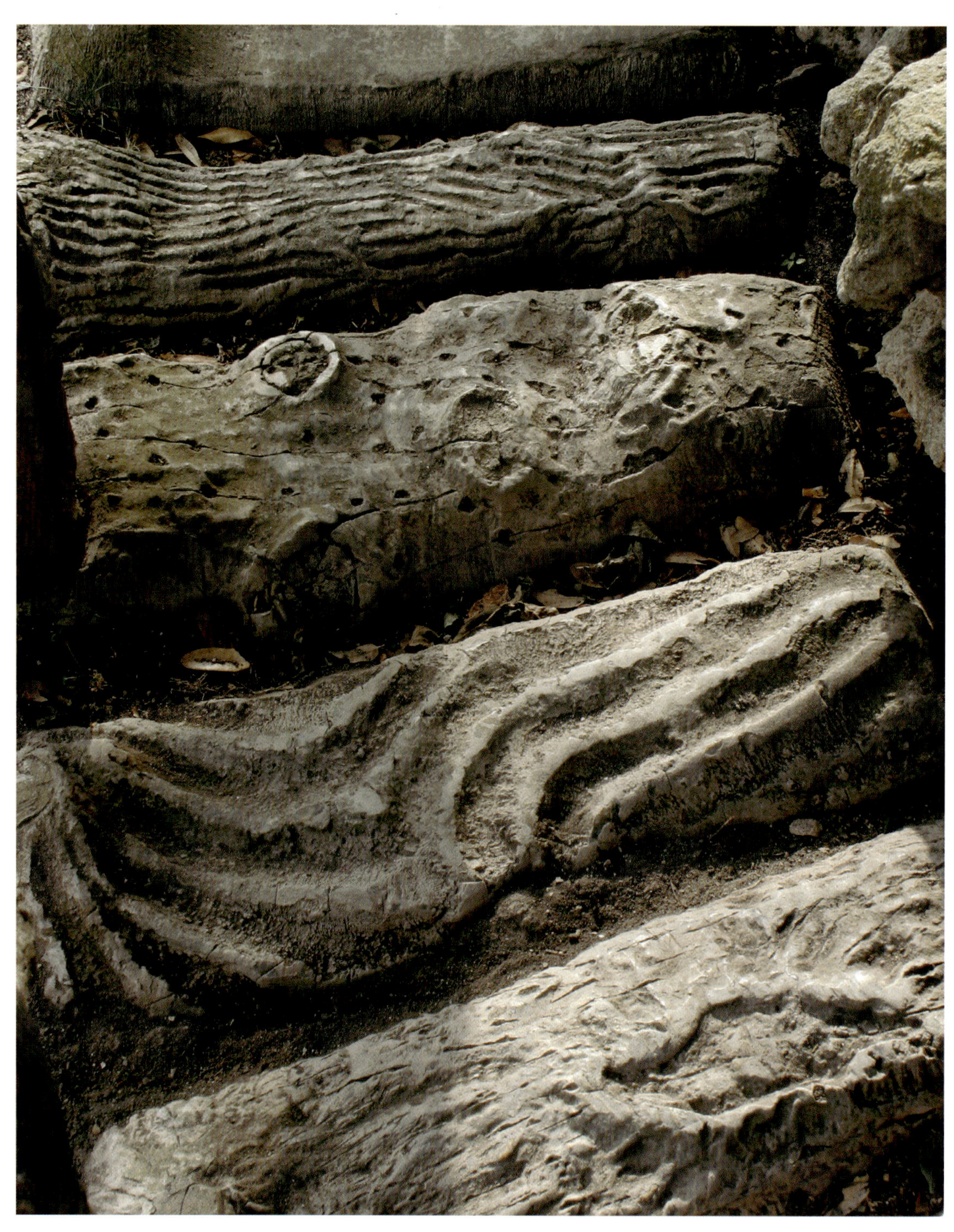

Wooden log walk, palapa fountain,
Alamo Cement Company, San
Antonio. Photo: Bob Parvin.

Notes

Chapter 1

1. Dionicio represents the anglicized spelling of Dionisio, which Rodríguez used after he arrived in the United States.

2. John Beardsley, *Gardens of Revelation: Environments of Visionary Artists* (New York: Abbeville Press, 1995), 21, 81–84, 95–98, 114–20, 143–51, 163–70.

3. Faux bois artisans identified by the author as of 2007: Diane and Anthony Ciomperlik, Concrete Illusions, Pleasanton, Texas, tel. 830-769-2314; Joe Colvin and Daniel Hastings, Grotto, New Orleans, Louisiana, tel. 504-609-9247; Carlos Cortés, San Antonio, Texas, tel. 210-472-3966; Melinda LoPresto and Megan Lashaway, Frontier Rustic Sculpting, Frontier, Michigan, tel. 517-254-4384; Meg Morley, Branch Studio, Pontiac, Michigan, tel. 248-874-1314; Alex and Jason Perakis, Unique Stone, Hamlet, North Carolina, tel. 910-582-5445; Frank Ramos, Houston, Texas, tel. 210-673-8419; Fabien Rochoux, Paris, France, tel. 011-331-4223-7216 (noted in Julia Morrill, "Faux Bois, for Real," *Garden Design,* August–September 1991, 51); Donald R. Tucker, Tomball, Texas, tel. 713-702-9932; Bob and Will Ziesmer, Pots Plus, Ltd., Danville, Kentucky, tel. 859-936-1922.

4. Carlos Cortés, personal interview, 20 Feb. 1998.

5. Bernard Dams and Andrew Zega, *Pleasure Pavilions and Follies: In the Gardens of the Ancien Regime* (Paris: Flammarion, 1995), 161.

6. George E. Woodward, *Woodward's Architecture and Rural Art No. 1, 1867* (New York: George E. Woodward, 1869), 56, 68, 119.

7. Calvert Vaux, *Villas and Cottages: A Series of Designs Prepared for Execution in the United States* (New York: Harper and Brothers, 1864), 288, 292.

8. Betsy Rogers, personal communication with the author, 1999.

9. "Cement," "Concrete," in *World Book Encyclopedia,* 1963 ed.

10. "Joseph Monier," in *New Encyclopedia Britannica* (Chicago: Micropaedia Ready Reference, 2002), vol. 8, 259.

11. Morrill, "Faux Bois, for Real," 48.

12. Beardsley, *Gardens of Revelation,* 130.

13. Rogers, personal communication, 1999.

14. Dan Hofstader, "Dreams of the Orient," *Conde Nast Traveler,* July 1997, 139–56.

15. Sharon Crutchfield of San Antonio related that she studied with a Japanese *giboku* artisan when she and her husband lived in Japan.

16. Don Morton referred me to Howard Christian of Trillage in New York City. Christian revealed that he had purchased faux bois planters, benches, and tables in Belgium that he believed were made ca. 1890–1920; telephone conversation with the author, 10 Aug. 2006. A collection of *adorno de jardin* (garden decoration), cement faux bois, and other sculptures from Buenos Aires, Argentina, was featured at Architectural Artifacts in Chicago in May 2006, according to Stuart Graham, who assembled the work. The exhibit and sale "Cemento!" included Argentinean work from the early 1900s through the present. Graham also related that the Buenos Aires Zoo possesses many faux bois pieces. Personal communication with the author, 12 May 2006.

17. Pat Jasper and Kay Turner, "Art among Us/Arte entre Nosotros: Mexican-American Folk Art in San Antonio" (article adapted from an exhibit catalogue of the same name), in *Hecho en Tejas: Texas-Mexican Folk Arts and Crafts,* ed. Joe S. Graham (Denton: University of North Texas Press, 1991), 51, 65.

18. Rosalind Rock, Ph.D., historian of the San Antonio Missions National Historical Park, personal communication with the author.

19. Adan Benavides, "Sacred Space, Profane Reality: The Politics of Building a Church in Eighteenth-Century Texas," *Southwestern Historical Quarterly* 107, no. 1 (2003): 15–17.

20. Joe S. Graham, Ph.D., "Tejano Folk Arts and Crafts in South Texas, Artesanía Tejana" (Kingsville: Texas A&I University, September 1989), catalogue for a traveling exhibit from the John E. Conner Museum, prepared by the University of Texas Institute of Texan Cultures. Courtesy of Cisi Canales Jary.

21. For the information on the artisans I am grateful to Curtis Hunt; Larry Peña Jr.; Susan Frost; Ted Voss; Suzanne Sheriff's 1989 dissertation "Este Soy Yo: The Politics of Representation of a Texas-Mexican Folk Artist," University of Texas, Austin; and Eleanor Johnson for sharing research on Revueltas by Dr. Robert Parker.

22. Rodríguez went to Nuevo Laredo, Mexico, where sixteen-year-old Rafael (Ralph) Corona was working in a restaurant, and brought him back to work in San Antonio; personal communication to the author in 1998 by Carlos Cortés, who interviewed Rafael Corona. George Cardosa was the brother of Sara, one of Rodríguez's wives; personal communication to the author from Mrs. Guadalupe Del Toro.

23. Ron Tyler et al., eds., *New Handbook of Texas History* (Austin: Texas Historical Association, 1996), vol. 6: 1103–1104.

24. Ron Bechtol, "Home Is Where the Art Is: A Tribute to San Antonio's Unheralded Artists," *San Antonio Light,* 1 Apr. 1984, 29–33.

25. Cortés interview, 1998.

26. Gregory Smith, "Carolina and Genaro P. Briones House," National Register of Historic Places, 1998, on file at the U.S. Department of the Interior, National Park Service, Washington, D.C. Smith related to the author that Mrs. Briones shared this information with him during taped interviews in August 1997.

27. Cyril M. Harris, ed., *Illustrated Dictionary of Historic Architecture* (New York: Dover Publications, 1977), 540.

28. Manuela Vargas Theall, taped interview, Arlington, Texas, 22 June 2000 (by special arrangement with Johanna Phelan); telephone interviews, 27 Mar. 2002, 3 Apr. 2002, 30 May 2002, July 2005; personal interview, 6 Jan. 2004; taped interview by Johanna Phelan, Aug. 2002; telephone conversations, Jan. 2006.

29. Rodríguez projects listed on the National Register of Historic Places are in Texas, Arkansas, and Tennessee. *Texas: San Antonio:* "Chinese Sunken Garden Gate" (thus on National Register; originally and presently named Japanese Tea Garden, known as Chinese Tea Garden 1942–84), "Dionicio Rodríguez Bridge in Brackenridge Park," "Buckeye Park Gate," "Stations of the Cross and Grotto at the Shrine of St. Anthony of Padua," "Fence at Alamo Cement Company," "Fountain at Alamo Cement Company," "Jacala Restaurant," "Trolley Stop in Alamo Heights," "Miraflores Park"; *Comfort:* "Gazebo for Albert Steves"; *Houston:* "Aviary at the Houston Zoo" (now the Flamingo Habitat at the Houston Zoo), "Woodlawn Garden of Memories Cemetery"; *Port Arthur:* "Eddingston Court"; *Sweeny:* "Gazebo for James Richard Marmion," "Palapa Table for James Richard Marmion." *Arkansas:* "The Arkansas Sculptures of Dionicio Rodríguez" in Little Switzerland, Couchwood, T. R. Pugh Memorial Park, Lakewood Park, and Crestview Park. *Tennessee:* "The Sculptures of Dionicio Rodríguez at Memorial Park Cemetery," Memphis.

30. Dionicio Rodríguez, letter to Clovis Hinds, 7 Jan. 1935. Courtesy of Katherine Hinds Smythe.

31. Theall interviews, 2000, 2006.

32. Information on Chavez from Marian Oppenheimer, telephone conversation, July 2005.

33. Letter from L. R. Clevlen to George Magher, 28 July 1937. Courtesy of Manuela Vargas Theall.

34. Letter from Dr. Aureliano Urrutia to Ray Lambert, 13 June 1924. Courtesy of Carlos Cortés.

35. Theall interview, 2000; Sam Murray, taped personal interview by Maria Pfeiffer and Patsy Light, 19 Feb. 1998; Mrs. Guadalupe Del Toro, telephone interview, San Antonio, Texas, 18 Dec. 1998, and taped interview by Maria Pfeiffer and Patsy Light, San Antonio, Texas, 21 Dec. 1998; Cortés interview, 1998.

36. Theall interview, 2005.

37. Theall interview, 2002.

38. Luis Robles Gil, letter of recommendation for Dionicio Rodríguez, 24 Mar. 1924; J. W. Douglas, letter of recommendation for Dionicio Rodríguez, 13 Mar. 1924. Both courtesy of Carlos Cortés.

39. Carlos Cortés, personal communication to the author, 2 June 2006.

40. Cortés interview, 1998.

41. *San Antonio City Directory, 1924–1925.*

42. Cortés interview, 1998.

43. Eldon Roarck, "Strolling with Eldon Roarck," *Commercial Appeal* (Memphis, Tenn.), 20 June 1935.

44. Clovis Hinds, letter to Dionicio Rodríguez, 15 Mar. 1939. Courtesy of Katherine Hinds Smythe.

45. Theall interview, 2005.

46. Del Toro interview, 1998.

47. Theall interview, 2000.

48. Theall interview, 2000.

49. Correspondence between Clovis Hinds and Dionicio Rodríguez, 1933–42. Courtesy of Katherine Hinds Smythe.

50. Rodríguez to Hinds, ca. 1939. Courtesy of Katherine Hinds Smythe.

51. Carlos Cortés, personal communication to the author, 2 June 2006.

52. Rodríguez to Hinds, 7 June 1938. Courtesy of Katherine Hinds Smythe.

53. *Statistical Abstract of the United States, 1941.*

54. *Statistical Abstract of the United States, 1956.*

55. Hinds to Rodríguez, 19 Oct. 1935. Courtesy of Katherine Hinds Smythe.

56. Theall interview, 2005.

57. *The Fifteenth Census of the United States: 1930* (Washington, D.C.: Government Printing Office, 1933), "General Report, Statistics by Subjects" enumerates the Mexican population in cities of 10,000 or more. There were 20 Mexicans in Birmingham; 7 in Memphis; 67 in Washington; 19,362 in Chicago (0.6% of the total population); 6,515 in Detroit (0.4% of the total population); 409 in the entire state of Arkansas; and 683,681 in Texas (11% of the total population).

58. Theall interview, 2005.

59. National Archives and Records Administration, microfilm A3379, 85. The author is grateful to O'Leen Stone of Congressman Lamar Smith's office, who helped determine Rodríguez's immigration status.

60. Theall interview, 2000.

61. Julie Vosmik, "The Sculptures of Dionicio Rodríguez at Memorial Park Cemetery," National Register of Historic Places, 1991, on file at U.S. Department of the Interior, National Park Service, Washington, D.C.

62. Stanley Schmidt, "Dionicio Rodríguez," manuscript, 29 Feb. 1980.

63. Vosmik, "The Sculptures of Dionicio Rodríguez at Memorial Park Cemetery," 37.

64. Schmidt, "Dionicio Rodríguez."

65. Carmina Danini, "Mexican, Local History Are in Stock during Pharmacy Estate Sale," *San Antonio Express-News,* 21 Feb. 1998.

66. Theall interviews, 2000, 2006.

67. Katherine Smythe and Dale Anthony, interview with John Richmond, Memphis, Tenn., 25 Mar. 1983. Courtesy of William Green, Ph.D.

68. Smythe and Anthony interview, 1983.

69. Sam Murray, taped interview by Maria Pfeiffer and Patsy Light, 19 Feb. 1998.

70. See chronology.

Chapter 2

1. David Uhler, "Behind the Tile Arch," *San Antonio Express-News,* 14 Sept. 1997, 1G, 9G.

2. Mary Carolyn Hollers George, *O'Neil Ford, Architect* (College Station: Texas A&M Press, 1992), 156.

3. Sarah C. Westkaemper, "Three Twentieth Century Gardens: A Heritage of Excellence in San Antonio," master's thesis, Louisiana State University, 1985, 49.

4. Dr. Aureliano Urrutia, letter to Ray Lambert, 13 June 1924. Courtesy of Carlos Cortés.

5. Amy Dorsett, "Legal Tug-of-war May Be Played Out on Tiny Park," *San Antonio Express-News,* 3 Aug. 2002, 1A, 2A.

6. Talavera refers to a type of lead-glazed tiles and ceramic ware that has been made in Puebla, Mexico, since 1531. The style originated in Spain and was known as Talavera de la Reina. Susan Frost generously shared this information about Talavera tile with the author.

7. Westkaemper, "Three Twentieth Century Gardens," 49.

8. Dr. A. A. Urrutia, telephone communication with the author, 14 Jan. 1998.

9. Urrutia, telephone communication, 1998.

10. The City of San Antonio researched the ownership of Miraflores and determined that a portion of the property had originally belonged to the City. It was auctioned off in lots that did not extend to the San Antonio River. At some point in time, the owners of these lots appropriated and incorporated city-owned property. In order for the City to acquire the entire parcel in 2006, it made an agreement with SBC and negotiated a settlement with the University of the Incarnate Word for the exchange of land on Hildebrand and Devine Road.

11. Uhler, "Behind the Tile Arch," 9G.

12. Beverly Bohancek, letter to author, 27 Jan. 2006.

13. Uhler, "Behind the Tile Arch," 9G.

14. Dr. A. A. Urrutia, telephone conversation with the author, 29 Mar. 2006.

15. Westkaemper, "Three Twentieth Century Gardens," 17.

16. Urrutia, telephone communication, 1998.

17. Dr. Aureliano Urrutia, *Pinacoteca* (San Antonio, Tex.: n.p., n.d.), 13. Courtesy of Chris Amberson (great-grandson of Dr. Urrutia) and Martha Utterback, Daughters of the Republic of Texas Library.

18. Theall interview, 2000.

19. Schmidt, "Dionicio Rodríguez."

20. Schmidt, "Dionicio Rodríguez."

21. Lloyd Jary, FAIA, architect for remodeling of Stone Werks (formerly the office of Alamo Cement). The author is grateful for his assistance.

22. *North San Antonio Times,* n.d.

23. It is unclear whether he was employed by the City of San Antonio or the San Antonio City Parks Department or was a contractor working for one of these entities.

24. W. E. Barker, "Beauty in Concrete and Wood," *Popular Mechanics,* Oct. 1927, 585–87. Park history is from Mike Greenberg, "Easier to Use, Prettier to See," *San Antonio Express-News,* 23 July 2006, 1J, 8J.

25. Bill Minutagllo [Minutaglio], "Sylvan Concrete That Could Fool a Termite," *San Antonio Express-News,* 18 Jan. 1981, 3M.

26. Esperanza Aguilar Flores, personal communication, 7 Feb. 2006. Mrs. Flores was born in one of these houses in 1927 and shared recollections of her family's life there. She recalled that after the Jingus were evicted, a Chinese family operated the concessions. Her father, Basilio Aguilar, was a trabajo rústico artisan, and several of his projects exist in San Antonio. Maria Watson Pfeiffer, former historian of the City Parks Department, personal communication, 4 Dec. 2006.

27. W. S. Delery, Park Engineer, San Antonio, Texas, "Prison Labor Used to Construct a Municipal Lily Pond and Japanese Garden," *American City* 20, no. 5 (January–June), 1919.

28. Scott Huddleston, "Then & Now; S.A. Treasure Garden," *San Antonio Express-News,* 21 September 2006, 2B; Jan Jarboe, "Apology Comes 42 Years Later," *San Antonio Express-News,* 14 October, 1984, 1C.

29. Minutagllo, "Sylvan Concrete."

30. Stephen Field, Ph.D., fax of the translation to the author, 2 Oct. 2001.

31. Lewis Fischer, *Saving San Antonio* (Lubbock: Texas Tech University Press, 1994), 123–27.

32. City of San Antonio Parks and Recreation records, Spanish Governor's Palace inventory, and architectural plan.

33. Paula Allen, "Cementville's Little Shrine is still a treasure," *San Antonio Express-News,* 23 Dec. 2001, 5G. Lloyd Jary, FAIA, provided history of the chapel.

34. Theall interview, 2000.

35. Sister Mary Ann Domagelski said the sisters now operate a home for retired priests, learning center, and retreat center.

36. Lucille Quiñones Hooker, telephone conversation with author, 20 Feb. 2003. Additional information from Adele Quiñones and Cyndy Roundtree.

Chapter 3

1. Cecilia Steinfeldt, *San Antonio Was* (San Antonio, Tex.: San Antonio Museum Association, 1978), 13, 14.

2. William F. Brogan, "Albert Steves Finds Joys on Farm," *San Antonio Light,* 9 July 1929, 1.

3. Margaret Lateer, telephone conversation with author, 1995.

4. Mrs. Richard Marmion, telephone interview, 4 June 2002.

5. Marmion interview.

6. *Houston: A History and Guide,* compiled by Workers of the Writers' Program of the Work Projects Administration in the State of Texas, American Guide Series (Houston: Anson Jones Press, 1942), 313, 314. Courtesy of Stephen Fox, Rice University.

7. Brian Hill, director of public affairs of the Houston Zoo, provided archival photographs and information about the aviary.

8. Letter courtesy of Carlos Cortés.

9. *Houston: A History and Guide*, 312.

10. Fred Maier, e-mail to author, 22 June 2004.

11. Del Toro interview, 1998.

12. Mrs. W. E. Shirley, "Eddingston Court," manuscript, vertical files, Port Arthur Public Library, Port Arthur, Texas, 1992.

13. "Port Arthuran of the Month: Harley Eddingston," *Port Arthuran*, Jan. 1956, 11.

14. Mrs. Margie Cook, telephone conversation, 13 Feb. 2004.

15. "Eddingston Leaves His Cayman Mark on PA," *Port Arthur News*, 28 May 1998, 4G.

16. *Texas General Contractors' Association Monthly Bulletin*, 1929, p. 32. Courtesy of Stephen Fox.

17. Stephen Fox, e-mail to author, 13 Oct. 2003.

18. Shirley, "Eddingston Court."

19. Jill Goldsmith, "Eddingston Empire: Ambrose T. Eddingston Brought Caribbean Flair to Port Arthur," *Port Arthur News*, 8 Apr. 1990, IC, 8C.

20. Christine Rappleye, "Southeast Texas Tales: Garden Spot of Texas on National Register," *Beaumont Enterprise* (Beaumont, Tex.), 31 Jan. 2005, IA.

21. Del Toro interview, 1998.

22. Mary Ellen Hunt, personal communication with the author, 1998.

23. Bradley Brooks, personal communication with the author, 1998.

24. Hunt, personal communication, 1998; on style shows, Emily Vaughan Jackson, personal communication to author.

25. David Charles Sloane, *The Last Great Necessity: Cemeteries in American History* (Baltimore, Md.: Johns Hopkins University Press, 1991), 88–181.

26. Lynda Seaman, personal communication to author.

27. Sloane, *Last Great Necessity*.

28. Theall interview, 2000.

29. Sister Margaret Riche, personal communication to author.

30. Congregation of Sisters of Divine Providence, *Family Circular*, Feb. 1946.

31. *Castroville Area Visitor Guide* (Castroville, Tex.: Castroville Chamber of Commerce, 2000), 23.

32. Ruth Aubey generously shared her collection of research notes, which includes photographs, notes, and maps of Eddingston Court and other sites of Rodríguez's work.

Chapter 4

1. Julie Vosmik, "The Arkansas Sculptures of Dionicio Rodríguez," National Register of Historic Places, Dec. 1986, on file at U.S. Department of the Interior, National Park Service, Washington, D.C. Vosmik's nominations include maps of Dionicio Rodríguez's nominated projects in Arkansas and Tennessee.

2. *The Old Mill* (North Little Rock, Ark.: Visitors Bureau, n.d.).

3. Tom Kazas, "Looks like Wood," *Americana*, Oct. 1989, 56–57.

4. Vosmik, "The Arkansas Sculptures."

5. "Pugh Park Is Dedicated in Lakewood Area: Picturesque Memorial Is Given to Public by Justin Matthews," *Arkansas Democrat* (Little Rock), Aug. 8, 1933, 10. The author is indebted to Sybil Crawford, who wrote "Dionicio Rodríguez: The Faux Bois Sculptor" for the *Pulaski County Historical Review* 50, no. 1 (Spring 2002), for mentioning the newspaper article, and to Raleigh Petersen in the Little Rock Main Library Reference Services Department for finding the article. The portrait of a suited Rodríguez reproduced in the present book appeared as an inset to a larger photo titled "Old Mill in Pugh Park," published on August 6, 1933, in the *Arkansas Democrat* (since 1991 the *Arkansas Democrat-Gazette*). The author is grateful to Robin Ward for her assistance.

6. *The Old Mill.*

7. Matthews is quoted in Vosmik, "The Arkansas Sculptures."

8. "Pugh Park Is Dedicated."

9. "Pugh Park Is Dedicated."

10. "Pugh Park Is Dedicated."

11. Sybil Crawford, "Dionicio Rodríguez: The Faux Bois Sculptor." *Pulaski County Historical Review* 50, no. 1 (Spring 2002): 13–24.

12. William E. Rutter, Bureau of History, Michigan Department of State, Inventory Form for St. Joseph's Church and Shrine, Apr. 19, 1990.

13. Quotation and source provided by Gladys Saborio from the *Brooklyn Exponent* (Brooklyn, Mich.), 14 Sept. 1933, in an e-mail to author, 19 Jan. 2006.

14. Gladys Saborio located an article in the *Michigan Catholic* dated 15 Aug. 1935, which she quoted as: "Working with the priests are Ralph Corona, a Mexican artist in stone-wood formations, and Leo Ouellette, who is in charge of construction. Both are parishioners. Dioysius Rodríguez, another Mexican artist, assisted with some of the stations completed first." E-mail to author, 3 June 2006.

15. Gladys Saborio, telephone conversation with author, 11 July 2006.

16. Rutter, Inventory Form.

17. Cortés interview, 1998.

18. Michelle T. Grigore, Ph.D., "The Past." Views from the Arb (Slayton Arboretum, Hillsdale College), 1 (Winter 2000): 2–3. Arlan Gilbert, Ph.D., "The Slayton Arboretum at Hillsdale College," manuscript, 2005.

19. Gladys Saborio, who researched the life and work of Rafael Corona, discovered the initials on the waterfall on a visit to the arboretum in 2006.

20. Rutter, Inventory Form.

21. Rutter, Inventory Form.

22. E-mail from Ina Hanel to Gladys Saborio, 11 June 2006, referring to a letter from Tom DeWald to Foster Fletcher, 5 July 1955, archived at the Ypsilanti Historical Museum; an interview with Mary Culver by Nazareth Barnabel Jr.; and Hanel's research about the Ford group who owned retreat cottages and the contractor, John Angellotti.

23. Theall interview, 2000.

24. Frank Tober, personal communication, 1998.

25. Carlos Cortés provided this information based on interviews with Albert Tober and his mother, 27 Nov. 2006.

26. Beardsley, *Gardens of Revelation,* 125–31.

27. Sloane, *Last Great Necessity.*

28. James Stevens Curl, *A Celebration of Death* (New York: Scribner, 1980), 156–60.

29. Sloane, *Last Great Necessity.*

30. Vosmik, "The Sculptures of Dionicio Rodríguez at Memorial Park Cemetery," section 8:1.

31. Rodríguez to Hinds, 1 Jan. 1938. Courtesy of Katherine Hinds Smythe.

32. Hinds to Rodríguez, 30 Nov. 1937. Courtesy of Katherine Hinds Smythe.

33. Carol Creighton, telephone conversation with author, 13 Oct. 2005.

34. Rodríguez to Hinds, 11 Jan. 1938.

35. Hinds to Rodríguez, 24 Oct. 1939. Courtesy of Katherine Hinds Smythe.

36. Hinds to Rodríguez, 22 Oct. 1938. Courtesy of Katherine Hinds Smythe.

37. *Memorial Park,* brochure, n.p., n.d. Courtesy Manuela Theall.

38. Roarck, "Strolling with Eldon Roarck."

39. Vosmik, "The Sculptures of Dionicio Rodríguez at Memorial Park Cemetery," section 9:1.

40. Genesis 25:9, 10.

41. Clovis Hinds's notes indicate his interest in this coffin's discovery near Copenhagen in 1935, and he included this replica in the burial tomb. Included in his notes was this quote: "Without vision and interest in history, the people perish." Courtesy of Manuela Theall.

42. Beardsley, *Gardens of Revelation,* 196.

43. See II Samuel 4:12.

44. According to Clovis Hinds's notes, which were given to the author by Manuela Theall, the chair is a replica of the Annie Laurie Wishing Chair built in the forecourt of the Wee Kirk at Glencairn, where Annie Laurie worshiped. He wrote: "In Scotland, they say the fairies have blessed this chair and tradition tells us that good fortune will forever smile upon the lad and lassie who sit here, hand in hand, and repeat the quaint Scotch [*sic*] verse on the tablet in front of the wishing chair." A plaque inscribed with the verse sited near an identical chair built by Rodríguez in Woodlawn Memorial Cemetery in Houston reads: "Dressed in our best and all alone. We sit within the wishing chair which bodes success for everyone exchanging bridal kisses there."

45. Lisa Simpson, "Memphis Memorial Park: A 20th Century Folk Art Collaboration," manuscript, Save Outdoor Furniture, Tennessee Survey, 1992. (Inventory of American Sculpture, Smithsonian American Art Museum). Courtesy of Nicole Semenchuk, Smithsonian American Art Museum, 1992.

46. Vosmik, "The Sculptures of Dionicio Rodríguez at Memorial Park Cemetery."

47. Clovis Hinds's notes. Courtesy of Manuela Vargas Theall.

48. Simpson, "Memphis Memorial Park."

49. "The Good Life," 1975, 8, 9 (article from unidentified Memphis magazine; no information available from the library).

50. Simpson, "Memphis Memorial Park."

51. Katherine Smythe and Dale Anthony, 1983.

52. Simpson, "Memphis Memorial Park."

53. Joe Thompson, telephone conversation, 11 June 2002.

54. Hinds to Rodríguez, 19 Oct. 1935.

55. Dorothy Richards, telephone interview with author, 17 and 18 Feb. 2005.

56. Rodriguez to Hinds, 3 June 1936, courtesy of Katherine Hinds Smythe; "Holding the Mirror up to Nature," Sunday Gravure Section of the *Washington Star*, 26 July 1936, 7.

57. Richards interview, 2005.

58. Tom Kazas, "Historic Sculptures to Die For," *Washington Post Magazine*, 21 Jan. 1990, 7.

59. Theall interview, 2000.

60. Theall interview, 2002.

61. Theall interview, 2002, and Carlos Cortés, personal communication with the author, Mar. 2006.

62. Theall interview, 2000.

63. Hinds to Rodríguez, 21 Dec. 1937. Courtesy of Katherine Hinds Smythe.

64. Wayne Guthrie, telephone conversation with author, 5 May 2002.

65. Miriam Easton Rutz, *Public Gardens of Michigan* (East Lansing: Michigan State University Press, 2002), 66–67.

66. Carol Hunt, "Art and Architecture at the Detroit Zoo, 2003," privately published. Courtesy of Marty Mitton of the Detroit Zoo.

67. J. M. Rocha Sr., to Hinds, 11 June 1938. Courtesy of Katherine Hinds Smythe.

68. Helen Sclair, "Dionicio Rodríguez, 1891–1955," *Association of Gravestone Studies Quarterly Newsletter* (Greenfield, Mass.) 22, no. 1 (Winter 1998): 13–15.

69. Helen Sclair, telephone conversation with author, 4 April 2006.

70. Hinds to Rodríguez, 24 Aug. 1939. Courtesy of Katherine Hinds Smythe.

71. Cortés interview, 1998.

72. Rodríguez to Hinds, 9 Oct. 1939. Text from a handwritten note from Hinds at the bottom of this earlier correspondence. Courtesy of Katherine Hinds Smythe.

73. Stephen Wilson, *Harvey Couch: An Entrepreneur Brings Electricity to Arkansas* (Little Rock: August House, 1986), 92–116; Winston P. Wilson, *Harvey Couch, the Master Builder* (Nashville, Tenn.: Broadman Press, 1947), 48–193.

74. Winston Wilson, *Harvey Couch, the Master Builder*; Stephen Wilson, *Harvey Couch: An Entrepreneur.*

75. Elizabeth Couch Dober (Couch's granddaughter), personal communication with the author, 21 May 2006.

76. Vosmik, "The Arkansas Sculptures."

77. Elizabeth Couch Dober, personal communication with the author, 8 Aug. 2005.

78. Catherine Remmel Matthews (Couch's granddaughter), telephone conversations with the author, 26 Feb. and 15 Apr. 2004.

79. Matthews telephone conversations, 2004.

80. Vosmik, "The Arkansas Sculptures."

81. Mike Bullock, "Cement Sculpture Adorns Colorful Clayton House," *Union County Leader* (Clayton, N.M.), 15 Nov. 1989.

82. Bullock, "Cement Sculpture."

83. Bullock, "Cement Sculpture."

84. Bullock, "Cement Sculpture."

85. Bullock, "Cement Sculpture."

86. Dora Rodríguez Garcia, personal communication, 26 Sept. 2006, courtesy of D. Ray Blakely

of Hertzstein Memorial Museum; Clifford Sampier, personal communication, 1 Dec. 2006, with John W. Murphey, State and National Register Coordinator, Historic Preservation Division, Department of Cultural Affairs, State of New Mexico.

87. Cortés, personal communication, 2006.

88. Rodríguez to Hinds, 2 Feb. 1941. Courtesy of Katherine Hinds Smythe.

89. Hinds to Rodríguez, 28 Feb. 1942. Courtesy of Katherine Hinds Smythe.

90. Tober, personal communication, 1998.

91. Theall interview, 2000.

92. Jerry Dean, "Motel Row Is Vanishing," *Arkansas Gazette* (Little Rock), 5 Sept. 1992, IC, 3C.

93. Murray interview, 1998.

94. William Green, Ph.D., personal files re: Dionicio Rodríguez.

95. Cortés interview, 1998.

96. Randy Mason, Michael Murphy, and Don Mayberger, *Rare Visions and Roadside Revelations,* video series by KCPT (Kansas City, Mo.) Public Television; also available on DVD. A book of the same title was published by Kansas City Star Books (2002).

Bibliography

Allen, Paula. "Cementville's Little Shrine Is Still a Treasure." *San Antonio Express-News,* 23 December 2001.

Alvarez, Marible. "Made in Mexico: Souvenirs, Artisans, Shoppers, and the Meanings of Other 'Border-Type-Things.'" Ph.D. diss., University of Arizona, 2003.

"Arkansas Historians Join in Rodriguez Search." *Seasons Newsletter* (Memorial Park and Funeral Home, Memphis, Tenn.) 7, Spring 1984.

Aureliano, Ramon, and Armando Marcial, Documentatistas, Museum of Natural History, Mexico City, Mexico. Letter to the author.

Barker, W. E. "Beauty in Concrete and Wood." *Popular Mechanics,* October 1927: 585–87.

Beardsley, John. *Gardens of Revelation: Environments of Visionary Artists.* New York: Abbeville Press, 1995.

Bechtol, Ron. "Home Is Where the Art Is." *San Antonio Light,* 1 April 1984.

Benavides, Adan. "Sacred Spaces, Profane Reality: The Politics of Building a Church in Eighteenth-Century Texas." *Southwestern Historical Quarterly* 107, no. 1 (July 2003): 15–17.

Beverly, Trevia Wooster. *At Rest: A Historical Discovery of Harris County Texas Cemeteries, 1882–1992.* Houston: Texas Publication and Research, 2001.

Bexar County Deed Records. Bexar County Courthouse. Vol. 2542: 472, roll 416; Vol. 2936: 358, roll 519; Vol. 642: 47; Vol. 722: 315; Vol. 37: 233; Vol. 1101: 385; Vol. 1319: 601; Vol. 1327: 413; Vol. 1459: 132; Vol. 1489: 440; Vol. 212: 170; WDVL & TRF: No. 42929, w/d; Vol. 5827: 923; Vol. 3036: 1156; Vol. 4540: 1755; Vol. 2127: 227–28. (WDVL = Warranty Deed with Vendor's Lien; TRF = Transfer; w/d = warrant deed.)

Brogan, William F. "Albert Steves Finds Joys on Farm." *San Antonio Light,* 9 July 1929.

Brooks, Bradley. "Owen Southwell, Architect, and the John Henry Phelan House." Paper presented at Beaumont Texas History Conference, Beaumont Independent School District Board Room, 9 January 1999.

"Buffalo Donated in 1920 by Government Started Zoo in City." *Houston Chronicle,* 22 January 1938.

Bullock, Mike. "Cement Sculpture Adorns Colorful Clayton House." *Union County Leader* (Clayton, N.M.), 15 November 1989.

Carson, Chris, and William McDonald. *A Guide to San Antonio Architecture.* San Antonio, Tex.: American Institute of Architects, San Antonio Chapter, 1986. 123, 127, 128.

Castroville Area Visitor Guide. Castroville, Tex.: Castroville Area Chamber of Commerce, 2000.

"Cement Sculptor Carlos Cortés Creates Work of Art." *Witte Museum Newsletter* (San Antonio, Tex.), Winter Quarter 1997.

Certificate of Declaration of Property for Cemetery Purposes. County of Harris, State of Texas, 12 March 1999. Filed of record in Harris County.

Chapman, Betty Trapp. *Historic Houston: An Illustrated History and Reference Guide.* San Antonio, Tex: Historical Publications, a Division of Lammert Publications, 1997. 73, 80–81.

Ciarrochi, Maria. "A Place to Pray." *Today's Catholic* (San Antonio, Tex.), 15 March 1996.

City of San Antonio Parks and Recreation Department Records. Spanish Governor's Palace inventory and architectural plan.

"City to Spend More than $33,000 on Improvements at Hermann Park This Year." *Houston Chronicle,* 7 January 1925.

Congregation of Sisters of Divine Providence, San Antonio, Tex. *Family Circular,* February 1946.

Crawford, Sybil. "Dionicio Rodriguez: The Faux Bois Sculptor." *Pulaski County Historical Review* (Pulaski County Historical Society, Little Rock, Ark.) 50, no. 1 (Spring 2002): 13–24.

Curl, James Stevens. *A Celebration of Death.* New York: Chas. Scribner's Sons, 1980.

Dams, Bernard H., and Andrew Zega. *Pleasure Pavilions and Follies: In the Gardens of the Ancien Regime.* Paris: Flammarion, 1995.

Danini, Carmina. "Mexican, Local History Are in Stock during Pharmacy Estate Sale." *San Antonio Express-News,* 21 February 1998.

Daughters of the Republic of Texas Library, San Antonio, Texas. Vertical files: Alamo Cement Company, Alamo Plaza, Brackenridge Park, Japanese Sunken Garden, Dionicio Rodríguez, Urrutia family, Urrutia house.

Dean, Jerry. "Motel Row Is Vanishing." *Arkansas Gazette* (Little Rock), 5 September 1992.

Delery, W. S., Park Engineer, San Antonio, Texas. "Prison Labor Used to Construct a Municipal Lily Pond and Japanese Garden." *American City* 20, no. 5 (January–June), 1919.

Dorsett, Amy. "Legal tug-of-war may be played out on tiny park." *San Antonio Express-News,* 3 Aug. 2002.

Druse, Ken. "Concrete Dreams." *Horticulture* 103, no. 2 (Spring Planting Issue, 2006): 60–63.

Fifteenth Census of the United States: 1933, vol. 2: Population. Washington, D.C.: Government Printing Office, 1933.

Fischer, Lewis. *Saving San Antonio.* Lubbock: Texas Tech University Press, 1996.

Forum of Civics. *Civics for Houston* 12, no. 6 (June 1928): cover, 12.

Fox, Stephen, Gerald Moorehead, and Nancy Hadley, eds. *Houston Architectural Guide 46* (1985): 144–45.

George, Mary Carolyn Hollers. *O'Neil Ford, Architect.* College Station: Texas A&M University Press, 1992.

Goetz, Robert. "Wood-Like Sculptures Fate Uncertain." *North San Antonio Times,* November 1986. 1, 3.

———. "SACS Joins Mission to Save Cement Sculptures." *North San Antonio Times,* 12 February 1987.

Goldsmith, Jill. "Eddingston Empire: Ambrose T. Eddingston Brought Caribbean Flair to Port Arthur." *Port Arthur News,* 8 April 1990.

Gordon, Debora. "The Pilgrimage: Visionary Worlds in Six Southern States." *Visionary Art* (Memphis, Tenn.), Spring 2001, 4, 8, 39, 914, 915.

Graham, Joe S. "Tejano Folk Arts and Crafts in South Texas, Artesanía Tejana." Kingsville: Texas A&I University, September 1989. Catalogue for a traveling exhibit from the John E. Conner Museum, prepared by the University of Texas Institute of Texan Cultures. Courtesy of Cisi Canales Jary.

Greenberg, Mike. "Easier to Use, Prettier to See." *San Antonio Express-News,* 23 July 2006, 1J, 8J.

Grigore, Michelle. "El Trabajo Rustico: The Rustic Work." *Views from the Arb* (Slayton Arboretum, Hillsdale College) 2 (Spring–Summer 2001): 2–4.

———. "The Past." *Views from the Arb* 1 (Winter 2000): 2–3.

Harris, Cyril M., ed. *Illustrated Dictionary of Historic Architecture.* New York: Dover Publications, 1977.

Hatton, Jim, and Jim Henderson. *Houston: A History of a Giant.* Tulsa, Okla.: Continental Heritage, 1976. 266, 277.

Hermanson, Renee. "Shelter May See Trolley Lines Again." *North San Antonio Times,* 6 November 1980.

Hofstader, Dan. "Dreams of the Orient." *Conde Nast Traveler,* July 1997: 139–56.

Holly, Henry Hudson and Michael Tomlan. *County Seats and Modern Dwellings: Two Victorian Domestic Architectural Stylebooks.* Watkins Glen, N.Y.: American Life Foundation and Study Institute, 1980.

Houston: A History and Guide. Compiled by Workers of the Writers' Program of the Works Project Administration in the State of Texas. American Guide Series. Houston: Anson Jones Press, 1942.

Houston City Directory, 1931–1932. Texas Room, Houston Public Library.

Huddleston, Scott. "Then & Now; S.A. Treasure Garden." *San Antonio Express-News,* 21 September 2006, 2B.

Hunt, Carol. "Art and Architecture at the Detroit Zoo, 1993." Courtesy of Marty Mitton, Detroit Zoo.

Jarboe, Jan. "Apology Comes 42 Years Later." *San Antonio Express-News,* 14 October, 1984, 1C.

Jasper, Pat, and Kay Turner. "Art among Us/Arte entre Nosotros: Mexican-American Folk Art in San Antonio." In *Hecho en Tejas: Texas-Mexican Folk Arts and Crafts,* ed. Joe S. Graham. Denton: University of North Texas Press, 1991.

Jefferson County Deed Records. Jefferson County Courthouse. Vol. 308: 311.

Johnston, Marguerite. *Houston, the Unknown City, 1836–1946.* College Station: Texas A&M Press, 1991, 185, 193, 194, 247.

Kazas, Tom. "Looks Like Wood." *Americana,* October 1989, 56–57.

———. "Historic Sculptures to Die For." *Washington Post Magazine,* 21 January 1990, 7.

King James Version of the Holy Bible. Oxford: Oxford University Press, n.d.

Lambeth, Laura. "Old Cement Plant Site Rescued." *San Antonio Express-News,* 11 February 1993, 1, 8.

Light, Patsy Pittman, and Maria Pfeiffer. National Register of Historic Places nominations. *San Antonio, Texas:* "Chinese Sunken Garden Gate" (now restored to its original name, "Japanese Tea Garden"), "Dionicio Rodriguez Bridge in Brackenridge Park," "Buckeye Park Gate," "Stations of the Cross and Grotto at the Shrine of St. Anthony of Padua," "Fence at Alamo Cement Company," "Fountain at Alamo Cement Company," "Jacala Restaurant," "Trolley Stop in Alamo Heights," "Miraflores Park." *Comfort, Texas:* "Gazebo for Albert Steves." *Houston, Texas:* "Aviary at the Houston Zoo" (now the Flamingo Habitat at the Houston Zoo), "Woodlawn Garden of Memories Cemetery." *Port Arthur, Texas:* "Eddingston Court." *Sweeny, Texas:* "Gazebo for James Richard Marmion," "Palapa Table for James Richard Marmion."

Maier, Fred. "History of the Houston Zoological Gardens." Manuscript.

———. "A History of the Houston Zoological Gardens." Manuscript.

Mason, Randy, Don Mayberger, and Michael Murphy. *Rare Visions & Roadside Revelations.* Kansas City, Mo.: Kansas City Star Books, 2002. 134, 178, 183. Video series and DVDs by KCPT (Kansas City Public Television) by the same title.

McAshen, Marie Phelps, and Mary Jo Bell, eds. *On the Corner of Main and Texas: A Houston Legacy.* Houston: Hutchins House Publishing, distributed by Gulf Publishing, 1985. 200, 294.

McComb, David. *Houston: The Bayou City.* Austin: University of Texas Press, 1969. 117, 122.

———. *Houston: A History.* Austin: University of Texas Press, 1969. 81.

Metes and Bounds Description of Woodlawn Cemetery. Russ Standley Surveying Company, Houston, Texas, 5 March 1999.

Minutagllo [Minutaglio], Bill. "Sylvan Concrete That Could Fool a Termite." *San Antonio Express-News,* 18 January 1981.

Morrill, Julie. "Faux Bois, for Real." *Garden Design,* August–September 1999.

The Municipal Book City of Houston, Period Ending December 31, 1928 (annual report of city government, including reports of various departments; Parks Department report credited to C. L. Brock). Houston, 1929.

The Old Mill. North Little Rock, Ark.: Visitors Bureau, n.d.

"Port Arthuran of the Month: Harley Eddingston." *Port Arthuran* (Port Arthur, Tex.), January 1956, 11.

"Pugh Park Is Dedicated in Lakewood Area: Picturesque Memorial Is Given to Public by Justin Matthews." *Arkansas Democrat* (Little Rock), August 8, 1933, 10.

Rappleye, Christine. "Southeast Texas Tales: Garden Spot of Texas on National Register." *Beaumont Enterprise* (Beaumont, Tex.), 31 January 2005, 1A.

Roarck, Eldon. "Strolling with Eldon Roarck." *Commercial Appeal* (Memphis, Tenn.), 20 June 1935.

Rutter, William E. Inventory Form for St. Joseph's Church and Shrine, Bureau of History, Michigan Department of State. 19 April 1990.

———. "W. H. L. McCourtie Estate." National Register of Historic Places, 24 January 1992. On file at U.S. Department of the Interior, National Park Service, Washington, D.C.

Rutz, Miriam Easton. *Public Gardens of Michigan.* East Lansing: Michigan State University Press, 2002.

San Antonio, as Seen by a Northern Visitor, pamphlet. St. Louis, Mo.: Kansas-Texas Railroad, 1930. 14, 21.

San Antonio Central Library, Texana/Genealogy Department. Vertical files: Alamo and Portland Cement Company, Brackenridge Park, Chinese Tea Garden, Carlos Cortés, Dionicio Rodríguez, Dr. Aureliano Urrutia.

San Antonio City Directory, 1924–1925, 1955–1956.

San Antonio Conservation Society Library. Vertical files: Alamo and Portland Cement Company, Dionicio Rodríguez, Brackenridge Park.

Schmidt, Stanley. "Dionicio Rodriguez." Manuscript, 29 February 1980.

———. "The Concrete Art of Dionicio Rodriguez." Manuscript based on interviews with J. R. Kagay and Richard Rodriguez Sr., n.d.

Sclair, Helen. "Dionicio Rodriguez, 1891–1955." *Association of Gravestone Studies Quarterly Newsletter* (Greenfield, Mass.) 22, no. 1 (Winter 1998): 13–15.

"Search for Rodriguez Starts Nationwide." *Seasons Newsletter* (Memorial Park and Funeral Home, Memphis, Tenn.) 6, Summer 1983.

Sheriff, Suzanne Katherine. "Este Soy Yo: The Politics of Representation of a Texas-Mexican Folk Artist." Ph.D. diss., University of Texas, Austin, 1989.

Shirley, Mrs. W. E. "Eddingston Court 1992." Manuscript, Port Arthur Public Library, Port Arthur, Tex., 1992.

Sloane, David Charles. *The Last Great Necessity.* Baltimore, Md.: Johns Hopkins University Press, 1994.

Smith, Bradley. *Mexico: A History in Art.* Mexico, D.F.: Editoria Cultural y Educativa, 1968. 148, 167.

Smith, Gregory. "Carolina and Genaro P. Briones House." National Register of Historic Places, August 7, 1998. On file at U.S. Department of the Interior, National Park Service, Washington, D.C.

Smithsonian Research Information System, Long View for Smithsonian American Art Museum. Inventories of American Painting and Sculpture.

Spanish Governor's Palace Inventory. San Antonio Conservation Society records in the Spanish Governor's Palace.

Standifird, Beth. "Statement of Significance: Miraflores Alumni Park (formerly known as Pioneer Park), 2002." San Antonio Conservation Society files.

Steinfeldt, Cecilia. *San Antonio Was.* San Antonio, Tex.: San Antonio Museum Association, 1978.

Survey Map of Woodlawn Garden of Memories. E. S. and Robert M. Atkinson, Civil Engineers, Houston, Tex., 28 August 1948. Courtesy of Provision Surveyors, Houston.

Sutherlin, Yvonne. "From the Cayman Islands to Port Arthur, Texas: The Eddingstons. A Family Makes More Than a Name of Themselves—They Make History." *News* (Beaumont, Tex.), 12 June 2005, CI, 3.

Texas General Contractors' Association Monthly Bulletin, 1929. Courtesy of Stephen Fox.

"The City Buys a Park." *Houston Daily Post* (Houston, Tex.), 25 June 1899, 11.

Tibbits, Ann Cain. "Stone Werks: A Successful Adaptation." *San Antonio Conservation Society News,* 1995.

Tyler, Ron, Douglas E. Barnett, Roy R. Barkley, eds. *New Handbook of Texas History.* Austin: Texas Historical Association, 1996. Vol. 3: 570, 721, 722; Vol. 5: 652, 653; Vol. 6: 1103–1104.

Uhler, David. "Behind the Tile Arch." *San Antonio-Express News,* 14 September 1997, IG, 9G.

———. "Family Tree." *San Antonio-Express News,* 13 August 1995, 1H, 4H.

———. "Gate Inches Its Way to Art Museum." *San Antonio Express-News,* 29 September 1998, 1B, 3B.

University of Texas at San Antonio Institute of Texan Cultures, Archival Photography Department, Tom Shelton photo archivist.

U.S. Bureau of the Census. *The Fifteenth Census of the United States, 1930 Population.* Vol. 2. Washington, D.C.: Government Printing Office, 1933.

U.S. Department of Commerce, Bureau of the Census. *Statistical Abstract of the United States, 1941.* Washington, D.C.: Government Printing Office, 1942.

———. *Statistical Abstract of the United States, 1956.* Washington, D.C.: Government Printing Office, 1957.

Urrutia, Dr. A. A. *Bodas de Oro del Doctor Aureliano Urrutia.* San Antonio, Tex.: Artes Graficas, 1946.

———. *Pinacoteca.* San Antonio, Tex.: n.p., n.d.

Vaux, Calvert. *Villas and Cottages: A Series of Designs Prepared for Execution in the United States.* New York: Harper and Brothers, 1864. Reprint Dover Publications, 1970.

Vosmik, Julie. "The Arkansas Sculptures of Dionicio Rodriguez." National Register of Historic Places, 4 December 1986. On file at U.S. Department of the Interior, National Park Service, Washington, D.C.

———. "The Sculptures of Dionicio Rodriguez at Memorial Park Cemetery." National Register of Historic Places, 31 January 1991. On file at U.S. Department of the Interior, National Park Service, Washington, D.C.

Walker, Tom. "Father and Son Team Creates with Concrete." *San Antonio Light,* 12 February 1989.

Weber, Tanya, and Tom Kazas. "Sleuth Uncovers Mystery of Artist." *Chronicle* (Quapaw Quarter Association, Little Rock, Ark.), February–March 1987.

Westkaemper, Sarah C. "Three Twentieth Century Gardens: A Heritage of Excellence in San Antonio." MA thesis, Louisiana State University, 1985.

Wilson, Stephen. *Harvey Couch: An Entrepreneur Brings Electricity to Arkansas.* Little Rock: August House, 1986.

Wilson, Winston P. *Harvey Couch, the Master Builder.* Nashville, Tenn.: Broadman Press, 1947.

Winn, Eliza Jane, and Julia Jones. "Houston, Texas, District 6, Points of Interest: Hermann Park Zoo." WPA Writers' Project. Houston Metropolitan Research Center, Houston Public Library.

Woodward, George E. *Woodward's Architecture and Rural Art No. 1, 1867.* New York: George E. Woodward, 1889.

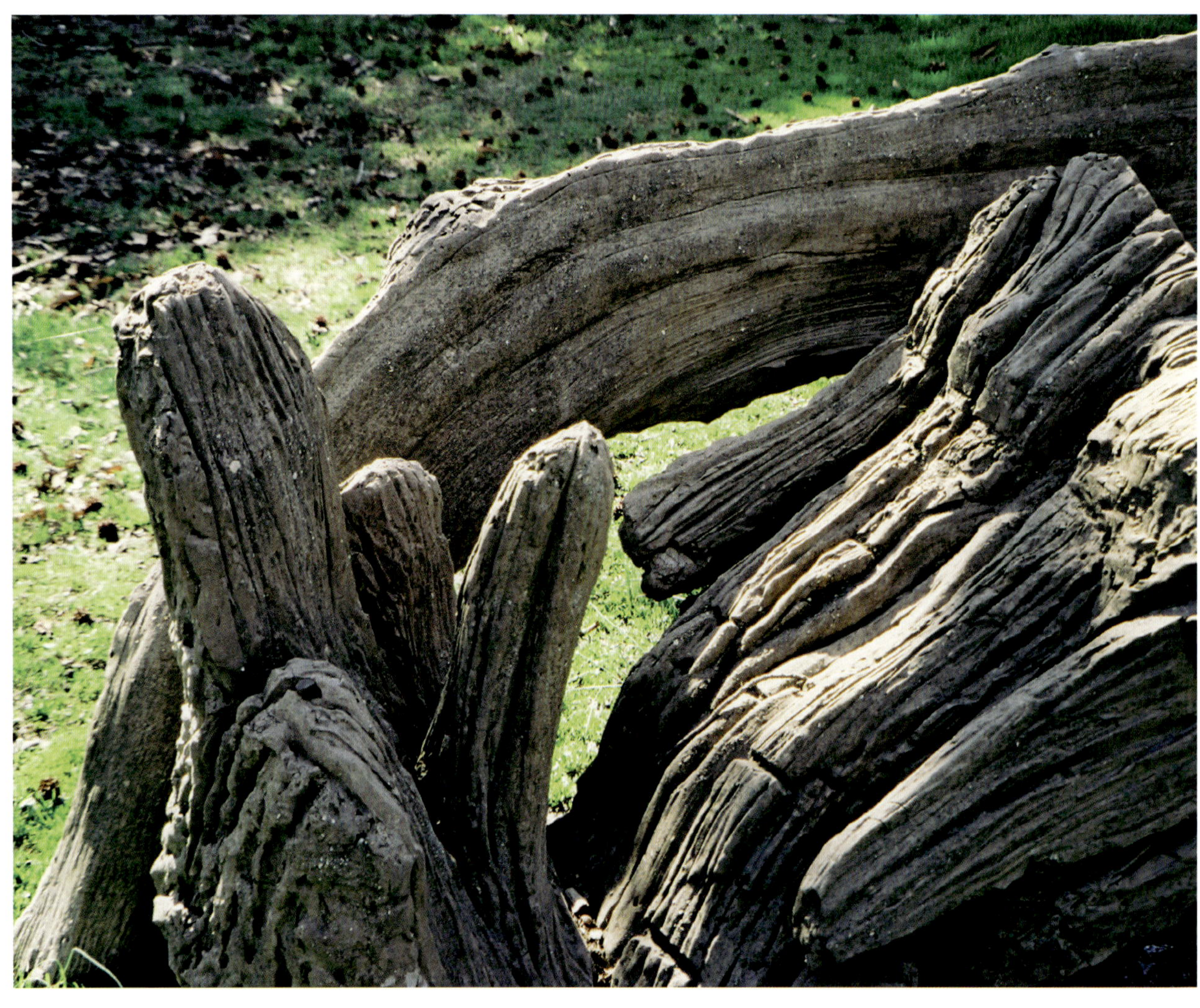

Fallen log bench texture, Cedar Hill Cemetery,
Suitland, Maryland. Photo: Maria Watson Pfeiffer.

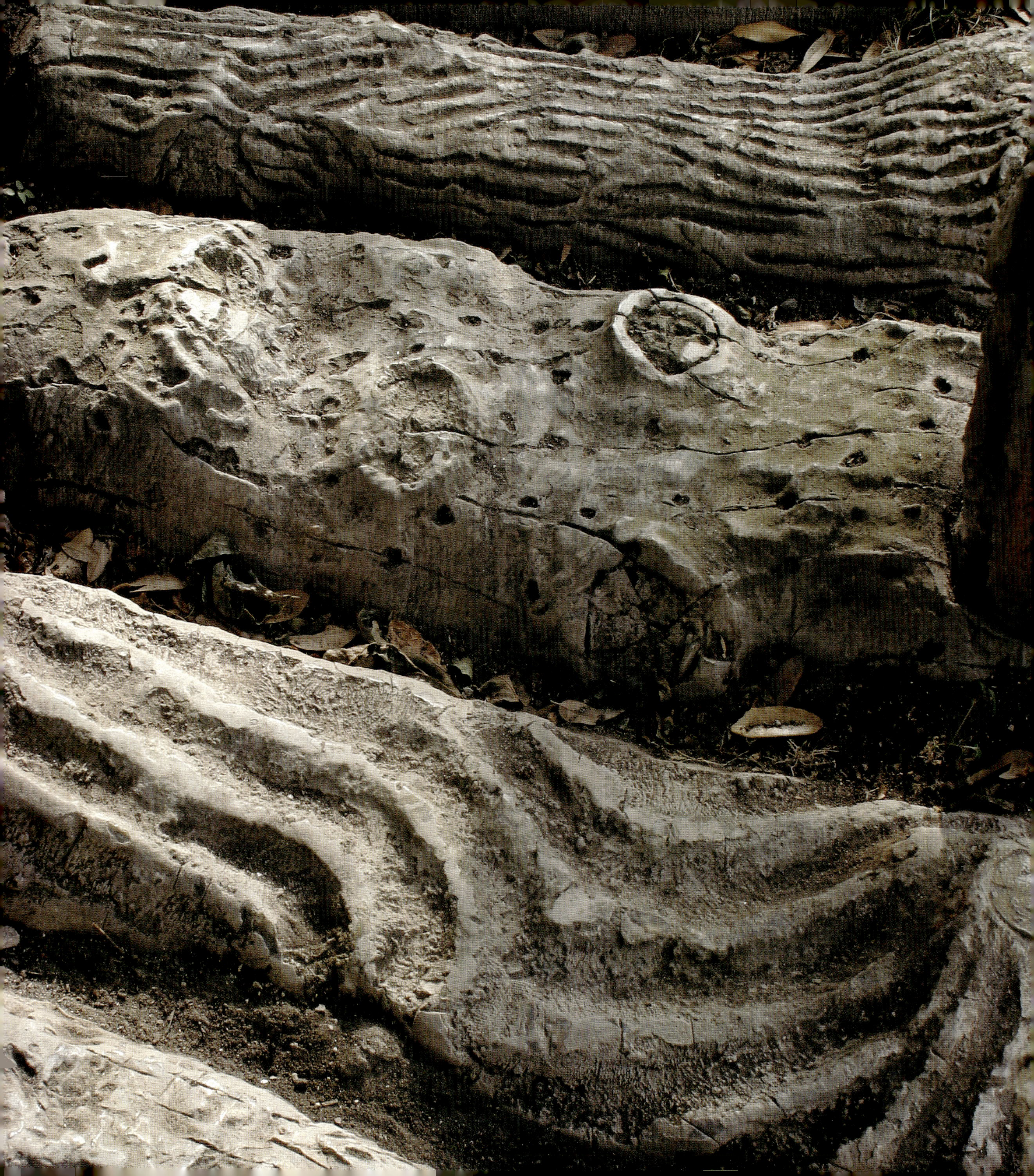